W9-BLQ-285

Redesigning Higher Education: Academic
Producing Dramatic Gains in Student Learning Affairs

by Lion F. Gardiner

ASHE-ERIC Higher Education Report 7, 1994

New Jersey Institute
for Collegiate
Teaching and Learning

*This report is a special cooperative project
between the New Jersey Institute for Collegiate Teaching
and Learning and the ERIC Clearinghouse on Higher Education*

Prepared by

*Clearinghouse on Higher Education
The George Washington University*

In cooperation with

*Association for the Study
of Higher Education*

Published by

*Graduate School of Education and
Human Development
The George Washington University*

Jonathan D. Fife, Series Editor

Cite as

Gardiner, Lion F. *Redesigning Higher Education: Producing Dramatic Gains in Student Learning.* Report No. 7. Washington, D.C.: Graduate School of Education and Human Development, The George Washington University, 1994.

Library of Congress Catalog Card Number 96-75971
ISSN 0884-0040
ISBN 1-878380-63-X

Managing Editor: Lynne J. Scott
Manuscript Editor: Barbara J. Fishel/Editech
Cover design by Michael David Brown, Rockville, Maryland

The ERIC Clearinghouse on Higher Education invites individuals to submit proposals for writing monographs for the ASHE-ERIC Higher Education Report series. Proposals must include:
1. A detailed manuscript proposal of not more than five pages.
2. A chapter-by-chapter outline.
3. A 75-word summary to be used by several review committees for the initial screening and rating of each proposal.
4. A vita and a writing sample.

ERIC Clearinghouse on Higher Education
Graduate School of Education and Human Development
The George Washington University
One Dupont Circle, Suite 630
Washington, DC 20036-1183

This publication was prepared partially with funding from the Office of Educational Research and Improvement, U.S. Department of Education, under contract no. ED RR-93-002008. The opinions expressed in this report do not necessarily reflect the positions or policies of OERI or the Department.

Since the late 1960s and early 1970s, American colleges and universities have been profoundly changed by the huge influx of "nontraditional" students who have increasingly characterized our campuses—women, people of color, and part-time and older students. These "new" students are far more representative of Americans as a whole than were their predecessors. They are often less well prepared for college than their relatively more privileged peers, and the goals to which they aspire, their styles of learning, and their educational needs often differ from those of more traditional students. Projections suggest our students will continue to increase in diversity far into the future.

A series of critical reports by authorities on higher education, political leaders, and businesspeople, published since the mid-1980s, have claimed that we in higher education have not responded effectively to the needs of our students of the last 25 years and that many of our graduates' knowledge and skills do not meet society's requirements for well-educated citizens.

How valid are these claims? How effectively are we educating our students? Because relatively few colleges or universities broadly assess what their graduates know and are able to do, we have limited evidence with which to answer these now-urgent questions, and no comprehensive statewide or national assessment exists that might provide this evidence. The research literature of higher education, however, now contains many valuable findings, albeit widely scattered, that can help us answer these questions and provide essential guidance to significantly improve our students' learning. *Redesigning Higher Education* gathers the findings of many of these studies to make them readily accessible.

What Are the Critical Competencies and How Do They Develop?

Scholars and leaders in business and government most frequently identify the skills and dispositions essential to society's economic and democratic success to include the capacities for critical thinking and complex problem solving, respect for people different from oneself, principled ethical behavior, lifelong learning, and effective interpersonal interaction and teamwork. These crucial skills and dispositions presuppose cognitive abilities studies have shown are poorly developed in many college and university students. These underpinnings of advanced intellectual performance, as well as effective interpersonal interaction and teamwork, require for their development continuous active involvement in learning and with other students and faculty, together with regular assessment and timely feedback on performance.

What Are the Effects of Our Curricula?

The limited research on curriculum is increasingly useful. Although our 3,600 colleges and universities differ in many other ways, over 90 percent use distribution systems of curriculum, in which students select courses from lists, often with considerable diversity of choice. Research reveals that men and women take significantly different courses, that groups of courses are correlated with gains, or declines, in specific competencies for groups of high- and low-ability students, and that student outcomes are not necessarily related to required courses. Thus, research has questioned the developmental value of distributional curricula; curricula need to be adapted to the specific needs of different students. Types and breadth of courses available, specific courses in the curriculum, and degree of choice may make relatively little difference in educational outcomes, although a true-core curriculum, found in a few institutions, can be positively associated with many valued outcomes. How an institution provides its curricula can be more important than its curricular structure and content.

Studies suggest, overall, that undergraduate liberal arts curricula tend to lack coherence and have limited breadth and depth. A liberal arts emphasis, however, as compared with more vocationally oriented curricula, can increase women's choice of gender atypical careers and African-American males' choice of higher prestige, typically majority careers, reduce authoritarianism, and increase capacity for principled ethical reasoning.

How Effectively Do Our Courses Develop Students' Intellectual Abilities?

Faculty aspire to develop students' thinking skills, but research consistently shows that in practice we tend to aim at facts and concepts in the disciplines, at the lowest cognitive levels, rather than development of intellect or values. Numerous studies of college classrooms reveal that, rather than actively involving our students in learning, we lecture, even though lectures are not nearly as effective as other means for developing cognitive skills. In addition, students may be attending to lectures only about one-half of their time in class, and retention of information from lectures is low.

Studies suggest our methods often fail to dislodge students' misconceptions and ensure learning of complex, abstract concepts. Capacity for problem solving is limited by our use of inappropriately simple practice exercises.

How Hard Do Students Work?

Although quality of effort is key to accomplishment, studies consistently show that students generally study far less than necessary to learn effectively, although in many cases they have considerable discretionary time. The limited evidence available on college outcomes reveals disappointing levels of knowledge and skills among students, consistent with the less than optimal methods we often use and the modest efforts of most students.

What Do Tests and Grades Tell Us?

Classroom tests often set the standard for students' learning. As with instruction, however, we tend to emphasize recall of memorized factual information rather than intellectual challenge. Taken together with our preference for lectures, our tests may be reinforcing our students' commonly fact-oriented memory learning, of limited value to either them or society.

Virtually all American colleges and universities employ grades as indicators of students'—and the institution's—accomplishment. Student retention, advancement, honors, and graduation, and therefore key public policy decisions, depend on these important symbols. Yet grades are often based on tests of uncertain technical quality and other, unknown components; they individually carry little information and, combined into averages, correlate poorly with success after graduation. Grades further provide for many students a strong antidevelopmental inducement to the pervasive cheating on campus studies consistently find.

How Does the Campus Climate Affect Our Students' Development?

The climate of a campus can welcome new students into what is for many an unfamiliar and threatening culture; provide the social interaction, emotional support, and personal integration and validation needed for learning and retention on campus; and inspire each person to high effort. In many cases, however, research reveals little involvement between students and the faculty, staff, or other students, a climate of limited intellectual stimulation, and a climate that tolerates widespread cheating and alcohol abuse. Studies frequently reveal campus environments where women and minority-group members are regularly devalued and overtly discriminated against. Together, this array of environmental conditions can powerfully militate against students' success.

How Well Do We Guide Our Students' Development?

Authorities widely agree that academic advising is a powerful tool for improving students' success, providing influential opportunities for out-of-class contact between students and faculty and personalized guidance for negotiating a new and complex culture, achieving self-understanding, and planning one's own development. Today, high-quality advising focuses on each student's specific developmental needs. High-quality advising is correlated with increases in students' self-esteem, satisfaction with college, and persistence in school. Yet national surveys reveal that on most campuses academic advising, when it occurs at all, tends to be primarily clerical in character rather than developmental, focusing as it does on registration.

Can Today's Students Learn?

Given our students' diverse backgrounds, frequent underpreparation, and limited academic success, with about half withdrawing before graduation, some faculty believe many lack the ability to learn. But striking success with elementary and high school students of modest academic origins and high-quality methods of instruction in college both demonstrate students' potential for high achievement, provided we adapt to their needs rather than demand they adapt to our traditions. *The higher the quality of instruction, the lower the correlation between students' assessed ability and the quality of their learning.*

How Can We Improve the Quality of The Student Outcomes We Produce?

Research now available on the student experience in colleges and universities shows we must make substantial changes if we are to serve society's needs for highly educated employees, citizens, and leaders. Significant steps we can take are to develop clear missions, carefully define our intended outcomes, hold high expectations for our students and ourselves, comprehensively assess both students and institutions, use research on student learning and organizations, integrate our curricula, systematically design instruction that will involve students actively at every point, teach students how to learn, develop a campus climate that challenges and supports each person, and ensure each student has high-quality developmental academic advising.

Our widespread problems in enabling all our students to succeed require vigorous, systemic responses. Research on student development, coupled with modern educational methods and quality improvement principles, *can enable us for the first time in human history to educate all of the people to a high level.* We will, however, have to use, rather than ignore, research. Informed, committed, and sustained leadership at all levels will be required, and institutions will have to invest in significant leadership training. Graduate schools will have to provide thorough, demanding professional training as educators for the future faculty, and the current professoriat will require significant assistance in developing the diverse professional knowledge and skills now required to educate our students. Professionally prepared and accountable leadership and faculty can develop a more positive and supportive culture on campus, build community and improve faculty and staff morale, and produce the high-quality results society now urgently needs and is asking us to provide.

CONTENTS

FOREWORD

It was fully a generation ago that sociologist Martin Trow first alerted us to the imminent transition of American higher education from an elite system organized to educate but a fraction of the populace to one guided by the democratic ideals of universal access, the gateway to a learning society. And that transition in access would, Trow predicted, bring with it radical shifts in the social purposes of a college education (lifelong learning), academic standards (greater heterogeneity), curriculum and instruction (flex time and place), faculty and administrative roles, and the politicization of the campus—or, more accurately, the dissolution of the boundaries between the campus and the polity.

We have been living, and continue to live, that transition. With one hand, American higher education clings to the faculty- and discipline-centered model of academic work (Jencks's and Reisman's academic revolution) that took shape after World War II and crystallized in the 1960s and 1970s; with the other, it gropes toward a more learner-centered model of collegiate education that can provide the broad human resource platform needed to support the information society we are becoming. How this dilemma resolves itself, and what role each of us can play in that resolution, is in the largest sense the question of the hour for American higher education. How will the transition be managed and how will each of us—as faculty members or administrators—contribute to managing it?

What resources do we have at our individual and collective disposal to address such pressing professional, and ultimately social and political, questions? We have searching and scathing (usually more of the latter than the former) critiques of the faculty-centered model, including *ProfScam* and *Impostors in the Temple* on the one hand and some visions of desirable learner-centered models on the other, among the most balanced of which is the work of the 1984 NIE Study Group on the Conditions of Excellence in American Higher Education.

Redesigning Higher Education is distinctive in that it focuses neither on critique nor on prescription alone, but on the theoretically grounded links between the two. Within the context of contemporary theory on student development, Lion Gardiner, associate professor of zoology at Rutgers University, examines the growing body of knowledge about student learning, college outcomes, and the effectiveness of various options for instruction and assessment as the basis for identifying an empirically grounded set of practices that we know lead to better learning for students. The challenge in moving to a more student-centered model is first clarifying what the basic elements of that model would be. And here Professor Gardiner scours the readily available and the more arcane sources, the widely published and the more and less scattered literatures, and melds them into a coherent and consistent portrait of how we might conduct our instructional mission.

But faculty roles and instructional strategies are, as Professor Gardiner recognizes, embedded in our organizational arrangements and cultures. And it is to the matter of effecting the organizational changes that will support the redesign of college teaching that he devotes the latter part of the monograph. These changes include how we train our college teachers, how we develop our faculty and academic administrators, and, ultimately, how we set our institutional priorities. He concludes with an institutional agenda for beginning to move forward.

Professor Gardiner's work was originally developed during his tenure as a Faculty Fellow at the New Jersey Institute for Collegiate Teaching and Learning, one of a growing number of state and regional initiatives to support and integrate the efforts of individual faculty who continue to struggle between the norms of their socialization and the needs of their students. This volume will, I hope, serve as a resource for that journey.

Martin J. Finkelstein
Director, New Jersey Institute for
Collegiate Teaching and Learning

Seton Hall University

 New Jersey Institute
for Collegiate
Teaching and Learning

Mailing address: Seton Hall University, S. Orange, NJ 07079
E-mail: finkelma@lanmail.shu.edu

ACKNOWLEDGMENTS

Many people have contributed to the development of this monograph. Martin J. Finkelstein of the New Jersey Institute for Collegiate Teaching and Learning suggested I write about student development in college, and he has provided ideas and encouragement, various information and materials, and support for some release time to assist the process. He also read various drafts of the manuscript and provided many helpful suggestions.

Other colleagues have provided stimulating and informative discussions that have influenced my thinking, and several of them contributed materials that have further aided my work: Howard B. Altman, Ralph Blair, Madan Capoor, Robert A. Cornesky, Robert M. Diamond, Mary Diez, Robert G. Fuller, Joanne Gainen, Thomas J. Grites, Wesley R. Habley, Rachel Hadas, Gary R. Hanson, Mark J. Huisman, Kathleen M. Kies, Steven P. McNeel, Theodore J. Marchese, Robert J. Menges, Barbara J. Millis, William S. Moore, Douglas W. Morrison, Alan Oppenheim, Rosa Oppenheim, Alton O. Roberts, Frederick R. Schram, Myrna Smith, and Vincent Tinto.

Barbara Bretcko, Daniel Burke, Linda Dye, Eamonn Kelly, Mary Mowry-Raddock, John Pesda, and Myrna J. Smith read and commented helpfully on various early drafts. Frances Bartkowski, Douglas W. Morrison, Nancy Omaha Boy, and Raymond T. Smith read parts of the manuscript, and Jonathan D. Fife, Dorothy J. Harnish, Lynn A. Wild, and four anonymous reviewers read the entire manuscript. Each person offered many detailed and helpful suggestions, which have substantially improved the final result.

The participants during three semesters in the Rutgers University–Campus at Newark Teaching Excellence Center Faculty Seminar on Students, Learning, and Teaching contributed various data, as did hundreds of Rutgers students in my classes.

The following people provided specific information or data and helpful materials from their own research and writings: Clifford Adelman, Nancy V. Chism, James A. Eison, Peter A. Facione, Donald R. Gallagher, Patricia A. Hutchings, Glenn R. Johnson, Christine A. Karatka, Archie Lapointe, Sherry Levy-Reiner, Karron G. Lewis, Georgine Loacker, Ann F. Lucas, Donald L. McCabe, Jacqueline McCaffrey, Marcia M. Mentkowski, Michael Moffatt, Patricia

H. Murrell, Leonard Ramist, James L. Ratcliff, Bernice R. Sandler, and Michael R. Winters.

Jeanne R. Baptiste, Carolyn Foote, and Wanda J. Gawienowski secured innumerable materials from various libraries both within and beyond the Rutgers University library system. Michael T. Bowman loaned me useful materials from his personal library.

I am grateful to each of these people. Without their concern for students and higher education and support for the project, my work would have been very difficult indeed. I especially thank those many dedicated and tireless researchers without whose work on students, teachers, and colleges there would be little new to say and far fewer useful insights to share. Their work permits us to develop a new vision of human development and of the higher education enterprise.

And, finally, thanks are due Rutgers University, without whose support I could not have undertaken this endeavor.

INTRODUCTION

The world is far smaller today than it was at the end of World War II. Transportation and communication link us firmly with other nations. Trade and finance are global. The last decade witnessed an extraordinary movement toward democracy, and many other nations now seek, through education and technology, benefits for their people we have long enjoyed. Some of these nations now press us economically and even threaten to outpace us. Leaders in business and government have warned for some time that we may have become complacent.

Technology is changing society. The U.S. Department of Labor projects a 22 percent increase between 1988 and 2000 in jobs requiring education beyond high school ("Demand" 1990). By 2000, a majority of *all* new jobs in the United States will require education beyond high school (National Task Force 1990). We in higher education have been asked to respond vigorously to prepare our students for this technological environment, an environment very different from the one many of us faced at graduation.

White males, the historic mainstays of technological professions, today account for an increasingly smaller part of the workforce. From 1985 through 2000, they will number a mere 15 percent of new workers (Pool 1990). Women, members of racial and ethnic minority groups, and foreigners will have to make up the difference. Many more mathematics and science teachers—teachers in those disciplines that will be essential to our technological advance—could be needed over the decade ahead (Darling-Hammond and Hudson 1990).

Educating All the People

During the three decades following World War II, U.S. college and university populations expanded far more than at any previous time. Between 1947 and 1963, enrollments increased more than twofold, by 1977 an additional fivefold (Pew 1990). The wave of servicepeople returning from the war was later followed by another—their children, the baby boomers of the 1960s.

The late 1960s and 1970s brought with them another development that profoundly affected institutions of higher education. Efforts to increase social equity, particularly by state governments, led to large numbers of so called "new" students, who began to appear on campuses across the country (Cross 1971). Women, people of color, and part-time and older students all made their presence felt in institutions long overwhelmingly the preserve of white, male, "academically adept adolescents" (Pew 1990, p. 1). By 1984, 19.7 percent of college students were nonwhite; by 1985, 42 percent were older than 25, 52 percent were women, and 42 percent attended part time (Smith 1989). Today, these new students have swollen student populations until, together, they number over 14 million people (National Center 1993). Moreover, whereas previous generations of students overwhelmingly lived on campus, today 80 percent of undergraduates in this country commute to college (Jacoby 1989).

The new students, far more representative of Americans as a whole than their predecessors, were also less well educated and thus less well prepared for college than their relatively more privileged peers. Therefore, they brought with them to college challenges quite different from those their institutions had previously confronted. In many cases, these students came from families less economically well off. The goals to which they aspired, their styles of learning, and their needs were all significantly different from those of more traditional students.

These changes in our students have continued apace. Traditional, first-time, full-time, undergraduate students who enroll in college directly from high school will soon be outnumbered by a new "emerging majority": students who are part time, 25 years of age or older, and who have not come to college directly from high school or who have stopped out of college for longer than a year (Pew 1990). In 1960, students of Caucasian ancestry made up 90 percent of undergraduates at the University of California–Berkeley; in 1980, they accounted for 66 percent and, more recently, about 45 percent (Duster 1991). In 1991, entering first-year students at Berkeley were for the first time primarily people of color. Asian-Americans alone constituted 35 percent of the class, whites a mere 30 percent. This trend will continue. In 1988, 20 percent of children under age 17 were members of racial minorities; by 2000, they will make up one-third (Commission on Minority 1988).

Today, we are being asked to educate all of the people to a very high level. Society depends on us to develop people who can, as employees, meet the needs of business for the international competition of the 21st century. In addition, our graduates will be central to solving every major social problem that faces us—ineffective schools, unstable families, drug abuse, crime, international conflict, environmental degradation. We are witnessing a proliferation of partisan strife worldwide and an explosion of intolerant ideological division at home. Society depends on us to produce graduates who have a sophisticated understanding of themselves and others who differ from them, who have the values and intellectual, professional, and social skills required as teachers, social workers, criminologists, ecologists, businesspeople, and citizens to lead our democracy into the new century and to create a peaceable and economically productive national and world community.

Many observers believe higher education has entered a period of change as great as any it has ever experienced. Although our system of higher education may be the best to have been developed by any nation, many question whether we continue to meet society's needs. They believe we will have to alter fundamentally many of the ways we conduct our affairs if we are to produce the quality of graduates society now requires. Although students of the last quarter century have in many ways been very different from their predecessors and although society has much higher expectations for their educators than ever before, many of our constituents believe we in higher education have not responded well to our students' needs and have fallen far short of society's expectations. In 1983, *A Nation at Risk: The Imperative of Educational Reform* (National Commission 1983) called attention to widespread educational problems in this country. Since then, a series of highly critical reports have focused specifically on quality in higher education, expressing a growing sense of urgency about perceived inadequacies and necessary changes (Bennett 1984; Boyer 1987; Cheney 1990; Commission for Educational 1994; Project on Redefining 1985; Study Group 1984; Wingspread Group 1993; Working Party 1986).

Purpose and Scope of This Report
How valid are these public perceptions? How effective are we at educating our students? Unfortunately, because few colleges or universities assess in detail what their students know and are able to do, either when they arrive on cam-

Many observers believe higher education has entered a period of change as great as any it has ever experienced.

pus or when they graduate, they have limited information on which to base answers to these questions. Further, no comprehensive state or national assessment provides this evidence. The professional research literature on higher education, however, now contains much valuable information, albeit widely scattered, that can help us answer these questions and provide essential guidance to learn how effective we are and to improve the quality of our students' learning.

This monograph brings together in one place the findings of hundreds of studies on various aspects of higher education and attempts to make them readily available. Its purposes are to help readers better understand their institutions by providing a basis for continuously improving the quality of their students' learning and to stimulate informed discussion about students and learning everywhere. The primary focus is the status of four core areas central to the quality of student development (used throughout this monograph to refer broadly to any desirable and natural change in students' cognitive, affective, or motor capacities) in higher education: curriculum, instruction, campus psychological climate, and academic advising. It reviews empirical research that illuminates the impact of each core area on students' learning and accomplishment of missions and that can (1) guide readers' thinking as they reflect on the current quality of their own courses, programs, institutions, and systems; (2) help them discover fresh insights and new ways of viewing their work and organizations; and (3) enable them to identify areas where they can improve quality on campus. The report also provides numerous specific suggestions on how to improve the contribution of each core area to students' development and suggestions concerning issues of leadership and management.

The report is addressed to the following audiences:

- Faculty members who, although well trained in the content of their disciplines, may be less familiar with the professional literature on student development or educational processes and wish to enhance their own professional knowledge and skills, thereby helping their students learn more effectively;
- Trustees and academic administrators—presidents, provosts, deans, department chairs—responsible for

accomplishment of missions, who might gain deeper insight into what does, does not, and should go on inside—and outside—the classroom and into methods of leadership that can more effectively meet the educational needs of all their constituents;

- People responsible for faculty, instructional, and leadership development, who might identify specific areas on which to focus their efforts and key issues to raise, and find empirical support for various practices and a rich collection of written resources to help in solving problems;

- Student affairs professionals, who can gain insight into their students' experiences, particularly in their academic activities, thereby more effectively helping them to integrate their education (see Bloland, Stamatakos, and Rogers 1994 for a critique of student development efforts in student affairs);

- Government leaders—elected officials, members of their staffs, and members of higher education coordinating agencies—charged with guiding public higher education, ensuring taxpayers a high return on their investment, and overseeing an enterprise central to the future well-being and economic success of the states and the nation;

- Journalists who interpret higher education to their communities, who can find up-to-date information on important research, issues, and social concerns affecting colleges and universities and can discover ideas and a wide array of resources to aid them in their work; and

- Concerned citizens—business leaders, taxpayers, parents, and students—who are our customers and pay our way, who can gain insight into human development and an overview of the higher education enterprise, which will have an increasingly powerful impact on society.

In every case, readers can use the report as a resource to inform decision making and action.

The section following this introduction reviews the most important abilities society requires of students today, the results of research describing how certain of these crucial abilities develop, and the conditions that are now believed necessary to produce them. The following four sections examine the four core areas central to student development and the contribution research suggests they now make to this development: curriculum; instruction (methods, the intellectual climate of the classroom, students' involvement, classroom tests, and grades); the campus climate; and academic advising.

The final four sections lay out the challenge to higher education and describe rich opportunities for producing dramatic gains in students' learning, examining evidence about the relative capacity of students to learn at a very high level; describing seven specific changes we can make, each one of which can improve students' learning and together can lead to significant gains in an institution's overall capacity to produce learning; and addressing overarching issues of leadership, management, and professional development necessary to foster the essential changes and link everything together in a systemic whole. The final section presents a vision and a challenge to develop a new kind of community on campus.

WHAT IS STUDENT DEVELOPMENT AND HOW DOES IT HAPPEN?

What Are the Critical Competencies?

Leaders in business, industry, and government have identified certain knowledge, skills, and dispositions as especially important for personal, business, and national economic and democratic success in the years ahead:

- Conscientiousness, personal responsibility, and dependability
- The ability to act in a principled, ethical fashion
- Skill in oral and written communication
- Interpersonal and team skills
- Skill in critical thinking and in solving complex problems
- Respect for people different from oneself
- The ability to adapt to change and
- The ability and desire for life-long learning (Candy and Crebert 1991; Carnevale, Gainer, and Meltzer 1990; "Challenge" 1995; Marshall 1989; Van Horn 1995; Wingspread Group 1993).

The amount of information being created today is enormous compared to any time in our history. Over a decade ago, an estimated 6,000 to 7,000 papers in science alone were being written daily, and information in science and technology was doubling every 5.5 years, a rate of increase that was projected to "jump to perhaps 40 percent per year" (Naisbitt 1982, p. 24) because of computer manipulation. As a result of this high rate of discovery, knowledge today becomes relatively quickly obsolete, and "in this era of the knowledge explosion, what students know when they leave college will not be nearly as important as what they are capable of learning" (Cross 1986, p. 10). Learning must continue throughout life.

How closely do the outcomes we in the academy desire for our students compare with the abilities required today in the world of work? Faculty agree almost universally that the development of students' higher-order intellectual or cognitive abilities is the most important educational task of colleges and universities. These abilities underpin our students' perceptions of the world and the consequent decisions they make. Specifically, critical thinking—the capacity to evaluate skillfully and fairly the quality of evidence and detect error, hypocrisy, manipulation, dissembling, and bias—is central to both personal success and national needs. A 1972 study of 40,000 faculty members by the American Council on Education found that 97 percent of the respondents indicated the most important goal of undergraduate education is to foster students' ability to think critically (Milton 1982). We also value highly creative problem solving and invention. In a 1989 survey of 5,450 faculty members from all types of institutions by the Car-negie Foundation for the Advancement of Teaching, 70 percent of the respondents stated that enhancing creative thinking in undergraduate education is very important (Boyer 1989). Bowen's Catalog of Goals, based on his review of 1,500 goal statements he found in the literature of higher education, includes such widely accepted cognitive outcomes as skill in written and oral communication, quantitative skills involving (among others) elementary mathematics and statistical reasoning, and rationality—logical, objective thinking, a "disposition to weigh evidence, evaluate facts and ideas critically, and . . . think independently," and a developed "ability to analyze and synthesize" (Bowen 1977, p. 55). Also important are the tolerance of or openness to novel ideas, a "willingness to question orthodoxy," the capacity "to deal with complexity and ambiguity," and "appreciation of intellectual and cultural diversity" (p. 55).

College and university faculty by no means limit the outcomes they value to the cognitive domain. Primarily affective outcomes include an appreciation of esthetic expression in literature, art, and nature; intellectual integrity; and a desire for lifelong learning (Bowen 1977). Explicitly emotional and moral concerns include sensitivity to feelings and emotions, emotional stability, assertiveness, self-confidence, acceptance of self and others, the capacity for empathy (putting oneself in the place of another), respect and tolerance for and cooperation with diverse people, a democratic, nonauthoritarian point of view, the belief in internalized and nondogmatic moral principles, and a sense of social responsibility (Bowen 1977).

Faculty also usually desire their graduates to have substantive knowledge about both western and nonwestern traditions, philosophy, natural and social science, and literature and art, as well as knowledge, skills, and values appropriate to some area of concentration. "Education of the whole person" is a goal many of us hold dear.

Clearly, the faculties of U.S. colleges and universities and leaders in various sectors of society agree substantially on the desired outcomes of student development. Acquiring the kinds of knowledge, skills, and values we ourselves respect should well equip our graduates for the realities they will face as citizens and workers, and for meeting the nation's increasingly urgent need for a highly educated citizenry.

How Do the Critical Competencies Develop?

Research conducted during the last three decades has illuminated key dimensions of our students' development central to producing these important abilities, enriching our understanding of what schools and colleges can do for their students. For example, many laypeople conceive of intelligence, the ability to learn and engage in cognitively complex behavior and abstract problem solving, as being primarily determined by unchangeable genetic characteristics. Although it is *influenced* by heredity, however, many cognitive psychologists understand intelligence more flexibly in terms of dynamic intellectual processes that can be developed and significantly improved (Baron 1985; Binet 1909, cited in Covington 1985; Ceci 1990; Cronbach 1984; Gardner 1985; Linn 1989; Plomin 1990; Schaie and Parr 1981; Sternberg 1985, 1986). "Intelligence is achievement—the result of past learning as well as a predictor of future learning" (McKeachie et al. 1990, p. 5). "Intelligence is education's most important product, as well as its most important raw material" (Snow 1980, p. 185).

This new knowledge about student development has become essential if colleges are to understand their diverse student clients and design educational experiences that can meet their needs (Chickering and Associates 1981; Delworth, Hanson, and Associates 1989; Fried 1981; Hood and Arceneaux 1990; Knefelkamp, Widick, and Parker 1978; Parker 1978; Pascarella and Terenzini 1991; Rodgers 1989; Upcraft, Gardner, and Associates 1989). To develop an essential conceptual foundation for discussion throughout this report, this subsection briefly reviews four key aspects of student development: the capacity for abstract reasoning, epistemology, the capacity for principled ethical reasoning, and the ability to work cooperatively in groups. Together with other dimensions of development, these four aspects make key contributions to that educational outcome without price—wisdom (Sternberg 1990).

Capacity for abstract reasoning: A foundation of higher-order abilities

All types of complex, higher-order reasoning, such as critical thinking, the creative solution of problems, and principled ethical reasoning, require as their prerequisite the capacity to manipulate abstractions—value, change, good and bad, purpose, trust, responsibility, democracy—not to mention myriad technical concepts like balance of payments, organic evolution, social class, and force, constructs that permit us to comprehend the world, contribute to its well-being, and enjoy it fully. In other words, we must be able to think with abstract symbols that stand for complex meanings and be able to manipulate these symbols, singly and with others, to construct new meaning for ourselves. Every discipline and professional field represented in the curricula of colleges and universities presupposes students' capacity to manipulate its abstractions.

Piaget discovered that not until about age 11 are children first able to reason with abstractions, a process known as "formal reasoning" (Inhelder and Piaget 1958; Piaget 1972). The reasoning or cognitive operations of younger children are thought to be limited to a concrete world of real objects, people, and situations. Later studies of college students, however, have repeatedly demonstrated in various fields that, despite their age and regardless of our own perceptions of their reasoning ability, a majority of our students are still concrete operational or transitional thinkers, somewhere between concrete and formal in their reasoning abilities (Dunlop and Fazio 1976; Hardy-Brown 1981; Kolodiy 1975; Kuhn et al. 1977; McKinnon and Renner 1971; Robbins 1981; Tomlinson-Keasey 1978). For example, a study of first-year physical science students at Rutgers University and Essex County College, all but a few of whom stated an interest in science-related majors, found that at least two-thirds of the students had not yet become formal thinkers (Griffiths 1973). Among 53 Rutgers students, of whom 3.8 percent were members of minority groups, only 34 percent were fully formal operational thinkers; 66 percent were not yet formal. Of 59 Essex students, who included among them 57.9 percent minority group members, 27 percent were categorized formal operational and 73 percent were nonformal. Studies further suggest that, without specific assistance from teachers, students may remain thus cognitively limited throughout their lives.

The study also discovered that many of the nonformal students, 55 percent at the university and 23 percent at the community college, depended (many of them presumably successfully) on the memory and recitation of technical jargon, such as mass, force, and momentum. These nonformal operational students did not understand the concepts represented by the terms they used. The rest of the nonformal students, 11 percent and 50 percent at the two institutions, respectively, lacked even technical terms to use and were helpless (see also "The problem of misconceptions" on p. 47 and "Development of higher-order cognitive abilities" on p. 50).

Concrete operational students "will consistently be unable to follow many lines of argument" in lectures; students in transition to formal operational reasoning "will frequently encounter difficulties" (Robbins 1981, p. 209). Only fully formal students "will in general have no difficulty following the abstract reasoning found in the average . . . lecture" (p. 209). Nonformal thinkers will have difficulty imagining possibilities that could exist now, in the past, or in the future; engaging in propositional, probabilistic, and correlational reasoning; considering relevant variables separate from each other; and conducting mental operations, such as in mental experiments. Such students may be unable to engage in *metacognition*—the critical examination of their own thinking for inconsistencies and for appropriateness of explanation—and the ability to compare and contrast different approaches to solving problems (Karplus et al. 1977). Their limits in thinking hypothetically and deductively compromise their understanding of many essential components of college-level reasoning; experiments in science—not to mention much that is central to mature understanding in other fields—may be beyond their ken.

These studies raise serious questions about what nonformal students, who in many institutions constitute a majority, might be learning in their courses and about what kinds of knowledge and skills tests assess. Studies show striking correlations between students' capacity for formal operations and success in college courses (Hardy Brown 1981; Hudak and Anderson 1990).

Research generally shows inconsistent patterns in the development of formal reasoning skills, or relatively small increases, over the college years (Pascarella and Terenzini 1991). Specially designed instruction, however, such as the ADAPT Program at the University of Nebraska–Lincoln (ADAPT 1978) and Project SOAR at Xavier University of Louisiana (Carmichael et al. 1978), have long been more successful than conventional instruction in fostering effective movement from concrete to formal reasoning. Such programs emphasize students' active involvement in learning and cooperative work with other students and deemphasize lectures, which consistently benefit only the most formal of students (Kolodiy 1975).

Epistemology: Precondition for critical thinking

A second dimension of cognitive development that is of great practical importance to college teachers is a student's epistemology: the assumptions he or she makes about the origin of knowledge and value and about the role of authority in learning and life.

A study of several cohorts of Harvard undergraduates (Perry 1970, 1981) identified nine distinct epistemologies or "positions" a student passes through during development and, therefore, different sets of beliefs he or she sequentially holds about content, activities, and roles central to the process of learning in college. Numerous other researchers have confirmed and expanded these findings (Baxter-Magolda 1990a, 1990b, 1992a, 1992b; Baxter-Magolda and Porterfield 1985; Belenky et al. 1986; King and Kitchener 1994; Moore 1989, 1991a). These nine positions are summarized here as four different, sequential levels.

A student currently at the first level, *Dualism,* understands the world in dualities: black-white, right-wrong, good-bad, "my group and its beliefs are good, other groups and their beliefs are bad." All questions, issues, or problems have one right answer or solution; all alternatives are wrong. One learns what is correct and what is the right thing to do from Authorities, because Authorities Know. The Dualist thus depends on authorities and tends to be docile, accepting, and therefore manipulable; "critical thinking" is an inscrutability. Self-critical metacognition, the capacity to examine and critique one's own thoughts, beliefs, and values, is impossible. Dualism constitutes a potential wellspring of ethnocentrism, fanaticism, and self-centered, intolerant ideology of every stripe. Submissiveness to established authorities and self-righteous feelings of superiority over people and groups dissenting from one's own viewpoints characterize dualistic authoritarianism, which can pose great danger to society (Altemeyer 1988).

The second epistemological level is *Multiplicity*. The Multiplist has come to understand that there can be more than one legitimate way to look at a situation, that competent authorities can disagree. But the Multiplist is trapped in subjectivity; in the absence of an agreed-upon Truth, one opinion is as good as another. To have an opinion makes the opinion right: "You have your opinion and I have mine, and that's cool." This shallow "tolerance" of dissent, however, is quite distinct from the thought-through and respectful acceptance of diversity we desire for our students and that society urgently needs. The Multiplist's key cognitive deficiency is not to comprehend the complex, contextual interrelationship of factors and the need to identify these factors carefully and evaluate critically the relative quality of evidence available in support of alternative opinions, ideas, or hypotheses.

Under appropriate conditions, Multiplists can move gradually into the third epistemological level, *Relativism*, whose meaning here is quite different from the common lay use of the term, which is more akin to the subjectivity found in Multiplicity. A Relativist understands the complex, contextual, interrelated nature of the world, and his or her gradually developing critical capacity is deliberately applied to evaluating the quality of evidence adduced in support of claims. Complex relativistic procedures underpin the thinking of all well-educated men and women and experts in every field, presupposing the developed capacity for formal, abstract reasoning. Metacognitive ability and empathy with others first appear at this time.

Finally, having entered the fourth level, *Commitment,* understood today as part of identity formation rather than epistemology per se, a student comes to realize that, despite living in a complex, contingent world, he or she must nevertheless *construct* personal values and principles for living and make personal commitments to people, causes, and career.

Dualism constitutes a potential wellspring of ethnocentrism, fanaticism, and self-centered, intolerant ideology of every stripe.

Clearly, a student's current epistemological level is a key factor affecting his or her response to efforts to induce learning. Dualists may eagerly take notes in traditional lectures but reject appeals for the critical thinking crucial to their development. They may resist cooperative group work with other students, whom they view as lacking credibility as authorities in the field. Both Dualists and Multiplists may be unable to understand the point of carefully collecting and evaluating evidence or of experimental thinking, the basis of much that we teach. Relativists may not yet see a personal need for the commitments that provide a foundation for adult behavior.

Studies consistently show that most of our undergraduates hold Dualistic and Multiplistic epistemologies at the lower end of the scheme. Most first-year students of traditional age are authoritarians (Sanford 1962); Relativists are rare. Sixty-eight percent of 101 Miami University (Ohio) first-year students in one study were Dualists (Baxter-Magolda 1992a). Although many or most students increase in epistemological complexity during college, the movement is slow and uneven. In studies of mostly college undergraduates in diverse institutions, the percentage of students moving one-third or more "Perry Position" (part of a "level" as used here) during one semester ranged from 27 to 56 (W. Moore 1991a). Another study showed an overall change from first year to graduation of less than one-half Perry Position (Mentkowski and Strait 1983). In fact, studies suggest most undergraduate students never reach Relativism. The percentages of undergraduate students testing as Relativists (Perry Position 5) in two samples were only 0.04 (N = 2,757) and 0.26 (N = 391) (calculated from data of William S. Moore, cited in MacGregor 1987). Relativists made up 2 percent of the Miami (Ohio) senior-year samples (N = 80); in the year following graduation, this number had increased to 12 percent (N = 70) (Baxter-Magolda 1992a). A sample of 264 Rutgers University students found no Relativists.*

The implications of these studies are important for the way we attempt to educate students and assess outcomes (King 1978; Knefelkamp and Slepitza 1978). For example,

---

* Contact the author for further information about the study at Rutgers.

why is students' epistemological development in college so slow? If most students do not understand the need for critical evaluation of evidence, how much do they understand (or what are they being asked to do) in their natural and social science courses, for example, and why are most of them not failing their tests in these courses? (See "What Do Classroom Tests Measure?" on p. 60.) If most graduate not yet Relativists, how well prepared are they to understand and deal skillfully with the competing points of view they will confront on important issues in all areas of their lives and professions? How many of our graduates can we claim are critical thinkers?

The percentage of incoming Canadian students who scored "at least 'slightly authoritarian'" increased markedly from 1973 to 1987, from 54 percent to 80 percent (Altemeyer 1988, p. 327), including the upper three of six categories. Altemeyer's work also, however, demonstrates a positive effect of college attendance on reducing authoritarianism. In a society and world increasingly racked by violent division among people based on differences of race, nationality, and religion, developing our students' epistemologies—their understanding of complexity and interrelatedness and their careful use of evidence—is surely one of our most important responsibilities and challenges.

Capacity for principled ethical reasoning: The basis for moral behavior

Higher education in this country has been involved in developing character and values since its inception in 1636 with the founding of Harvard College. Leaders in government, business, religion, and higher education, however, have for some time been urging us to redouble our efforts to ensure graduates have developed the capacity for ethical behavior. Many share this concern for moral education; 85 percent of respondents to the 1989 Carnegie faculty survey believed it was "very important" (41 percent) or "fairly important" (44 percent) to "shape student values in undergraduate education" (Boyer 1989). Many colleges and universities, although by no means all, have their students' moral development as a stated educational outcome. In one study, 31.6 percent of all 19 New Jersey community colleges had as a general education goal for their students to "demonstrate the ability to make informed judgments concerning ethical issues" (College Outcomes Evaluation Program 1990a, p. 47). On the other hand, only one in 12, or 8.3 percent, of public four-year institutions in New Jersey reported having such an intended outcome.

Moral development can be partitioned into four separate but related components: (1) moral or ethical sensitivity—recognizing a situation contains moral issues; (2) moral judgment—determining right action; (3) moral motivation—caring to do the moral thing; and (4) moral character—behaving in a moral way (Rest 1984, 1986, 1994a). The four components are by no means equal in their level of development in any person, but inadequate development in any one of the components can result in moral failure. The components can be assessed separately from each other, and they require different experiences for their development (Bebeau 1994).

Complexity of moral judgment is linked to moral behavior (Bredemeier and Shields 1994; Duckett and Ryden 1994; Ponemon and Gabhart 1994; Rest 1994b; Thoma 1994), and research reveals common patterns in our reasoning about issues with moral content (Colby and Kohlberg 1987; Gilligan 1977, 1981, 1982; Kohlberg 1981; Kohlberg, Boyd, and Levine 1990; Kohlberg, Levine, and Hewer 1983; Nucci and Pascarella 1987; Rest 1979, 1986; Rest and Narváez 1994; Rich and DeVitis 1985). Knowledge of these patterns is essential for those who attempt to foster students' moral development. One's current reasoning about moral issues, situations, or problems depends upon the distance he or she has progressed through a series of discrete, sequential developmental stages, each representing a distinct moral philosophy. Researchers have investigated moral judgment in many diverse populations, among them urban and rural Americans, members of upper and lower social classes, adherents to various religions (Rest 1986, 1994a), and people of many different cultures (Snarey 1985). To the extent to which this conceptual framework remains consistent for such disparate populations, it could represent a truly objective, universal pattern of moral decision making. Knowing our own students' developmental levels provides a means of understanding them and their reasoning about issues with moral content, and it can enable us to develop educational methods effective for helping them continue their development.

At *Stage 1* moral judgment, one's orientation is to punishment and obedience. What is right action is behavior that will avoid punishment and trouble from powers superior to one's own. *Stage 2* moral judgment views right action as serving one's own desires and needs, and sometimes others'. A person adapts to his or her perceptions of what others want: "You scratch my back and I'll scratch yours." Mutual advantage of this sort defines reciprocity, not principles of justice, loyalty, gratitude, or responsibility.

Stage 3 reasoning is sometimes referred to as a "good boy–nice girl" orientation. What is right is what will gain one favor or approval in the eyes of important others. Students at Stage 3 often support stereotypes of majority or "natural" behavior.

Stage 4 judgment supports a law-and-order perspective. A relatively rigid respect for authority and duty, abiding by fixed rules, and maintaining the social order are primary concerns for Stage 4 students. At *Stage 5,* however, students understand the relativity of values in the epistemological sense described earlier. As in Stage 4, the law is important, but morality is here understood more flexibly as based on social consensus; laws are capable of change in response to social need. The official moral philosophy of the United States as expressed in its Constitution resides at Stage 5.

The "autonomous" morality of *Stage 6* is based on universal ethical principles. People reasoning at this stage consider what is right a matter of individual conscience as defined by self-chosen, abstract, and universal ethical principles or values, as distinct from rigid, concrete, Stage 4 laws—the Golden Rule rather than the Ten Commandments. These principles articulate justice, reciprocity, equality, and responsibility among people. Respect for all persons as human beings, regardless of race, ethnic group, or creed, is important to students at this stage. Stage 6 requires the hypothetical reasoning characteristic of abstract, formal operations and a Level 3 relativistic epistemology. Gilligan suggests that women tend to emphasize quality of interpersonal relationships and care-giving responsibilities in considering moral issues (Gilligan 1977, 1982), although most studies do not show gender differences (Thoma 1994). Stages 1 and 2 are Preconventional, Stages 3 and 4 (the modal stages of moral reasoning of most people) Conventional, and Stages 5 and 6 Postconventional.

As one moves through the stages toward more complex, abstract postconventional or principled moral reasoning, thinking is increasingly less selfishly oriented and more able to recognize the rights and needs of others. Most undergraduate college students reason primarily at conventional Stages 3 and 4. Thus, they often learn principled solutions to ethical problems "largely by rote," "have trouble extending principles beyond the cases specifically taught," "are baffled when ideals conflict," and "oversimplify life situations" (Rest 1994b, p. 214). Thinking about moral issues generally increases in complexity and percentage of postconventional principled reasoning through the college years, albeit often relatively slowly (Mentkowski and Strait 1983; Pascarella and Terenzini 1991). Specific educational interventions in college can increase the modal stage of moral reasoning (Bebeau 1994; Duckett and Ryden 1994; McNeel 1994; Rest 1986, 1994b; Self, Olivarez, and Baldwin 1994; Sprinthall 1994; Whiteley 1982; Whiteley and Yokota 1988). Ensuring all our students have ample opportunity to consider relevant moral dilemmas in many different courses, and thus develop their capacity for reasoning about the worth and ethical treatment of others, is crucial to fitting them for effective citizenship and leadership in the state, nation, and world.

Implications for students' development

The ability of our students to increase in these three types of cognitive and ethical development during their college years holds great significance for our diverse, multicultural society. The increased cognitive complexity that attends this development, and thus the capacity for self-knowledge and self-control, brings with it the potential for significant improvement in mutual understanding and respect among disparate groups and the creative solution of our pressing social problems, not to mention superior technological, economic, and artistic productivity. Planned and systematic development of these complex abilities is now essential if our society is to continue to flourish.

How are these abstract cognitive and ethical capacities developed? The cognitive complexity necessary for advanced formal operations or problem-solving ability "is developed . . . through hard, disciplined work in self-critical pursuit of high standards" (Lerner 1989, p. 174). The several major cognitive reorganizations that underpin mature, relativistic epistemology and the capacity to engage in principled ethical reasoning are difficult transformations to make. Authorities agree movement through these interconnected developmental sequences entails the gradual and repeated reconstruction of the way a student views the world.

The development of cognitive complexity happens slowly, involves potential emotional obstructions, and is thought to require extensive practice in reasoning, together with regular assessment, prompt feedback, and reflection. For example, students who use primarily Stage 3 conventional moral reasoning cannot understand and therefore respond to or profit from illustrations, examples, or problems that require postconventional, principled ethical reasoning. If these students are to benefit from our instruction, research suggests they must be approached only slightly above their current level. Further, scant evidence exists that this increase in cognitive complexity can be developed passively through lectures, automatically through the steady acquisition of facts and concepts, or through learning "steps" in "how to think." "There is little doubt that higher levels of cognitive and moral reasoning cannot be directly taught" (Johnson and Johnson 1989, p. 49).

The evidence that people cannot understand epistemologies or moral reasoning more than one level or stage beyond their own—the concept of "plus one"—suggests our instruction needs to be carefully designed so that, wherever he or she is developmentally situated, a student can engage in personally meaningful activities in a broad diversity of disciplinary, moral, emotional, and social contexts that can ease movement toward the next higher level of complexity. We need to know at what point students are in their development if we are to achieve the educational effects we want. We also need the essential body of professional knowledge and array of skills that can enable us to accomplish this difficult developmental task, the central core of the teaching profession.

Ability for cooperative work: The basis for community
Developed interpersonal skills and the ability to work effectively in teams with others have become high priorities for employers. What does research tell us about the value of cooperation? To what extent should we emphasize coop-

eration as compared to primarily individual work or competition? (Kohn 1992; Rich and DeVitis 1992). A meta-analysis of 521 studies comparing the relative effects of cooperative, competitive, and individualistic behavior on many different outcomes, 40 percent of which were conducted in college and university settings, found individual efforts consistently outperformed competitive efforts where the two approaches were compared (Johnson and Johnson 1989). Cooperation, however, was generally more effective than either competition or individual work in producing desired outcomes. Fifty percent of the studies produced statistically significant effects in favor of cooperation; only 10 percent favored competition or individual effort.

The meta-analysis showed that cooperative learning, as compared to competitive or individual learning, led to higher-level reasoning ability and greater retention of learning for students at all levels of schooling. Students showed both movement among Piagetian stages of cognitive development and an increase in their level of moral reasoning. These effects are induced, not by discussion among students per se, but by intellectual conflict between alternative explanations—argument and counterargument. Learning that occurs in groups can transfer to individual students when they are tested later by themselves. The difference in impact between cooperative and individual learning is particularly notable for the higher-level thinking skills of analysis, synthesis, and evaluation as compared with low-level recall, comprehension, and plug-and-play formula application (see "Understanding cognitive outcomes" on p. 41).

Cooperative activities overwhelmingly more often had a positive effect on self-esteem than did competitive or individual activities. A number of studies in the meta-analysis examined the personality characteristic of competitiveness versus the degree of success achieved in many diverse endeavors. In every case, for every group of people, a negative correlation existed between competitiveness and accomplishment. Studies showed that competition lowers artistic performance and undergraduates' ability to solve problems. Moreover, competition breeds a number of untoward emotional symptoms. Competition is usually adverse to community: For one to win, others must lose.

A cooperative effort among students can also provide an opportunity to develop not only skill in critical, evaluative thinking, but also skill at what has been called "connected knowing" (Belenky et al. 1986; Clinchy 1989). Rather than focusing on judgment and evaluation, skills of critical thinking, the focus of connected knowing is on understanding another person and his or her perspective. Connected knowing or learning requires the key skills of placing oneself in another's stead, of listening carefully, of hearing accurately how another person is reasoning, understanding the world, and feeling. These skills are essential today, not only for academic, intellectual effectiveness, but also for comprehending and having an impact on an increasingly diverse, fractious, and violent world. They are essential for building community.

The Role of Students' Active Involvement

Considerable research over the last three decades has explored the relationship between students' active involvement in college—with academic work, intellectual issues, the faculty, and other students—and the development of various outcomes (Astin 1977, 1984, 1993; Feldman and Newcomb 1969; Pace 1984, 1990; Pascarella 1985; Pascarella and Terenzini 1991). Based on a review of 2,600 empirical studies of college's effects on students, "One of the most inescapable and unequivocal conclusions . . . is that the impact of college is largely determined by the individual's quality of effort and level of involvement in both academic and nonacademic activities" (Pascarella and Terenzini 1991, p. 610).

Involvement with people is one of the most important ways of inducing student development in college. Informal, out-of-class contact between students and faculty is correlated with many important outcomes, such as intellectual level, interpersonal skills, educational aspirations, autonomy and independence, and attainment and interest in scholarly careers (Pascarella and Terenzini 1991). "The most influential interactions appear to be those that focus on ideas or intellectual matters, thereby extending and reinforcing the intellectual goals of the academic program" (p. 620).

A study involving 24,847 students, 146 input variables, 192 college environment (process) variables, and 82 student outcomes (having statistically removed the effects of the input and environmental factors) concludes:

Student-faculty interaction has significant positive correlations with every *academic attainment outcome . . . ,* every self-reported area of intellectual and personal growth, as well as with a variety of personality and attitudinal outcomes . . . and . . . all self-rated abilities except physical health *(Astin 1993, p. 383, emphasis in the original).*

Thus, "frequent interaction between faculty and students" is desirable (p. 384).

Interaction between and among students shows a similar effect on development. "Once again, . . . a pervasive pattern of positive benefits [is] associated with frequent student-student interaction" (Astin 1993, p. 385). "The student's peer group is the single most potent source of influence on growth and development during the undergraduate years" (p. 398), and efforts "to find ways to engage students in extracurricular activities" (p. 386) are valuable.

The concepts of students' involvement (Astin 1984) and their quality of effort (Pace 1984) are similar to integration in campus life (Pascarella and Terenzini 1991), an important means for retaining students on campus until graduation (Tinto 1987, 1993). Put another way, in addition to its potent direct developmental effects, the involvement of students can serve to retain them on campus, an obvious precondition of development. "Involvement indices make up one of the most important and perhaps accurate ways of assessing quality" on campus (Kuh 1981, p. 2).

On the basis of these lines of research (and others), students of human development today generally view the process of cognitive development as a gradual one in which students construct an increasingly complex, finely textured, and abstract personal reality. This construction of knowledge can be envisioned as occurring through an active, dialectical process whereby a student continually interacts with his or her environment. The interaction can involve the interposition of concepts within a student's own mind or external phenomena, including other people (another student or a teacher). In college, as in life more generally, the process of construction often involves two or more people working together to understand and solve problems—*to make meaning.*

Conditions for Educational Quality: A Summary

A number of specific conditions, generally agreed upon by researchers (see Astin 1993; Chickering and Gamson 1987, 1991; Pascarella and Terenzini 1991; Study Group 1984), are thought to foster the development of these key college- and university-level competencies.

1. *Challenge.* Students need to be provided with activities aimed just above their current levels of cognitive development so they can both understand and be challenged by them (Sanford 1966). These activities can set up important tensions or conflicts—cognitive dissonances—with students' current understandings of the world and thus have developmental value by stimulating them to take one step beyond their present level.

2. *A supportive environment.* Both intellectual assistance in comprehending and emotional support when reflecting are required from teachers and peers alike (Sanford 1966). The cognitive changes students experience during development can lead to considerable inner turmoil as one view of the world is challenged and gradually replaced by another. The risks of damaging self-esteem, stalling development, or provoking outright retreat from painful confrontations with the world are always present (Perry 1970, 1981).

3. *Sustained, diverse, and appropriate active involvement in learning.* Students should be kept busy reading, writing, solving, designing, and interacting cooperatively with peers and professors, both in class and outside of class, and reflecting on these experiences. They should be kept constantly thinking and feeling. Two fundamental principles underlie the conditions of educational excellence (Study Group 1984). First, "the amount of student learning and personal development associated with any educational program is directly proportional to the quality and quantity of [students'] involvement in that program," and, second, "the effectiveness of any educational policy or practice is directly related to the capacity of that policy or practice to increase [students'] involvement in learning" (p. 19). Students learn what they study.

"The effectiveness of any educational policy or practice is directly related to the capacity of that policy or practice to increase [students'] involvement in learning."

4. *High expectations.* Expectations for quality of educational outcomes should be high. Considerable research has demonstrated that hard, challenging goals can substantially increase one's productivity, while no goals or easy goals may actually set low ceilings for performance and thus actually retard quality of effort (Locke and Latham 1984, 1990).

5. *Clearly defined outcomes, frequent assessment, and prompt feedback.* Knowing clearly what desired outcomes should be and having specific and timely knowledge of actual results achieved contribute powerfully to improving performance (Locke and Latham 1984, 1990). Students need to know what they should know and be able to do and, on a regular basis, how well they have succeeded in their efforts.

To what extent do our current practices in colleges and universities capitalize on this valuable knowledge about our students? To what degree do we now use methods that are known empirically to work? Do our educational processes conform to what experts today regard as high-quality, accepted professional practice? What is the quality of the outcomes we produce? Can we improve the quality of our educational processes by applying this research more actively and thus significantly improve the quality of our results?

The next four sections examine research exploring four core components of students' experiences on campus that are central to their development and therefore critical to maintaining and improving an institution's quality: curriculum, instruction, psychological climate of the campus, and academic advising.

THE CURRICULUM: Framework for Development

Based on an institution's own values and philosophy, the curriculum determines the pattern of courses a student takes and should thereby ensure, for each person, the intellectual rigor, depth, and balance among the types of learning needed for his or her effective personal and professional development. Students need to learn concepts and principles, to develop cognitive and motor skills, and to develop attitudes and values that will be important to them and to society. Central to their success is the selection of particular courses that will provide specific, developmentally appropriate experiences. The curriculum should be more than a sum of constituent parts. In both general education and a student's major field of concentration, it should serve as a map to integrate its parts and help construct a coherent, thought-out view of self and the world.

To what extent do students now engage in such experiences in a planned and systematic fashion? To what degree does the curriculum foster the kinds of learning most important for each person? Providing definitive answers to these questions has been difficult. Research on the structure and effects of curricula is limited (Stark and Lowther 1986). Relatively little research exists on patterns of courses taken and the specific outcomes these courses produce. "The prevalent way to view the college curriculum refers to its intentions, not (cf. p. 8) . . . its results" (Ratcliff and Associates 1990, p. 7). Although without research we cannot be sure our in-tended outcomes become our actual outcomes, it is generally perceived that U.S. college and department curricula generally are much less effective and efficient than they might be.

Difficulty in understanding the effectiveness of curricula is more basic than a lack of social science research, however. Few institutions specify in clear detail their intended educational results or outcomes—what their graduates should know and be able to do. Moreover, because most do not systematically assess how much their students have learned through their curricula, few colleges and universities have an accurate idea of their actual educational outcomes or results, much less which curricular processes have produced them. Assessment, of both outcomes and educational processes, can demonstrate that the curriculum is having its intended effects. The following discussion reviews findings of some of the limited studies available that suggest answers to several key questions about college and university curricula.

Design of the Curriculum: Focusing on Students' Development
Do distributional curricula serve students' developmental needs?

The "distribution" system of general education curricula, in which students fulfill requirements for graduation by choosing from menus of courses, is used by over 90 percent (Astin 1993) to 97 percent (Hutchings, Marchese, and Wright 1991) of U.S. colleges and universities. A majority of these curricula are similar to each other. In a study of 303 institutions with distributional curricula, over half (53 percent) of the curricula could not be "distinguished by any unique features" (Hurtado, Astin, and Dey 1991, p. 145).

Distributional curricula ordinarily provide students with considerable latitude when choosing their courses. High-quality, development-oriented academic advising is therefore essential to enable our diverse, often seriously under-prepared and naive, students to choose wisely among potentially confusing curricular options so they can meet their own developmental needs.

A comprehensive national study of thousands of students found, for curricula that allowed students to choose among various distributional general education courses, that the specific curricular structure in an institution made little difference for most of the 22 general education outcomes studied (Astin 1993). The types and breadth of courses available to students, the specific courses included in a curriculum, and the relative freedom of choice had no "substantial effect on how students develop" (p. 425). Astin found, however, that a "true-core" interdisciplinary curriculum, characteristic of fewer than 2 percent of the hundreds of institutions in his sample, where all students take the same, identical general education courses, did have a positive effect on many developmental outcomes, as well as on several aspects of students' satisfaction with college. "Most of these effects appear to be uniquely attributable to having a true-core curriculum" (p. 332). Astin suggests that, consistent with his overall finding of a powerful influence on a student by his or her peers, "the beneficial effects of a true-core curriculum may be mediated by the peer group . . .

[by providing] a common experience that can stimulate student discussion outside class and facilitate formation of strong bonds among student peers" (p. 425). In other words, "how the students *approach* general education (and how the faculty actually *deliver* the curriculum) is far more important than the formal curriculum content and structure" (p. 425, emphasis in the original).

This true core may lead to learning that is superior to that produced by distributional curricula through adapting more effectively to students' diverse needs by providing the more frequent student-student contact and peer-based learning that may come through this widely shared, common educational experience. Such experiences therefore may not only lead to the development of a higher level of cognitive skill but also foster a stronger sense of community on campus, which may in turn produce the positive association Astin found between a true-core curriculum and students' satisfaction with and staying in college.

A study of the gains made in specific competencies at "Western University," a private research university, by graduating seniors who had scored relatively high or relatively low on their SATs found that various groups of courses were correlated with gains, or declines, in specific competencies for high- and low-ability groups of students (Jones and Ratcliff 1990). The researchers suggest their results are consistent with and support the development of different curricular patterns for various types of students, depending on the specific competencies to be developed. This research does not support the developmental value of distributional curricula, but it does emphasize the importance of adapting curricula to the individual needs of different kinds of students.

> *[It] does not support the current use of a wide range of options in a distributional general education requirement. Instead, it suggests that discrete arrays of coursework be identified [that] are more appropriate and productive for different ability levels of students. . . . In the majority of cases, Western University coursework chosen by high-ability students led to gains in learned abilities, as measured by the GRE. The converse was true for the low-ability students; here the majority of coursework chosen did not lead to gains in general learning. Nevertheless,*

discrete sets of coursework were identified that were beneficial to these students. These results suggest the need for greater academic advising in the undergraduate course selection or greater prescription in the curriculum (Jones and Ratcliff 1990, p. 37, emphasis in the original).

Unfortunately, academic advising at most institutions lacks a developmental focus (see "Academic Advising: Guiding Development" beginning on p. 87). Students often pick courses without the essential developmental context skilled guidance could provide. Lack of careful advising, coupled with ill-defined outcomes for both curricula and courses, may have serious educational results.

Student transcripts often reflect a sense of educational wandering, if not drift. By graduation most have come to understand that their degrees have more to do with the successful accumulation of credits than with the purposeful pursuit of knowledge. At most selective institutions, attrition rates remain stubbornly high, with most of the loss occurring in the first year of instruction ("Learning Slope" 1991, p. 3A).

"At far too many institutions, the distribution requirements of general education are unfocused. They encourage randomness, not coherence . . ." (Boyer 1990a, p. 14). "We're kind of like a McUniversity, a smorgasbord of fast food," one student told Carnegie researchers.

Are liberal arts programs practical?

A few studies compare outcomes for students in liberal arts curricula with those in narrower, vocationally oriented programs. In one study, an emphasis on liberal arts significantly increased African-American male students' choice of higher prestige, more demanding, and typically white careers, and attending a liberal arts college increased women's selection of gender-atypical careers (Pascarella and Terenzini 1991). In another study, students enrolled in liberal arts curricula showed over twice the reduction in authoritarianism of other students. Although, as first-year students, they started with lower scores on authoritarianism than nursing and business majors, the decrease in the scores of liberal arts majors over four years of university coursework was "particularly dramatic . . . and significantly greater than the others" (Altemeyer 1988, p. 92).

Liberal arts students also show greater gains in moral judgment (McNeel 1994). In fact, some vocationally oriented major programs may actually produce a decrement in moral development. "Business and education majors were much more likely to show significant decreases in principled reasoning" (McNeel 1994, p. 34). Accounting majors generally have lower scores on moral judgment than other, nonbusiness majors in several studies (Ponemon and Gabhart 1994)—with even lower scores found among senior accountants and partners in CPA firms. In other studies, " . . . veterinary medical education appears to inhibit the increase in moral reasoning . . ." (Self, Olivarez, and Baldwin 1994, p. 166), and medical students tended not to increase in the quality of their moral reasoning (Self and Baldwin 1994, p. 160). What may be the impact on society, especially on its school children, if vocational curricula preparing teachers and other professionals retard their moral development? The potential for moral development in college is suggested by average effect sizes revealed to be among the largest college impacts examined (McNeel 1994). What would be the effects on society if we agreed to define moral development as a formal outcome goal and resolutely set about to produce it across the curriculum?

While careful design of the curriculum can lead students through a rational and relevant sequence of experiences that can lay out for them a clear and appropriate developmental map, the results of a detailed study by the Association of American Colleges of curricular focus, breadth, and depth based on the transcripts of all 19,086 1987 graduates from 30 diverse colleges and universities suggest that "the undergraduate curriculum in the liberal arts lack[s] . . . sufficient breadth of study, particularly in the natural sciences and mathematics, and . . . substantial depth . . ." (Zemsky 1989, p. 36). "In common sense terms, there is a notable absence of structure and coherence in college and university curricula" (p. 7).

Do students share a common educational experience?
Are certain outcomes of such personal and social importance that all students should have achieved them? Are certain formative experiences for students so central to their

development that everyone should share them? If common learning is important, is the curriculum now providing it? And do other curricula provide for students the important shared experiences of peer groups suggested for true-core curricula?

Students at the previously mentioned "Western University" shared very little of their formal learning with each other (Jones and Ratcliff 1990). Only 15 to 20 percent of a student's courses were taken in common with at least five other students in the same high- or low-ability sample of students. Thus, although diverse curricular options can be an institutional strength, it can also be a weakness. The central concern is the extent to which diversity in the curriculum enhances or dilutes the quality of student outcomes. The good effects of a "true-core" curriculum relative to distributed curricula stand out prominently here.

One striking discontinuity in students' educational experience emerges from an analysis of transcripts including 485,000 courses taken by 12,600 American undergraduates (Adelman 1990). Men and women students take very different sets of courses: "From high school through graduate school there is a men's curriculum and a women's curriculum" (p. 242). And nearly two-thirds of the 82 college outcomes in one study reflected "significant gender effects" (Astin 1993). What might be the implications for students' and society's development of such a striking disjunction in the college experience?

Effects of the Curriculum's Courses
Should "general education" be confined to the first two years?
Some four-year institutions encourage students to finish their required general education courses during their first two years. Often students regard most of the curriculum not related to their major as a necessary evil, as something they must sit through to get a college degree (Moffatt 1989, p. 282). In a survey of Harvard seniors who expressed disappointment with their courses, however, almost every one "chose classes in [the] freshman year 'to get the requirements out of the way'" (Light 1992, p. 53). Many students do not understand the importance of the general education curriculum, possibly because of poorly defined outcomes and lack of developmental academic advising.

Beyond the unfortunate implication of the personal irrelevance of general education compared to the more narrow, specialized, and professionally oriented learning associated with a major, if our focus is on students' development rather than the mere fulfillment of requirements, such a policy could be counterproductive. While certain important competencies are developed in lower-division courses, upper-division courses "[contribute] strongly to the development of specific learned abilities, particularly analytic reasoning" (Jones and Ratcliff 1990, p. 38). Quantitative abilities, for example, are developed not only by lower-division mathematics courses, but also in certain applied courses in business and in the natural and social sciences, suggesting that general education "should . . . extend vertically, from the freshman to the senior years" (Boyer 1987, p. 101). The slow development of higher-order cognitive skills and other important, slow-to-develop skills should be fostered deliberately—in general education courses and in the major as well, and not only during the first and second years, but throughout the college experience.

What is the role of introductory courses?
Introductory courses underpin a student's understanding of the various disciplines and professional fields, and many students never take later, advanced courses in fields outside their majors. Yet most faculty in a national study said material that would familiarize students with the modes of inquiry characteristic of their fields should be left for advanced courses (Stark et al. 1988). If faculty practice what they believe, how can the undergraduate general education curriculum enable students to understand and use effectively the diverse epistemologies of these fields? In most cases, are these ways of reasoning not precisely the most important contributions to the curriculum expected of these introductory courses?

Do required courses have their intended effects?
Although the actual assessed achievement of outcomes for students in one study at four diverse institutions was not necessarily related to the courses required by the institution, it was related to other patterns of courses (Ratcliff and Associates 1990). And our general failure to specify clearly the outcomes or results we expect from either curricula or

courses could be significant here: Planning, implementation, and assessment become difficult without clear direction. (See also "Instruction: Teaching, Testing, and Communicating Outcomes" beginning on p. 37 for other possible reasons for this disjunction between curricular requirements and results.)

Overall Effects of the Curriculum
How much is learned through the curriculum?

A study of the transcripts of 73 graduating university seniors, some of whom had high scores on their SATs and some of whom had low scores, that involved over 4,000 courses examined students' "general learned abilities" upon graduation (Jones and Ratcliff 1990). Students' abilities were assessed by GRE general test results after the effects of precollege learning, as assessed by the SAT, were statistically removed. The study revealed that, once students' precollege learning had been removed, neither students in the high-score group nor the low-score group showed strong positive gains from their college experiences. In both groups, some students had gained in general learned ability, while others had actually declined in ability. The results of the study led the investigators to conclude that the average student at that university did not select coursework associated "with gains in general learned abilities" (p. 20). They further concluded that different curricular patterns could contribute to general learned abilities in different ways and that courses at different levels throughout the curriculum are correlated with gains in students' abilities. Similarly, some groups of courses were associated with declines in specific abilities, such as analytic reasoning. Further research would be required to explain why certain courses are associated with gains or declines in particular competencies.

What does a transcript of courses signify?

The research reviewed here calls into serious question the widespread practice of mechanically certifying students for graduation on the basis of the number of credits they have accumulated. The effects of individual courses on different students can be quite diverse. For example, students are at very different stages with respect to a number of dimensions of their development and thus their capacity to understand and profit from specific courses. "Exposure" to these activities is not enough. "Simple counts of the number of credits or courses a student has taken in a particular subject may not be a reliable proxy of general learning in the attendant subject area" (Ratcliff and Associates 1990, p. 43). More effective would be the use of high-quality developmental advising coupled with defining clearly the specific competencies to be developed—student outcomes rather than educational processes—and then assessing achievement of the actual outcomes. Here the emphasis is placed squarely on results of both students and institutions rather than on the time spent in courses.

Once students' precollege learning had been removed, neither students in the high-score group nor the low-score group showed strong positive gains from their college experiences.

How well do our curricula serve society's needs?
America's college curricula undeniably play a key role in ensuring society's well-being. Much evidence now suggests, however, that they are not contributing what they are capable of and what is needed.

> *Much about postsecondary learning is inappropriate for adult learners . . . , [including] insufficient individualization, needless repetition, and inadequate recognition of prior learning. . . . Higher education institutions themselves remain a major impediment to addressing the nation's needs for resources for adult learning. . . . There is significant resistance in many four-year colleges and universities to making the accommodation necessary* (Commission on Higher 1984, p. 7).

Further, a consortium of top-level leaders in American higher education notes that although "there has been great interest in curriculum revitalization, the sense lingers that results have been disappointing. Core issues have too often been avoided. Hodgepodge courses and experiences have passed for undergraduate education" (Irvine Group 1990, p. 2).

> *Over the past decade, undergraduate renewal has relied on curricular patterns that have not worked well. Outmoded distribution requirements, for example, where students select courses from broad academic fields, usually have failed to accomplish what is intended. These courses amount to electives, not general education. . . . Merely reconfiguring the undergraduate curriculum, dropping*

*or adding elements without addressing fundamental top-
ics, achieves little* (p. 2).

To express its perceived incoherent, hodgepodge character,
this distribution system has been variously and irreverently
dubbed a supermarket, cafeteria, grab bag, or green-stamp
endeavor (accumulate credits, paste 'em in, and redeem
'em for a diploma).

Although prominent critiques of college curricula are perhaps most widely known (e.g., Project on Redefining 1985),
concern about curricular quality is not limited to general
education, the liberal arts, or the undergraduate level. Many
specialized undergraduate and graduate curricula, from
accounting to veterinary medicine, have been criticized as
well (see, e.g., Evangelauf 1989 and Wyer 1993 [account-
ing]; American Institute 1990 and Committee on Education
1984 through 1990 [biology]; Field 1995 [dentistry]; American
Economics 1990 [economics]; Blum 1992, Johnston, Shaman, and Zemsky 1987, and "Universities Need" 1995 [engi-
neering]; Commission on Admission 1990 [graduate man-
agement]; "Better History" 1992 [history]; Project on the
Future 1984 [journalism]; Burrows 1990 and Panel 1984
[medicine]; Project on Liberal Education 1990 [natural sci-
ence]; Altman 1989 [premedicine]; Holmes Group 1995,
Lively 1993, Olson 1986, and Winkler 1985 [teacher educa-
tion]; Aerospace Education Foundation 1989 [technology];
and Monaghan 1988 [veterinary medicine]).

Conclusions

Although much more research is needed to help us understand the effects of curricula, the results reviewed here are
both instructive and consistent. This research suggests that
college and university curricula, as they now function, in
many cases do not produce the results we intend and that
"the curriculum is no longer achieving its intended purpose" (Fife 1991, p. xiii). In most cases, curricula unfocused
by clear statements of intended outcomes that permit naive
students broad choices among courses result in markedly
different outcomes from those imagined.

We should pay much more attention to the way the curriculum is presented and how students interact with it
(Astin 1993). Institutions need far better information about
their students' developmental needs as they enter the insti-

tution and their achievement as they move through their curricula. Essential are a clear definition of intended outcomes, knowledge of how each course or curricular component interacts with students' developmental levels, learning styles, developed competencies upon entrance, and other important variables, and specific information on how these components contribute to each outcome produced. Do some courses contribute especially to the development of important outcomes? Do some contribute little? Do certain groups of courses, when taken in sequence, have predictable, significant effects on students' development greater than the sum of their individual contributions? Regular assessment is essential to students' development. In addition, advising must be far more sophisticated to orient and guide our widely diverse students as they construct curricular paths most appropriate to their individual development.

INSTRUCTION: Teaching, Testing, and Communicating Outcomes

What Do We Teach and What Do They Learn?

A college's courses are the flesh on its curricular frame, and curricula produce their developmental effects through the courses they comprise. A larger and more specific body of research exists on instruction than on curricula. This section reviews studies related to several key aspects of instruction, each of which has important effects on our capacity to produce learning: instructional methods and the intellectual climate and degree of active involvement students experience; the quality of assessment of learning outcomes; and faculty grading practices.

What professors and students do in the classroom

Courses are a college's primary means for helping students to develop. Many instructional methods are available today, and the efficacy of a number of them for enhancing students' development is well documented. To what extent do the courses we teach employ established principles of quality instruction—principles of professional practice accepted by experts? In other words, to what degree are the courses we teach characterized by clearly defined outcomes, effective means of assessing results, and timely feedback for students on their progress; high expectations; a challenging environment for the development of higher-order skills; and a sustained high level of diverse and active involvement in learning for students?

Instructional design. High-quality instructional design is characterized by, among other features, clearly stated outcome goals and objectives that describe the specific curricular outcomes a course attempts to produce; it is also characterized by the educational activities capable of developing them. A national study of faculty teaching introductory courses reveals that effective thinking was the "overwhelming choice" of educational purpose stated by respondents (Stark et al. 1990). When asked open-ended questions about goals for their courses, however, of 4,000 goals provided by these same faculty, the most frequently mentioned was "teaching the concepts of the field"; relatively few goals mentioned intellectual development. In addition, "very few faculty members contributed goals focused on value development or 'learning the great ideas of humanity'" (p. 115). Detailed interviews with 89 faculty members about the processes they use to plan courses found only 35 percent strongly emphasized their program's or the college's curricular goals, only 12 percent used feedback from previous students, and 8 percent emphasized the views of experts in instruction (Stark et al. 1988). Further, "they rarely mentioned making choices among alternative instructional strategies" (p. 227). Thus, "the faculty interviewed seemed to teach as they had been taught and to have acquired course-planning skills on the job" (p. 227).

The Lecture System. A study of nearly 1,800 faculty members at five different types of institutions found that, regardless of institutional type (large or small, public or independent, community college or research university), an average of 73 to 83 percent of respondents chose the lecture as their principal instructional method over discussion, recitation, lab/shop, applied instruction (in music), and individualized instruction (Blackburn et al. 1980). "Give . . . faculty almost any kind of class in any subject, large or small, upper or lower division, and they will lecture" (p. 41). Other studies have repeatedly confirmed the pervasiveness of the lecture. Recent research by Thielens found the lecture method was the modal instructional method used by "89 percent of the physical scientists and mathematicians, 81 percent of the social scientists, and 61 percent of the humanities faculty (although 81 percent of the art historians and 90 percent of the philosophers lectured)" (Bonwell and Eison 1991, p. 3). A report by the Association of American Medical Colleges points out that 37 percent of North American medical schools scheduled over 1,000 hours of lectures for the first two-year, preclinical medicine curriculum, and another 42 percent scheduled between 800 and 1,000 hours (Panel 1984). With "abundant evidence [indicating] that the educational yield from lectures is generally low" (p. 12), the report recommends reducing scheduled lectures by one-third to one-half and allowing students unscheduled time for more productive learning activities.

Since the medieval universities of Paris and Bologna (Haskins 1957), the lecture has shown remarkable durability in the face of technological advances and the often sharp attacks of its critics, themselves dating back almost as far (McLeish 1968). But how effective are lectures in fostering important outcomes for students? A review of five different studies concludes that students learn more from reading complex material than they do from listening to lectures about it (Davis and Alexander 1977a). Further, two of the studies reviewed conclude that the process of trying to take notes from a lecture, although useful for aiding recall later on and in raising test scores, can interfere with immediate retention of information communicated in a lecture (Davis and Alexander 1977a).

A review of 17 studies comparing lectures to discussions concludes that lectures are as effective as discussions for learning low-level factual material (McKeachie 1986), but research clearly favors discussion over the lecture as an instructional method when the variables studied are retention of information after a course is over, transfer of knowledge to novel situations, development of skill in thinking or problem solving, or achievement of affective outcomes, such as motivation for additional learning or change in attitudes—in other words, the kinds of learning we most care about. A review of seven additional studies (Davis and Alexander 1977a) supports this finding.

Other studies suggest further limitations of lectures as means of student development. A review of four studies (Davis and Alexander 1977a) reveals that students who benefit most from lectures are those who are "brighter," better educated, and from families of higher socioeconomic status, in other words, presumably those students with relatively highly developed abstract reasoning skills. (The studies on which these statements are based were all completed when students were better prepared for college than they often now are, long before the opening in the 1960s and 1970s of colleges and universities to all citizens, and the appearance on campuses of large numbers of students from disadvantaged backgrounds.) But two other studies cited by Davis, Fry, and Alexander (1977) suggest that even more able students gain more from discussions than from more directive methods, such as lectures.

Virtually every model for teaching thinking and fostering intellectual development advocates extensive student-teacher and student-student discussion. But engaging students in classroom dialogue is not always easy. Dialogue in college classrooms is scarce; teachers' questions are dominated by requests for factual information. . . . Class discussions often stay at the level of "quiz shows," "rambling bull" sessions, or "wrangling bull" sessions (Kurfiss 1988, p. 66).

In a "quiz show," teachers merely ask students for information and, by doing so, may reinforce a concrete, fact-oriented, dualistic epistemology. "Rambling bull sessions" consist of students multiplistically sharing unchallenged opinions, "wrangling bull sessions" of students dogmatically arguing their opinions on a controversial topic. Both types of bull sessions may reinforce rather than challenge cognitively simplistic dualist or multiplistic epistemologies by failing to demand carefully reasoned contextual evaluation of evidence.

Samuel Johnson long ago produced his own straightforward critique of lectures:

> *People have now adays . . . got a strange opinion that every thing should be taught by lectures. Now, I cannot see that lectures can do so much good as reading the books from which the lectures are taken. . . . Lectures were once useful; but now, when all can read, and books are so numerous, lectures are unnecessary* (Boswell's *Life of Samuel Johnson, LL.D.*, pp. 144, 471).*

The intellectual climate of the college classroom

Among the outcomes most widely desired by faculty, and of highest value to both students and society, are the higher-order cognitive skills and dispositions of critical thinking, complex problem solving, and principled ethical reasoning. These abilities and orientations depend on high levels of abstraction and are characterized by their use of analysis, synthesis, and evaluation. These skills require for their development the explicit teaching of specific ways of thinking (heuristics), copious practice (students' active involvement), frequent assessment of progress, and timely corrective feedback (McKeachie et al. 1990; Woods 1987). What does research tell us about the effectiveness of college courses in fostering intellectual development? Are some disciplines more productive than others? Do the intellectual

---

*James Boswell, *Life of Samuel Johnson, LL.D.* (Chicago: Encyclopedia Britannica, 1952).

challenges we give our students increase as the semester progresses? Are the cognitive demands more rigorous in advanced than in lower-level courses? Does class level or institutional size or type make a difference for students' intellectual experience?

Understanding cognitive outcomes. In an attempt to clarify thinking and communication, many have tried to classify the specific competencies we seek to develop in students (Lenning 1977). The model of cognitive behavior that has received the widest use in educational planning and practice—and that has over the last four decades become for many educators one of their most highly valued professional tools—is the Taxonomy of Educational Objectives or "Bloom Taxonomy" (Bloom 1956). This model is commonly used in the research discussed in the following paragraphs and thus is briefly described here. Teachers can also easily use to good effect the techniques found in these studies when defining their intended outcomes as learning objectives and when assessing the actual outcomes their courses produce.

The taxonomy organizes cognitive behavior into six levels:

1. Knowledge, here referred to as *Recall* (Paul 1995, chap. 10), requiring memory alone;
2. *Comprehension*, which includes acquisition of concepts and principles;
3. *Application*, in which concepts and principles are used in new, albeit straightforward situations;
4. *Analysis*, which involves the disassembly of wholes to identify their constituent parts, themes, or organizing principles;
5. *Synthesis*, in which novel wholes are assembled from parts; and
6. *Evaluation*, which involves judgment of relative value or quality.

The last three levels are all involved in critical thinking and complex problem solving, including principled ethical reasoning. They are thought of as constituting higher-order intellectual processes—the skills we value most.

The taxonomy is valuable for our work as teachers. With its use, any question asked of or by a student, or any problem, activity, or assignment, can be rated as to its probable cognitive requirements for a successful answer or solution or its completion. The taxonomy has long been used to control the cognitive level of each item in assessments of students' learning. Collectively, a test's overall cognitive demands can be determined directly and easily.

Students' active involvement with thinking. When students are in class, how much of the time are they actively involved in thinking? Is the time they spend in class correlated with the development of their cognitive skills? A series of studies of the verbal and intellectual dynamics in various undergraduate and graduate learning situations provides insight into the cognitive character of our instruction (Ellner and Barnes 1983).

An analysis of audiotapes of 155 class sessions in 40 undergraduate courses at two private and two public institutions used a modified version of the Taxonomy of Educational Objectives to examine the intellectual climate and the quality of questioning in the classes (Fischer and Grant 1983). Talk in the classroom primarily involved the transmission of facts; recall-level discussion was almost twice as common as discussion rated at all five other cognitive levels together. This result held true regardless of discipline, time in the semester, or institutional size.

Although professors in classes of all sizes mostly employed recall-level discourse, class size significantly affected the cognitive skills used by students. Students in small classes (15 students or fewer) used an average median thinking level of analysis, those in medium-size classes (16 to 45 students) used comprehension, and those in large classes (46 to 300 students) used recall. Thus, the thinking level expressed orally by students in small and medium-sized classes was higher than that of their professors. As professors became more direct in their teaching style, giving students less choice on how to respond, students' level of thinking decreased; as professors became more indirect, students' cognitive level rose. "Despite a ratio of 47 [students] to 1 [professor], professors talked four times more frequently than students" (Fischer and Grant 1983, p. 56). Further, "as professors talked more, students reduced their use of cognitive skills" (p. 56).

From antiquity, questions have been one of a teacher's choicest professional tools. An analysis of professors' questioning behavior, based on the same audiotapes described earlier, concludes that the professors teaching those 155 classes spent little time questioning students (Barnes 1983). The percentage of class time devoted to questioning ranged from 0.2 percent to 9.2 percent (if the single lowest and single highest percentages, 0.03 and 20.8, respectively, were dropped). No significant difference occurred regardless of institutional type or size, level of course (beginning or advanced), or discipline.

Questions asked in class were analyzed for the level of thinking skill required for students to answer them. Memory-level (recall) questions accounted for 89.3 percent of all questions asked. Results did not differ between public and private institutions or between large and small institutions. Evaluation-level thinking, the highest level in the Taxonomy of Educational Objectives, occurred only 0.3 percent to 2.5 percent of the time.

As the cognitive level of instructors' questions rose, the level of students' responses also rose. As professors asked more recall-level questions, students' cognitive level decreased. Almost a third (31.9 percent) of all questions asked by faculty resulted in no participation by students. "Not only were many of the classes void of intellectual interchange between professor and students, but they also lacked excitement and vigor" (Barnes 1983, p. 79). Other studies support this finding. A study of 19 University of Texas–Austin faculty members found their most common questions had to do with mechanical issues, such as time or handouts, or were rhetorical, where students' responses were unnecessary (Lewis 1984). Most content-related questions involved recall and comprehension.

A study of audiotapes and 138 student questionnaires from the classes of 12 professors evenly divided among the humanities and natural and social sciences at a small liberal arts college noted for its use of diverse teaching styles found significant changes in students' critical thinking ability (Smith 1983). Based on scores achieved on critical-thinking tests during the semester, changes in students' ability were significantly and positively correlated with levels of praise from faculty, interaction among students, and high-level cognitive responses from students in class. As

Small classes used an average median thinking level of analysis, medium-size classes used comprehension and large classes used recall.

these latter processes rose, behaviors involved with memorizing decreased. "We can see that the amount of time spent listening is negatively related to change in critical thinking and positively related to memorizing" (p. 100). Students' active participation constituted only 14.2 percent of the time in these classes, however. Questioning (2.6 percent) and encouragement by the professor (3.7 percent) took up 6.3 percent of the time. Of time spent on questions asked of students (2.6 percent), 49 percent involved memory alone (recall); 4 percent of the questioning time involved questions requiring evaluation. "The differences in critical-thinking scores and in critical-thinking behaviors between classes with low- and high-level participants were dramatic. . . " (p. 111). Although other estimates of students' involvement in high school classes are far higher, "the active intellectual interchange, which one often imagines when envisioning a college classroom, does not take place on the average" (p. 110).

A different study, of audiotapes of 19 classes from the liberal arts, natural science, engineering, and business colleges at the University of Texas–Austin, using the Cognitive Interaction Analysis System (Johnson 1986, 1987a; Lewis 1986; Lewis and Johnson 1986), found that teacher talk made up 88.5 percent of class time, student talk 5 percent, and silence, owing to pauses in what the instructor said or to quizzes, 6.4 percent (Lewis 1984). Overall, the faculty lectured 80 to 90 percent of the time. This pattern differed little among the four colleges.

Are graduate courses different? To what extent is the intellectual climate in graduate professional courses different from the one experienced in many undergraduate courses? Studies are few, but research in U.S. medical schools reveals a similar pattern of students' minimal involvement and an emphasis on memorizing facts (Foster 1983). In a study of the instruction of 380 faculty members at seven medical schools, one-third of the faculty used no "thought-provoking" questions. Many of the professors who used such questions "did so in a formalized or mechanical manner—producing boredom, irritation, [and] anxiety rather than interest and stimulation" (p. 121). Four other studies "found a paucity of student participation in classes and an emphasis by the faculty on factual information rather than higher-order thinking. Students were not challenged to pursue inquiry in depth or to approach clinical problems with intellectual curiosity" (p. 121).

Overall, medical training consists of "a multitude of disjointed facts . . . [that could] exceed what students can learn in a four-year period" (Burrows 1990, p. B1), and tests tend to focus on facts as well. A calculation at one state veterinary medical school showed students were required to learn 216,000 facts, or 200 facts each day, seven days a week (Monaghan 1988).

In summary, the research on college classes is consistent: Faculty can strongly influence the amount of students' active involvement and the cognitive level of the classroom. Nevertheless, faculty overwhelmingly lecture, primarily transmitting facts requiring low cognitive levels to students who function as passive listeners. Our primary stock in trade might, after all, be "'inert ideas'—that is to say, ideas that are merely received into the mind without being utilized, or tested, or thrown into fresh combinations" (Whitehead 1929, p. 1).

The impact of our methods

How effectively do our current methods keep students focused on their tasks? To what extent do students benefit from our efforts?

How much do students hear in our lectures? If the conclusions of the research reviewed above are valid, our students spend most of their time in class learning facts. How closely do they pay attention to what we are saying? How much of what we say do they actually hear, and how much of this low-level material do students retain for use at some time after the class, or course, is over?

After only 15 to 20 minutes in a lecture, students' minds begin to wander, and retention of information begins to fall off (Davis and Alexander 1977a). More recent studies confirm that attention drops off after 10 to 20 minutes (Bonwell and Eison 1991). A study of both observed and self-reported on-target classroom (lecture) behavior found great similarity in observed behavior among both learning-oriented and grade-oriented students (Milton, Pollio, and Eison 1986). Average observed on-target behavior—for example, attending to the lecturer, taking notes, or asking or answering questions—was only 49 percent. About half the time in lectures was spent thinking about people, time, body, and mood; up to 15 percent of the time in class involved fantasy.

How much do they remember? Studies of the retention of course material (Gustav 1969; McLeish 1968) at all levels of schooling generally show rare high values of as much as 50 percent retained, but results frequently drop below 20 percent (Brethower 1977). The published values for remembering are probably overestimates, as the student has often forgotten some information by the time the initial measurements are taken and presumably will continue to do so after the final post-test (Brethower 1977).

One carefully designed study at Norwich (England) University tested students almost immediately following a specially designed lecture (McLeish 1968). Students were tested on their recall of facts, theory, and application of content they had just heard, and they were allowed maximum use of the lecture notes they had just taken, knowing they would be tested, and a printed summary of the lecture. The average for students' recall of this information was only 42 percent. One week later, a subgroup of these students was retested with the same test they had already taken, presumably making them beneficiaries of test practice effects. Although recall among the students varied (with some remembering three times as much as others), they remembered an average of only 20 percent of the lecture content, having forgotten in one week an additional 50 percent of what they had remembered earlier from the lecture. A second study, of Northern Polytechnic University architecture students, also found that students recalled only 42 percent of a lecture's content when tested almost immediately after the lecture (McLeish 1968).

"In general, very little of a lecture can be recalled except in the case of listeners with above-average education and intelligence" (Verner and Dickinson, cited in Bonwell and Eison 1991, p. 9). "Given the placement scores of many freshmen, this statement should give pause to most instructors in higher education" (p. 9). One can only imagine the effect on current students of what has become the Lecture System. If higher-order thinking skills "are retained and used long after the individual has forgotten the detailed specifics of the subject matter taught in schools" (Bloom 1984, p. 14) and if, as the old adage suggests, education is what remains after the facts are forgotten, what does the accumulated research reviewed here imply for the quality of our graduates? Would it not be wiser to focus less on facts and more on developing these higher-order skills?

How much of their coursework do students retain and how much of it can they use after graduation, the outcome that is, after all, the major purpose of the college experience? In a study of how much students retained of their two-semester introductory economics course compared to other students who had never taken the course (Saunders 1980), 1,220 sophomores were given a test to determine their ability to comprehend and use economics in realistic situations. As sophomores, those who took the introductory economics course scored 18.7 percent higher than those who did not, immediately after having completed the course, 14.4 percent higher two years later as seniors, and only 9.8 percent higher as alumni, seven years after having taken the course. A 10 percent long-term gain in ability after taking a year-long course seems slight, given the time, effort, and financial investment made.

Studies regularly reported in the media suggest students lack basic factual knowledge most educated people believe they should have. A national Gallup survey of 696 college seniors, for example, revealed 42 percent of respondents were unaware the Koran is the sacred scripture of Islam, 42 percent could not locate the Civil War between 1850 and 1900, and 31 percent placed Reconstruction after World War II. Only two of five items from the test for U.S. citizenship were correctly answered by "a high percentage" of students (Heller 1989). The "most comprehensive survey of Ivy League students ever conducted" reveals that 50 percent of 3,119 students at eight elite, highly selective institutions were unable to name their own two U.S. senators, 23 percent did not know the number of members on the U.S. Supreme Court, and 59 percent could not name four justices on the Court ("Big Gaps" 1993; "New Poll" 1993).

The problem of misconceptions. The difficulty in educating our students runs deeper than the common factual knowledge they should learn. Students entering a course often understand the phenomena they study quite differently from the frequently more complex and abstract ways in which faculty experts conceive them (Gardner 1991; Helm and Novak 1983; Pfundt and Duit 1991). These misconceptions are thought to stem from students' early attempts to understand a very complex world. The naive (or layperson's) hypotheses they form, however, can often become significant obstacles to accurate understanding of the disciplines and effective living. Unfortunately, these misconceptions, often unknown to teachers, are highly resistant to change, especially by abstract verbal explanations in lectures, although those students who have developed abstract reasoning skills have fewer misconceptions than their peers without such skills (Lawson 1988). Identifying misconceptions and correcting them through students' active exploration of phenomena with peers are therefore essential aspects of effective instruction. Students can better confront and falsify their theories by active involvement than by "teachers' simply making lecture-style presentations of correct information" (Mestre 1987, p. 5).

Taken together, the studies reviewed so far suggest many of our passive students' misconceptions—their erroneous ideas about the world—can slip through our educational net. For example, beliefs in the paranormal—astrology as a predictor of personality, Bigfoot, the Loch Ness monster, ancient astronauts, the Bermuda triangle, ghosts, communication with the dead, UFOs as spacecraft—often go undisturbed, suggesting the ineffectiveness of our current methods of instruction (Bainbridge 1978; Eve and Harrold 1986; Feder 1986, 1987; Gray 1984, 1987; Harrold and Eve 1986, 1987; Hudson 1987). In one comparison of the beliefs of 979 college students in three different regions (Connecticut, California, and Texas), for example, at least one-third of the respondents believed in the paranormal claim for about half the questions (Hudson 1987, p. 59).

In comparison, the theory of organic evolution, a highly complex, abstract, and counterintuitive concept, is the intellectual foundation for modern life science, with innumerable implications for understanding the natural world and human behavior and with many practical applications in medicine (disease), agriculture (breeding, pest control), and social relations (race). Today, organic evolution is one of the best supported and most firmly established theories in the history of science.

How effective, then, are our current methods in correcting students' misconceptions about this important theory? A survey of students at Ohio State University explored their attitudes toward and knowledge of evolution (Fuerst 1984). Of 735 undergraduates in physical anthropology and biology courses for majors in these fields, 75.1 percent "believed in" the theory of evolution, but of these undergraduate students, only 41.9 percent both agreed that evolution was scientifically valid and understood the basis of this validity. Of 90 students in graduate genetics courses, only 55 percent responded similarly, although 84 percent "believed in" evolution. Another item in the survey probed comprehension of a key—but elementary—aspect of the theory, differential production of offspring. Only 7.5 percent of the undergraduate students and 21 percent of the advanced, graduate students responded correctly. It would appear that "current mass biological education is not very successful in conveying the scientific basis of evolutionary biology" (Fuerst 1984, p. 218). If these results in any way represent learning in science courses, the implications for teachers' effectiveness could be devastating.

Oberlin College, a small, private liberal arts institution, is much more highly selective of its entering students than Ohio State, and its students are therefore on average better prepared than and thus significantly different in a number of ways from students at Ohio State. A parallel study at Oberlin reveals that, of 102 advanced biology majors, only 61.2 percent understood the scientific basis for the validity of evolution, and a mere 16.4 percent understood the evolutionary role of differential production of offspring (Zimmerman 1986).

The practical implication of such misconstruction of science is suggested by the further discovery that fully 17.4 percent of the Ohio State life science undergraduates and 11 percent of the life science graduate students agreed that teaching concepts relying on a naturalistic explanation of the world, such as the modern theory of evolution, would lead to society's "decay"; 8.8 percent of Oberlin students in the study agreed with this proposition.

The results of the study at Ohio State "lead us to wonder about the level of understanding of evolutionary biology. . . among high school teachers of biology" (Fuerst 1984, p. 227), who are, of course, all educated in colleges and universities. A survey of 404 teachers of biology in Ohio high schools using some of the items from the previous two studies found a little over half (54 percent) of the biology teachers understood the basis for the validity of evolution; a mere 11.6 percent of respondents understood the role of differential reproduction (Zimmerman 1987). For the high school biology teachers in the sample, "Science as process, as a method of better understanding the world, is not adequately appreciated. Instead, science is viewed as a compilation of 'facts'" (p. 123). In yet another study, fewer than 2 percent of 336 Ohio school board presidents understood the scientific basis for evolution, a matter with serious implications for effective learning of biology in the schools, given recent pressure to give equal time to "creation science" in science classes (Zimmerman 1988). Surely unclarified misconceptions and faulty understanding of concepts in college courses are not limited to evolution or biology. Current teaching methods in higher education could have widely ranging, untoward social impacts.

Development of higher-order cognitive abilities. Students develop their capacity for abstract thinking, epistemology, and competence in moral judgment during the college years (Pascarella and Terenzini 1991). Studies consistently show, however, that growth is slow and limited. Our all-too-common focus on specialized facts dispensed in lectures undoubtedly retards what might otherwise be more rapid and extensive development of these key cognitive abilities. Indeed, we might actually reinforce simple, inflexible, concrete modes of thinking, a Dualistic world view, and Conventional moral reasoning patterns. In addition, students' consistent lack of vigorous intellectual interaction with other students or faculty could significantly limit development of their social, interpersonal competence.

In life generally, as in most disciplines and professional fields, problem solving—the ability to solve complex, highly abstract, and ill-defined, ill-structured, or "messy" real-world problems—is essential to success. If our instructional methods are often unable to help students grasp abstract concepts like organic evolution, located on only the second (Comprehension) level of the Taxonomy of Educational Objectives, what are the effects of our efforts to teach complex problem solving? Some disciplines, notably the physical sciences, mathematics, and technology, are often characterized by students' solving many problems. How effective is this common practice in developing these crucial skills?

Although a majority of engineering students in one study could use memorized formulas correctly to solve physics "problems," when asked for "coherent verbal descriptions" of the abstract concepts involved, "widespread misconceptions" suddenly appeared (Clement 1981, p. 161). A study of engineering undergraduates at McMaster University reports that, over four years, the students watched the faculty solve more than 1,000 problems and they themselves solved another 3,000 problems as homework (Woods 1987), "yet despite all this activity, they showed negligible improvement in problem-solving skills. . . " (p. 59). Students were "excellent at recalling memorized procedures for solving one type of problem" (p. 58), but of the 3,000 problems solved by students, only 20.6 percent required for their solution the higher-order processes of Analysis and Synthesis. Woods terms them "problems" rather than lower-level "exercises," adding "both faculty and students rarely distinguish between these two processes." The "problems" professors gave their students were, for the most part, only at the Application level of cognitive complexity, one step beyond Comprehension. Students were therefore incapable of developing true problem-solving skills. Fortunately, stunningly better results are possible using methods consistent with research on students' learning (Van Heuvelen 1991a, 1991b).

How much work do students do? Serious learning requires students' sustained effort outside the classroom. Most of what effective students learn they generally learn outside of class meetings through reading, working on problems, reviewing, and other activities. An informal survey of 20 faculty members from diverse disciplines at Rutgers University and Essex County College indicates they expect their students to study an average of 2.1 hours for every hour they spend in class. It appears, however, that students spend far less time studying than is necessary for them to learn.

Among undergraduates living both on and off campus at the University of Rhode Island, students studied about one hour for each hour of class time; socializing was a major use of students' discretionary time (Brittingham 1988). Fewer than a quarter (23 percent) of student respondents to another survey claimed to devote 16 or more hours per week to studying; employment and social activities, not intellectual, academically relevant activities, dominated students' out-of-class time (Boyer 1990a). In a Massachusetts study, full-time students claimed to study an average of six hours per week (Hutchings, Marchese, and Wright 1991). The 1986 American Council on Education–UCLA CIRP study of a national sample of 204,000 first-year students reveals that 50.5 percent of respondents claimed to spend five or fewer hours per week on "study or homework"; only 3.2 percent spent 20 or more hours ("Hours" 1987). Only 33.7 percent of 1993 CIRP respondents spent six or more hours studying, continuing a four-year decline (Cage 1994). Of hundreds of Rutgers University undergraduate students in residence halls who completed 24-hour, mostly midsemester, weekday time reports, 60 to 70 percent reported studying only two hours a day (Moffatt 1989). "About a quarter . . . hardly studied at all on a day-to-day basis but relied on frenetic cramming before exams" (p. 32). These study habits in college seem to be continuing a pattern established earlier. High school students spent a "mere four or five hours per week" on homework (Walberg 1984, p. 22), as contrasted, for example, with 28 hours on television.

A Carnegie study reveals that over a quarter of undergraduate students ordinarily spent no time weekly in the library, and most undergraduates considered the library merely a quiet place in which to study (Boyer 1987). More than half did not use the library to look at specialized bibliographies or follow up on works cited by writers; 40 percent did not search for additional references. In another national study, only 10.1 percent of first-year student respondents claimed to have studied in the library in the last year (Dodge 1991). It follows that one reason for most students' low level of use of the library could be their generally low investment of time in studying.

With the small amount of time most undergraduates seem to devote to intellectual work, what do they do with their often considerable discretionary time? One-quarter of residential undergraduates at Rutgers University devoted one or two hours daily to "organized extracurricular activities, mostly to fraternities or sororities, less often to other student groups" (Moffatt 1989, p. 33). One-tenth were involved in various athletic activities, personal or intramural. Most of the remainder of students' discretionary time was devoted to "friendly fun with peers"—hanging out, gossiping, fooling around, snacking with friends, visiting bars, flirting, engaging in sexual activity—and "students managed to find an impressive amount of time for such diversions" (p. 33). In fact, students spent an average of over four hours daily on friendly fun during midsemester weekdays. A sample of 28 students attended an average of 2.5 parties for the previous week, for an average of 11.5 hours invested in parties. "Class is the tediousness that the student body goes through between weekends" (p. 32). Fully 37.6 percent of the 1986 ACE–UCLA CIRP respondents spent six or more hours weekly partying, 81.6 percent spent the same amount of time socializing with friends (37.3 percent spent 16 or more hours), and 39.1 percent spent six or more hours watching television ("Hours" 1987).

This low level of intellectual effort by students is very discouraging to faculty members (Brittingham 1988). But the apparent ease with which students are able to pass through American colleges and universities surely reflects the lectures they attend requiring only modest intellectual effort in class and out. A moderate level of attention and skill in taking notes in class and effort to review before memory tests seems to ensure graduation for most. The influential report of the NIE Study Group refers to students' time as "one of our most precious educational resources" (Study Group 1984, p. 18), but given the findings reviewed here, one would be hard pressed to argue that our fact-dominated courses or, for that matter, our cocurricular activities make the best use of this time. Increasing students' effort would significantly improve both students' and the institution's productivity. It is up to us to develop a psychological climate that produces students' responsibility for high-quality effort (Davis and Murrell 1993). Two centuries ago, Adam Smith noted that "when the masters . . . really perform their duty, there are no examples, I believe, that the greater part of the students ever neglect theirs" (1976, p. 287).

Only 33.7 percent of 1993 CIRP respondents spent six or more hours [per week] studying, continuing a four-year decline.

The bottom line: How much value do we create?

Our students' demonstrated lack of adequate opportunity to practice important college-level thinking skills in their courses is consistent with, and might in large part explain, results of the New Jersey Test of General Intellectual Skills (GIS), an essay-format assessment of college-level, higher-order thinking skills, available as the ETS *Tasks in Critical Thinking*. The GIS indicated that, among New Jersey public college and university students at the end of their sophomore year, only 58 percent demonstrated proficiency in gathering information, 44 percent in analyzing information, 33 percent in quantitative analysis, and 51 percent in presenting information (College Outcomes Evaluation Program 1990b). Complicating interpretation of these data, however, is uncertainty about the degree to which higher education was responsible for these outcomes and to what extent students' characteristics upon entry to college or other life experiences during college contributed positively to these students' unimpressive levels of assessed thinking ability

No comprehensive national data on college outcomes are available. We have no national means of assessing and evaluating what students know and can do when they graduate from college, or how effective their institutions have been in educating them—nor do most institutions know. Results from the first comprehensive National Adult Literacy Survey, however, provide a useful, if limited, snapshot of college outcomes nationwide (Barton and Lapointe 1995). Based on a 1992 sample of over 26,000 native-born Americans aged 16 years or older, this study reveals that college graduates are, not surprisingly, more literate than people who have dropped out of college or have not attended at all. "Their *levels* of literateness[, however,] range from a lot less than impressive to mediocre to near alarming, depending on who is making the judgment" (p. 2, emphasis in the original).

The survey included three scales—prose, document, and quantitative literacy—with each scale having five levels of competence, level 5 being highest. For prose literacy, about half (47 percent) of four-year college graduates and 62 percent of two-year graduates could not, for example, state an argument presented in a newspaper article or contrast the points of view in two editorials (level 4); only 11 percent and 2 percent, respectively, could, for example, summarize two ways prospective jurors can be challenged by lawyers or compare two approaches described in an article on growing up (Level 5).

For document literacy, 53 percent of four-year graduates and 70 percent of two-year graduates, given certain conditions, were unable, for example, to use a bus schedule to identify the best bus to take, determine from a table a multiyear pattern of oil exports (both level 4), or write a paragraph summarizing a table containing parents' and teachers' agreement and disagreement on an issue (level 5). For quantitative literacy, 47 percent of four-year college graduates and 65 percent of two-year graduates could not, for example, calculate the cost per ounce of peanut butter from information on a supermarket shelf label (level 4) or explain how to compute total interest charges on a loan from a newspaper advertisement (level 5).

Again, we cannot tell how much of these modest assessed abilities were developed by the students' colleges and how much they brought with them to college or developed off campus. Certainly the skills assessed by the National Adult Literacy Survey and even more so the GIS are essential for all college graduates—and it still is some distance beyond to wisdom. We often claim far more for our institutions than the data support, and society requires far more.

A precondition for improving quality in the schools

The quality of our teaching reaches far beyond its direct effects on our own students. An ethnographic study of experienced, well-educated high school science teachers reveals that these professionals modeled their own teaching behavior on their university science professors and what they saw them do as teachers (Gallagher 1989); they teach as they were taught. These teachers did not stress logical organization of content or higher-order cognitive skills as important components of teaching. They believed their responsibility was "to present information to students and that it is the students' job to learn it" (p. 49). They did not recognize motivation as an important part of their role. "Many . . . view[ed] students as 'predestined' (p. 49); relatively few can succeed. Nearly all of the teachers lacked both concepts and vocabulary for deep discussion about students' learning and about teaching. All teachers studied

TABLE 1

NATIONAL EDUCATION GOALS

By the year 2000:

Goal 1. All children in America will start school ready to learn.

Goal 2. The high school graduation rate will increase to at least 90 percent.

Goal 3. All students will leave grades 4, 8, and 12 having demonstrated competency over challenging subject matter, including English, mathematics, science, foreign languages, civics and government, economics, arts, history, and geography, and every school in America will ensure that all students learn to use their minds well, so they may be prepared for responsible citizenship, further learning, and productive employment in our Nation's modern economy.

Goal 4. The Nation's teaching force will have access to programs for the continued improvement of their professional skills and the opportunity to acquire the knowledge and skills needed to instruct and prepare all American students for the next century.
Objective. The number of teachers with a substantive background in mathematics and science, including the metric system of measurement, will increase by 50 percent.
Objective. The number of United States undergraduate and graduate students, especially women and minorities, who complete degrees in mathematics, science, and engineering will increase significantly.

believed they were performing well; few could identify ways to improve their performance (see also Stark et al. 1988, 1990).

Today, schools and colleges in this country are increasingly being thought of as "all one system," K–16 (AAHE Education Trust 1994; Commission for Educational 1994; Hodgkinson 1985; Plater 1995). Each part depends on the others, and all must function well together if the nation's needs are to be met. We in higher education are being urged to show far more interest in the schools than we have in the past and to play an active, indeed crucial, role in the urgent process of school reform, improved quality, and the achievement of our eight national goals for education (see table 1) ("Alliance for Learning" 1994). "The perception persists that higher education is 'sitting on the sidelines' in the current school reform effort," however

Goal 5. United States students will be first in the world in mathematics and science achievement.

Goal 6. Every adult American will be literate and will possess the knowledge and skills necessary to compete in a global economy and exercise the rights and responsibilities of citizenship.
Objective. The proportion of the qualified students, especially minorities, who enter college, who complete at least two years, and who complete their degree programs will increase substantially.
Objective. The proportion of college graduates who demonstrate an advanced ability to think critically, communicate effectively, and solve problems will increase substantially.

Goal 7. Every school in the United States will be free of drugs, violence, and the unauthorized presence of firearms and alcohol and will offer a disciplined environment conducive to learning.

Goal 8. Every school will promote partnerships that will increase parental involvement and participation in promoting the social, emotional, and academic growth of children.

Note: The objectives listed with these goals relate to higher education; the goals have other objectives not included here.
Source: National Education 1994.

("AAHE's New Agenda" 1993, p. 10). Beyond any specific efforts on our part to help the schools, the results of the studies reviewed in this monograph suggest that transformation of elementary and secondary schools will depend on our first significantly improving the quality of our own work as educators.

Teachers' perceptions of the quality of their teaching

Professors rate very highly the quality of their own teaching. Nearly 90 percent of almost 1,800 faculty members at five types of institutions rated themselves "above average" or "superior" (Blackburn et al. 1980). In two other studies cited, 99 percent of faculty rated their teaching ability "above average."

What type of feedback do we receive on our professional work as educators? Given our often-noted isolation from each other as colleagues and what is on many campuses and in many departments a nearly total lack of reflective conversation about students and learning, desired outcomes, and actual results, students' evaluations of courses can be a primary—sometimes the only—source of feedback to us on the quality of our work. In contrast to some academic folklore, however, students' evaluations of teaching tend to be relatively mild and complimentary. In one study at the University of Michigan, for example, students evaluated 90 percent of the faculty as being in the upper two categories on the questionnaire (Blackburn et al. 1980). Feedback of this type can reinforce our self-perception of relatively uniform high professional quality; "faculty don't believe they have any problem with their teaching" (p. 35).

Faculty respondents in this study, however, were less confident about the teaching abilities of their departmental colleagues, rating them as lower by 10 percent (selective liberal arts colleges) to over 30 percent (research universities) than they rated themselves. (That only 31.9 percent of respondents in a 1989 UCLA survey of 35,478 faculty members at 392 colleges and universities believed faculty respect each other on their campuses could provide additional evidence of lack of communication among colleagues as well as a negative psychological climate unconducive to fostering community for staff and students alike [*Chronicle* 1994].)

How do we arrive at our judgments of our abilities?

> *In the main [faculty] base their self-ratings on self-assessment and the performance of their students. Informed student opinion is taken into consideration, but they value [colleagues'] feedback much less so and administrative response the least of all. In fact, research university faculty essentially find it valueless.*
>
> *In short, faculty apparently have a highly internal set of criteria for judging their classroom performance, one [that] is supported by their personal experience with students but is relatively free from colleagues' and supervisors' opinions* (Blackburn et al. 1980, p. 35).

The results of classroom tests, one of the few means of obtaining feedback on teachers' work, may, with their tendency to focus on facts and their common problems of validity and reliability (see "What Do Classroom Tests

Measure?" on p. 60), seriously mislead us, and others, about the quality of our own and our institutions' educational performance.

Conclusions

On the basis of these studies, what can be said about the experiences of our students in their college courses? To what extent do our educational processes—the activities we choose for students—enhance their development in directions we value?

Across studies, at least about 50 percent of first-year students' to seniors' gains in abstract reasoning, critical thinking, and conceptual complexity are made during a student's first year (Pascarella and Terenzini 1991, p. 155). Could this result be because of the greater intellectual rigor of college generally than high school, the benefit of which difference is reaped early but soon levels off to become a low ceiling retarding further significant development?

Instead of providing students with a consistent diet of challenging, intellectually complex situations that will help them develop higher-level cognitive skills and learn how our disciplines comprehend or construct the world, we instead too often give them what Joseph Schwab is said to have called a "rhetoric of conclusions." We assume students naturally develop certain complex, higher-order thinking skills by memorizing facts about a discipline and then somehow spontaneously learn to apply these newly developed cognitive skills (Fischer and Grant 1983). Instead, our academic practices may actually retard students' acquisition of facility for abstract thinking and their movement out of Dualism and Multiplicity into Relativism. Our methods may also limit their opportunity to confront and struggle personally with complex moral dilemmas and to develop valuable interpersonal and team skills.

If key misconceptions about the world pass through our courses undisturbed, if even the low-level factual content of our courses is relatively soon forgotten (as studies indicate most often happens), to what extent does our primary educational method, lecture-dominated courses, create value for our students? Without regular assessment of curricular outcomes, do we know? "It is nice to have faculty enthusiastic about updating their lecture notes and keeping abreast of their field, but there is not much evidence that lecturing is related in important ways to [students'] learning" (Cross 1976, p. x).

What Do Classroom Tests Measure?

The goals and objectives for courses provide essential guidance when we design activities in our courses and assessments to measure their results—the objectives our students actually achieve. These statements of *intended* outcomes also guide our students as they learn. It is important to set explicit goals that describe in specific detail the results we intend, to use these goals actively, and to develop goals that are challenging rather than easy to achieve (Locke and Latham 1984, 1990). It is also important to have specific and timely knowledge of the *actual* outcomes achieved. Actual results can be compared to intentions, and thus both students' and teachers' performance can be adjusted to improve the quality of results. Having studied, students need to know soon how effectively they have learned.

Assessing students' intellectual skills

Because most colleges do not systematically assess the outcomes their curricula produce, our perceptions of students'—and institutions'—accomplishments ordinarily depend on grades: the cumulative results of classroom assessment. Therefore, classroom tests become important for all users of grades: teachers, students, the institution as a whole, and higher-level policy makers. What classroom methods do we use to assess students' learning? Do our assessments reflect high expectations? To what extent are these assessments technically sound, and do they produce trustworthy, useful results? Do they themselves foster development of high-level reasoning skills and other important outcomes?

Test item types and cognitive levels. Milton (1982) surveyed the literature on classroom assessment of student outcomes; representative of the research he reviewed was a study of the types of pencil-and-paper test items employed by 1,700 University of Illinois faculty members. Types of recognition items used included multiple choice (14 percent), true-false (9 percent), and matching (7 percent). Production items requiring short written answers included short-answer essay (24 percent) and fill in the blank (12 percent). Only 17 percent of respondents used essay tests in their courses. In contrast, well-written multiple choice and essay items are best suited of these formats to assess all six levels of thinking skill in the Taxonomy of Educational Objectives (although most faculty members write multiple-choice questions requiring primarily cognitive levels 1 and 2, recall and comprehension). Other types of questions assess primarily recall. Overall, therefore, the results of this part of the study support the widely held perception that most tests college students encounter ask them only for factual recognition or recall and comprehension-level understanding.

Faculty respondents said they asked only 13 percent of "problem-solving" items. Of the 3,500 students queried in the study (from all classes, including juniors and seniors), 82 percent agreed that, "despite instructors' insistence that they do not teach facts, most grades are based on tests [that] are primarily factual in content" (p. 45). At the University of Tennessee, 87 percent of about 400 graduating seniors also agreed with this statement (Milton 1982). Tests written by 19 University of Texas–Austin faculty showed relatively few questions requiring analysis, synthesis, or evaluation (Lewis 1984).

Milton cites a study of 500 University of Illinois students, almost 90 percent of whom agreed with the statement, "Most objective examinations call for factual information" (Milton 1982), yet another, similar study, of "two highly regarded very small . . . liberal arts colleges" in the Midwest (p. 46), yielded percentages of test item types similar to those at the University of Illinois. These results suggest institutional size may not be a distinguishing variable when judging the quality of classroom assessment. Studies of 150 University of Tennessee faculty teaching introductory courses and of medical school faculty produced similar results—that most college and university classroom assessments ask students merely to "recall isolated facts or bits of information" (p. 49).

Essay examinations provide faculty with opportunities to have students exercise not only their higher cognitive abilities but also their skill in written communication. What can be said about the quality of essay tests? Of 4,500 students at five Nebraska institutions of various types, including the state research university, almost half of the students (47 percent) claimed never or only rarely ever to have had to write an

Most tests college students encounter ask them only for factual recognition or recall and comprehension-level understanding.

essay examination (Milton 1982). At the University of Illinois, 17 percent of faculty respondents claimed to use essay tests, but of four factors professors used to evaluate the quality of essays—organization, style, knowledge of facts, and originality—faculty from most departments considered knowledge of facts the most significant indicant of quality in students' essay responses. The inference is that most of the essay questions written by these faculty members probably requested isolated facts.

Students tend to prefer multiple-choice tests to essay tests, which might be because essay tests are rare, even in small colleges (Milton, Pollio, and Eison 1986, p. 167). This "preference reflects a common belief that [multiple-choice] tests are easier to take and to get good grades on" (p. 172), a belief consistent with the apparently low level of cognitive skill demanded for most multiple-choice items used by most professors.

Publishers' test-item banks. A further contributor to the low cognitive level required by many classroom tests may be the test-item banks in book or computer disk format textbook publishers supply free to professors. These gifts are inducements to professors to require their students to purchase the publishers' books. Using the items in these collections individually or having them automatically compiled into a test directly from the disk can save teachers considerable time. A rating of the quality, on several dimensions, of six randomly selected psychology textbook test-item banks, however, found common defects in design of the items (Evans, Dodson, and Bailey 1981). In addition, a rating of 276 items by two independent raters using the Taxonomy of Educational Objectives (with the raters in agreement 98 percent of the time) revealed that 83.3 percent of the items in one bank required recall only, in three banks the range was from 94.1 to 96.4 percent recall, and two banks required memory for 100 percent of their items. Only 10 items, or 2.8 percent of the total sample, were even at level 2, comprehension. And *only one* of the 276 items studied asked for any higher-order thinking, analysis. Concluding his extensive review of research on classroom tests, Milton (1982) notes, "Most test questions for undergraduates and for some advanced students require a grasp of factual information and little more. There is almost no emphasis [through] test questions on the higher-order mental processes" (p. 49).

The technical qualities of classroom tests

Among the characteristics used to judge the quality of assessment methods are their capacity to produce valid inferences when interpreted and their reliability. For example, a pencil-and-paper test that assesses what it is said to assess, and not something else, is able to produce evidence that can form the basis for valid interpretation. A test that assesses something other than what it is thought to assess produces results useless for decision making. Reliability is an assessment's stability or consistency of performance over time. For example, a test administered to different groups of people at different times, if reliable, tends to perform similarly during each administration. Because reliability of the instrument is a prerequisite for validity, a test that is unreliable also produces untrustworthy results.

Validity of classroom tests. At the University of Kansas, 17 faculty members in art and science disciplines indicated that 31 percent of their test items assessed "complex cognitive skills (such as problem solving) in their students" (Milton, Pollio, and Eison 1986, p. 21). Independent judges, however, found only 8.5 percent of the items were of this sort; 91 percent of the items asked for recall or recognition. In other words, the validity of any inferences the teachers may have made about their students' complex cognitive skills based on these tests was compromised by the assessments' inability to measure the behaviors claimed.

Reliability of classroom tests. A 1954 study of 1,000 faculty members in 28 colleges and universities concluded that little evidence existed of the teachers' deliberate efforts to design reliable tests (Milton 1982). Another study, of almost 200 classroom tests from diverse disciplines at Pennsylvania State University, found that after statistical analysis, "the reliabilities were found, on the average, to be very low" (p. 26).

Experience in colleges and universities and the many published studies consistently suggest that faculty in this country care deeply about their students' developing higher-order cognitive skills. It is equally clear from the studies reviewed here that our tests do not generally assess such skills. Our tests are thus in all too many cases unable to produce evidence relevant to our students' reasoning. Apparently, many of the professors in the studies described here were unaware of the technical properties of their assessments, which is not surprising, given that few of us have had the benefit of formal training for our work as teachers. For example, most faculty members in colleges and universities today are still unaware of the Taxonomy of Educational Objectives, for four decades the standard for controlling the cognitive demands of assessments. "Good teaching also means careful evaluation of the student. And yet it is for this important task most teachers are not well prepared" (Boyer 1987, p. 154).

Laying a firm foundation. The basis for planning effective assessments in courses is a set of explicit, written objectives that state the course's intended outcomes for its students' development in specific and behavioral language (Gardiner 1989). Each objective determines, among other things, the cognitive level at which students should be able to perform. But most college and university faculty members still do not develop formal instructional objectives for their courses. Consequently, their assessments frequently lack the solid foundation of clearly stated outcomes required for effective design. "If the teacher's thinking is not too clear about aims, there is no way that test questions can be prepared [that] will measure them" (Milton 1982, p. 25).

A comparison with commercial tests. With the remarkable increase of interest in assessment of all types in higher education over the last decade, certain widely used commercial tests have come under intense criticism. Concerns have been voiced about the capacity of these instruments to measure the complex kinds of learning in which our students engage and their alleged potential for producing biased results when taken by members of ethnic and cultural minority groups. Such instruments, however, are usually constructed with the greatest of care by some of the nation's most highly trained experts in assessment (Milton 1982). Each item is laboriously pilot tested, subjected to rigorous criticism, and revised, often several times, before use. These same concerns about commercial instruments have not generally been raised about college classroom tests, however, which are, through grades, usually the main form of evidence of both students' development and institutions' performance. American students take a vastly greater number of these faculty-designed tests each year than they ever do of commercial tests. "Classroom tests continue to reign supreme; it is as though they are error free" (Milton 1982, p. 4). Perhaps it is these tests that "should be the primary targets of criticism" (p. 4).

Conclusions

Very few of us have had formal training for the complex task of designing and interpreting assessments of students' work. Instead, our training in graduate school has generally been almost exclusively as researchers, as discoverers of knowledge in some relatively narrow, specialized area of a discipline. A study of graduate teaching assistants at the University of Tennessee–Knoxville, replicated at other institutions, showed that 91 percent of these students prepared, and 99 percent evaluated, tests and that 91 percent assigned final grades (Milton, Pollio, and Eison 1986). The training and guidance these student-teachers received for this complex, technically demanding psychometric work with high impact on students was "minimal or nonexistent" (p. 12). Almost three-quarters of University of Tennessee faculty members in one study claimed to have learned how to design tests without any formal training (Milton 1982), and over a quarter of the respondents claimed that intuition was responsible for any skill they had in developing tests. In another study, 82 percent of professors cited trial and error as their method of learning test design (Milton 1982).

Considerable literature exists that can help teachers design high-quality assessments of student learning (Angelo and Cross 1993; Bloom, Hastings, and Madaus 1971; Carey 1988; Cashin 1987; Clegg and Cashin 1986; Cronbach 1984; Hanna and Cashin 1987; Jacobs and Chase 1992; Mehrens and Lehmann 1984; Thorndike and Hagen 1986). But college faculty members do not generally read the professional literature in higher education. "Around 99 percent of faculty members do not read either the past or the current literature from which these investigations have been drawn" (Milton 1982, p. 33). The problems of validity and reliability described above can in large part be attributed to our lack of knowledge of how to assess our students' learning. Given such a foundation of sand as an underpinning for classroom assessment and grading, Milton asks, "What is the meaning of a GPA?" (p. 51).

To what extent do our attempts to assess actual outcomes affect the achievement of intended outcomes? The Uncertainty Principle, well known in the field of physics, states that the process of measuring a phenomenon will itself affect the phenomenon (Milton 1982). The Uncertainty Principle thus suggests that our attempts to assess students' developmental outcomes may affect the learning process itself. Students generally study what they believe will be on tests, as their grades and futures are at stake. Emphasizing facts on tests communicates to students that the Expert-Authority, the teacher, believes learning factual knowledge is what is most important. Thus, students emphasize the memorization of facts, most of which they will soon forget, and may thus be kept from using their learning experience to develop more sophisticated and important abstract reasoning skills and critical or creative competencies. Students are likely thus to be specifically retarded in their cognitive development and retained in place where they now are. The many who are Dualists, for example, may not only not be assisted in their needed move to Multiplicity, but also be actively reinforced in Dualism. The specific message they may receive in our courses is that facts are what count; get them passively from Authorities.

Overall, the low cognitive-level content of our classroom assessments and our lack of attention to questions of validity and reliability call into question the meaning of the results generally produced by these tests, as well as the manifold uses of these results by students, teachers, institutions, and policy makers.

What Do Grades Tell Us? Do Grades Affect Outcomes?

Grades are the chief means by which faculty in most U.S. colleges and universities signify to students and others, inside and beyond the institution, the quality of our developmental outcomes. A national sample of 6,165 students, parents, business recruiters, and faculty members discovered that most people place considerable faith in the capacity of grades to communicate effectively important characteristics of students (Milton, Pollio, and Eison 1986).

How well do grades communicate outcomes?

Grades are related to cognitive development and academic learning (Astin 1993; Hartnett and Schroder 1987; Smith

1992), but their meaning is often unclear and their interpretation difficult.

Research on grades extends back to at least the early years of this century (see, e.g., Starch and Elliott 1912, 1913a, 1913b), and a number of their serious conceptual and statistical weaknesses as means of communication have long been understood. More recently, grades have come under intense attack as being ineffectual in doing the work we ask of them as well as for actively retarding our efforts as educators (Battersby 1973; Kirschenbaum, Simon, and Napier 1971; Kohn 1993; Marshall 1968).

First, as single letters or digits, grades can scarcely communicate detailed, useful information about achievement of the diverse cognitive, affective, or motor outcomes we seek. Second, given the uncertain effectiveness as mental measurements of most classroom tests, the wide mixture of tests, class participation, attendance, and other components of grades, and the fact that the user of a grade rarely has any idea which of these variables went into a grade or in what proportion, the utility of grades as means of communication is deeply compromised. A grade is "an inadequate report of an inaccurate judgment by a biased and variable judge of the extent to which a student has attained an undefined level of mastery of an unknown proportion of an indefinite amount of material" (Dressell 1957, p. 6).

Third, the preeminent use of grades is not to give feedback to students on their development, but to provide a basis for those outside our institutions to sort, rank, and select those of our graduates whom they deem fit for their own purposes (Milton, Pollio, and Eison 1986). Employers and graduate schools rely on grades as important predictors of future success; thus, grades form a basis for high-stakes decisions about a student. Ironically, the predictive validity of grades is severely limited. Major reviews of 108 (Cohen 1984) and 150 (Baird 1985) different studies of the relationship between college grades and diverse types of adult achievement revealed it to be slight. Undergraduate grades do predict first-year graduate or professional school grades, their strongest predictive ability, but only at a median level of about 0.30; in fact, assuming the normal distribution of grades, only 60 percent of students will even have their graduate school grades in the same half of the distribution as their undergraduate grades (Warren 1971).

Rather than helping students develop, we may be generating grades for a professionally questionable weeding-out function for someone else's convenience by means of a statistically compromised method—and in so doing labeling many of our students "damaged goods." A high-quality educational process uses assessment formatively to ensure all "products" are of high quality and communicates results continuously to students in meaningful ways. The needs of other organizations too often take precedence over our educational responsibilities to our students.

Do grades affect moral development?
Faculty are often unhappy with students' frequently single-minded focus on grades rather than their own intellectual, affective, and social development. This orientation toward grades, presumably fostered by the high stakes associated with them, may have wider implications for students' development than distraction from significance and effort wasted on the irrelevant. Research suggests the emphasis on production of grades may create a psychological climate that retards rather than enhances students' moral development, a linchpin of mature human relations and prosocial behavior throughout life.

How much do students cheat? Fully 70 percent of faculty respondents in one survey agreed that undergraduates "have become more grade conscious," 42 percent agreed that undergraduate students "are more competitive," and 43 percent believe students are "more willing to cheat" (Boyer 1989). Grades provide for many students a rationale to engage in unethical behavior based on low-level, preconventional moral reasoning. When asked whether they had ever cheated to get a better grade, one-third of a national sample of 6,165 students and former students responded affirmatively (Milton, Pollio, and Eison 1986). Over half of current students in the sample said they had cheated. In a 1964 study, one-half of the students reported they had engaged in academic dishonesty, including over one-third of the respondents with A's and B+'s (Milton, Pollio, and Eison 1986). These findings are consistent with an estimate of a 40 to nearly 90 percent rate of cheating cited by Boyer (1990a) and considerable additional research.

Two-thirds of 117 Rutgers University students in one study claimed they had cheated in their courses, 95 percent of them more than once (Norman 1988). In another study at Rutgers, the researcher classified fully 50 percent of economics majors and 42 percent of communications, political science, and psychology majors as "hard core" cheaters (Moffatt 1990). Another study of 3,630 college students found that, during the previous year, 32 percent had cheated on an examination, 61 percent had lied to their parents, 16 percent had stolen items from a store, and about a third would lie to secure a job on their resume, on the application, or during an interview (Viadero 1992).

Other studies abound. Of over 6,000 students at 31 "highly selective" colleges, two-thirds of respondents claimed to have cheated on a test or major assignment at least one time when in college; one-fifth (19.1 percent) were "active cheaters," cheating five or more times (McCabe 1992). Over half (52.4 percent) of cheaters cited pressure to get good grades as a significant motivation behind their dishonest behavior.

Forty percent of 552 Concordia University students claimed to have cheated "in recent months"; 60 percent of engineering and computer science majors had cheated in the six months before the study ("Widespread Cheating" 1987, p. 47). A study of 234 first-year through senior students in introductory courses at Miami University of Ohio found that 72.1 percent of respondents claimed to have plagiarized class work. Based on an analysis of additional items in the questionnaire, other students, presumably unconsciously because of ignorance, were likely also plagiarizing, making a total of 91.2 percent who plagiarized ("Plagiarism" 1990). In another study, over 30 percent of the 200,000 student respondents had plagiarized in the previous year. This behavior is consistent with research on the moral development of college students. "*Perception* of some moral issues [is] distressingly low," and "students generally [show] insensitivity to the issue of promise keeping" (McNeel 1994, p. 46, emphasis added). Students' reasons for cheating demonstrate a variety of probable lower stages of moral judgment. We need to help students recognize ethical dilemmas and how to think effectively about them.

How effectively have we dealt with this apparent epidemic of antisocial behavior? Too often, little information is available to students or faculty about an institution's policy on dishonesty, resulting in confusion (Maramark and Maline 1993). Students "rarely report" others' dishonesty (p. 5), and as few as 20 percent of faculty who observed cheating complied with their institution's policies for handling it.

Does cheating have long-term developmental effects?
A meta-analysis of 521 studies on cooperative versus competitive and individual behavior cites various sources indicating the untoward effects of grade-induced competition (Johnson and Johnson 1989). In an effort to gain admission to medical school, students quoted in the *Chicago Tribune* claimed to "try to give the wrong information to other students. We take books from the medical library and destroy parts of them. We don't share information. We sabotage others' chemistry experiments" (Johnson and Johnson 1989, p. 32). "The university at the undergraduate level sounds like a place where cheating comes almost as naturally as breathing, where it's an academic skill almost as important as reading, writing, and math" (Moffatt 1989, p. 1). Indeed, this valued skill has justified at least two book-length treatises on its methodological subtleties (Baker 1989; M. Moore 1991). What is the intellectual and ethical quality of such a campus climate? And what, then, does a grade mean?

Entirely aside from the potential corrupting effects of cheating on the validity of a student's grade point average, what may be the long-term effects of a pattern of dishonesty consistently unchallenged in college? The president of the Association of American Medical Colleges stated in a speech to the association that cheating by premed students is "all too common" ("Does Research" 1988). Citing the association's investigation of 952 cases of dishonesty over the previous decade, he stated that dishonesty is repeated later in undergraduate and graduate medical training through residents' stealing supplies and possibly in research fraud and called for medical school admission committees to look at the "moral background" of applicants.

A state investigation discovered that, among partners in mostly New York City law firms, who are not required to pay withholding tax, almost 10 percent failed to file state income taxes for one or more of the previous three years, a rate about 20 times greater than the 0.5 percent rate for their employees, who do have to pay withholding taxes

(Kolbert 1989). Nearly 350 of these partners had failed to submit tax returns for three or more years, a felony for which conviction leads to automatic disbarment. Recall the relatively low moral judgment scores discovered among senior members of CPA firms (p. 29). These highly placed professionals are graduates of our institutions, many of the institutions prestigious and many of the professionals with both undergraduate and graduate degrees. What role did we play in their moral development? One study found that one-third of a sample of 39 college teachers had an average principled reasoning score "scarcely above that typical of incoming freshmen" (McNeel 1994, p. 42).

The media regularly describe yet other species of corruption among highly placed persons in business and government, almost all of them graduates of our institutions. They also frequently publish reports of scandals on campus associated with finances, research fraud, drugs, sexual violence, and athletics. Aside from the climate of moral laxity such events can engender, what will be the life-long consequences of the moral classroom climate we, members of the most highly educated sector of society, create through our toleration of widespread dishonesty during these formative years?

Speaking broadly of our responsibility for students' moral development, former Harvard president Derek Bok stated, "Despite the importance of moral development to the individual student and the society, one cannot say that higher education has demonstrated deep concern for the problem" (cited in Gold 1988). Frequently, "especially in large universities, the subject is not treated as a serious responsibility worthy of sustained discussion and determined action by the faculty and administration." Research on campus cheating seems consistent with this view.

Conclusions

Considering the widespread practice of summative, *defect-detecting,* for-grading-only assessment, the amount of resources in student, faculty, and administrative staff time and energy devoted to producing, communicating, and curating grades is enormous. Instead of focusing on bureaucratic number crunching, suppose we focused instead on personally meaningful learning aimed at specific, stated outcomes and assessed students regularly to provide formative feedback on their progress—*defect prevention*. Should we not be focusing on our students' development, including their moral development? And what would be the effect if we taught students how to recognize, reason skillfully about, and avoid unethical behavior?

THE CAMPUS CLIMATE: Context for Development

The quality of the psychological climate on campus can be a crucial factor in aiding or limiting a student's development. The extent to which our now-diverse students find a welcoming, intellectually stimulating, ethically principled, and emotionally supportive and caring environment when they arrive on campus can significantly affect both their decision to remain in school and their achievement of the desired developmental outcomes. Today, we understand better than ever the key roles played by social relationships, sense of community, and emotional support in effective learning. Lack of a sense of community among students had more powerful direct effects on their satisfaction with their college experience than many other of 192 environmental variables in Astin's major study (1993). With care, we can transform a potentially stressful transition to a new community—with its strange customs, more demanding tasks, and personal risks—into sustained, high-quality effort leading to personal and professional fulfillment, and we can do so by developing in each person an inspiring vision of his or her capacity for high-quality performance and potential impact on society.

What would be the effect if we taught students how to recognize, reason skillfully about, and avoid unethical behavior?

Climate and Student Development

Research on student outcomes demonstrates a clear association between psychological climate and students' academic performance, intellectual and personal growth, attitudes toward their academic programs, satisfaction with college, and voluntary persistence on campus (Pascarella and Terenzini 1991). Contact with other students and staff is key. "It is clear that many of the most important effects of college occur through students' interpersonal experiences with faculty members and other students" (p. 644). Students' experiences in the classroom are an important factor. The climate in the classroom, or "psychological morale" (Walberg 1984), has a strong effect, not only on cognitive but also on affective learning, increasing it by a full .60 standard deviation.

A pervasive interest in the world, an excitement with ideas, and an eagerness to learn can inspire new members of a campus community to high-quality intellectual effort. Many of our campuses, however, apparently fall short of this ideal, with instruction and assessment in many or most classrooms focusing on memorization of facts, grades dominating intellectual life on many campuses, and a climate that often tolerates widespread cheating.

Further, results of several major studies indicate "alcohol abuse is a common, not marginal, activity at most colleges" (Wechsler, Deutsch, and Dowdall 1995, p. B1). Eighty percent of fraternity and sorority residents binge. Of 17,592 students on 140 campuses in one study, representative of all four-year institutions, 44 percent of respondents reported binging at least once in the previous two weeks (Shea 1994). At institutions where half or more of students were binge drinkers, more than half of first-year students said they had binged in their first week on campus, two-thirds during the first semester (Gose 1995). Legal drinking age presents no obstacle to obtaining alcohol, and underage drinking is pervasive.

Drunkenness commonly leads to a campus climate characterized by vandalism, verbal and physical violence, unplanned, unwanted, and unsafe sex, disturbance of others' studying and sleep (87 percent of nonbingers in one study [Wechsler, Deutsch, and Dowdall 1995]), and relatively low academic achievement for bingers. Tolerance of this pattern of behavior creates a campus climate antithetical to intellectual work, civility, community, and human development.

Some colleges now experience violence from the presence of gangs, guns, and drugs on campus (Lederman 1994). Fully 7.5 percent of 29,935 student respondents in one study said they had carried guns, knives, or other weapons in the previous 30 days (*Chronicle* 1995b). MIT and Louisiana State now use walk-through metal detectors to screen out guns and knives at large parties given by student groups (*Chronicle* 1995a, 1995c).

Integration into the Community and Involvement
According to Vincent Tinto, integration is "the perception of being a member, of belonging to an institution where people value your presence" (Evangelauf 1990, p. A18). And what develops a community that integrates every person is a "high-quality, caring, and concerned faculty and staff" (Tinto 1993, p. 201). Students' academic and social integration affects positively their persistence on campus (Bean 1980; Cabrera et al. 1992; Cabrera, Nora, and Castañeda 1993; Tinto 1985, 1993).

Of college and university presidents surveyed by the Carnegie Foundation (Boyer 1990a), 97 percent "strongly believe[d] in the importance of community," and 71 percent of respondents (87 percent at research and doctoral universities) rated as "very important" the need for a greater effort to build a stronger overall sense of community on their campuses. In the 1989 Carnegie survey of faculty, 11 percent of respondents rated the quality of life at their institutions as "excellent," 50 percent as "fair or poor" (Boyer 1989). Only 9 percent of respondents said an "excellent" sense of community could be found on their campuses; 28 percent rated community as "good," 66 percent as "poor." Students feel the lack of community as well. About half of the students who responded to a 1984 Carnegie Foundation survey said they felt "like a number in a book," and about 40 percent claimed not to have any professor who was "interested in their personal lives" (Boyer 1989).

Research and observation bear out this sense of alienation. "At present our colleges do not on the whole ever take account of their students as persons, not even the colleges that claim to be small and personal" (Bowen 1980, p. 34). The "most notable decline during the college years" has been in students' sense of psychological well-being (Astin 1993, p. 397). Might this effect be related to the degree of support a student feels?

According to one study, a majority of 406 medical students at two different institutions claimed to have been subjected to physical or emotional abuse during their four years in medical school (Nicklin 1990). Abuse involved insults, rudeness, physical blows, and threats of bodily harm, and, for over half the women at one institution, sexual advances, in most cases from physicians and clinical staff.

The results of our neglect of students' emotional and social needs may be profound. Of 189 undergraduates at the University of Waterloo (Ontario), almost half claimed to have considered committing suicide during their stay at the university, 39 percent because of stress ("Half" 1985). Finding the campus "one of the more stressed environments in society," the researchers note that Canadian college and university students commit suicide at a rate 50 percent higher than nonstudents of the same age. Although the rate of suicides among college and university students in the United States is lower, after accidents suicide is nevertheless estimated to be the second cause of death for college students (Shea 1995).

Commuter and Part-time Students

Considerable evidence demonstrates that residing on campus confers on students considerable benefits compared to students who commute from off-campus housing (Chickering 1974; Pascarella and Terenzini 1991). "The most important determinant of college impact is living on campus, an experience that opens students to other forces for change" (Gamson 1991, p. 52). Yet most students live off campus. The prominence of commuter students on campus has changed dramatically over the last 30 years, partly as a result of the development of community colleges, virtually all of whose students commute. Today, about 80 percent of U.S. undergraduates commute from housing beyond their campus borders (Jacoby 1989; Stewart and Rue 1983). How responsive are we to the special needs of this large group of students? Sixty percent of college presidents at four-year institutions who responded to one survey reported inadequate—low-quality—services for commuters on their campuses (Boyer 1990a). Seventy-six percent of presidents stated students' lack of participation in campus events was one of the most serious problems affecting student life.

How do we respond to the needs of the almost one-half of our students who attend college part time? Many of them are older adults who hold full-time jobs in addition to raising families and therefore live off-campus. Despite the special needs that must be met if they are to have educational experiences in any way comparable to those of full-time students, all of us in academe know well the casual attention these students often receive. "The best universities especially continue to abhor part-time students, and some are almost cruel toward them" (Keller 1983, p. 14). We must be more careful to meet these students' needs.

Students' Involvement with Faculty

Large, impersonal lecture courses, ineffective responses to commuters' needs, and other deficiencies in climate can conspire to reduce students' crucial out-of-class contact with other students and the faculty, widening the gulf between them. At Rutgers University, for example, students

. . . had no idea of most of what the professors spent their time doing and thinking about: research, publication, and departmental politics. . . . Student friends were surprised to learn that I had written a book, or even that I had my Ph.D. Two . . . admitted . . . that they had always privately thought that "tenure" meant a faculty member had been around for "ten years" (Moffatt 1989, p. 25).

"Many faculty and academic administrators distance themselves from student life and appear to be confused about their obligations in nonacademic matters" (Boyer 1987, p. 5). A lack of faculty members' engagement with students of this magnitude mightily limits the positive developmental effects we can and should have.

The Climate for Women and Members Of Minority Groups

Of special importance to us should be the campus climate perceived by women and students from minority groups. Beyond our ethical responsibility to ensure a hospitable, nurturing environment for all our students, the success of these two student populations is especially important in a number of different fields crucial to the nation's future, given the urgent state and national need to graduate them in far greater numbers and in more diverse fields than we now do. The success of women and members of minority groups in college has become an urgent societal priority. Together these groups make up well over 50 percent of all students on most campuses, and research on the campus experiences of women and members of ethnic minorities can illuminate the quality of the campus climate for everyone. The capacity of the campus climate to inspire and sustain these students and to provide the essential personal validation they often require (Rendon 1994) can be a powerful tool for ensuring their retention and success in college.

Women on campus

In the decade from 1974 to 1984, the number of women in college increased nine times faster than the number of men (Bernstein 1990). In 1980, women for the first time made up fully half of all college undergraduates, finally achieving a level of attendance equal to that of men, although this proportional increase has primarily benefited white women rather than women of color (Bernstein and Cock 1994). During approximately this same period of rapid growth, from 1960 to 1986, however, women's colleges, whose historic contributions to the education of and provision of opportunities for women are well documented (Astin 1993; Pascarella and Terenzini 1991), decreased from 233 to 90 (Bernstein 1990). Women's colleges, as perceived by their students, tend to be more student-centered and civic-minded than coed institutions and to value multiculturalism more (Smith, Wolf, and Morrison 1995, p. 264). They involve their students more deeply and thus are more effective in producing several important outcomes among students. In fact, after removing the effects of college selectivity and individual factors, "graduates of women's colleges are strongly overrepresented in the high-status, male-dominated occupations of medicine, scientific research, and engineering" (Pascarella and Ter-enzini 1991, p. 601).

Now that their access to higher education has improved, what is the quality of the campus experience for women? Regrettably, the ways in which women and men are treated still differ significantly on many campuses (Hall and Sandler 1982), a continuation of a pattern established earlier, in elementary and high school (Rothman 1991). Women are still subject to a "chilly" climate in the classroom (Hall and Sandler 1982).

Studies demonstrate a consistent pattern of behavior that must surely significantly affect the development of our female students. For example, female students are called on in class less often than males and when called on are more often than men asked low, Recall-level questions; men receive more complex questions requiring higher-order thinking (Sandler 1986). Women students receive less encouragement than men; for instance, they are more often interrupted during discussions and receive less eye contact than men when a teacher asks a question (discouraging a response). Women's names are forgotten more often than men's, they are chosen less frequently as faculty assistants, and, despite the urgent need for women in the natural sciences and technology, their advisers sometimes openly discourage them from choosing traditionally "masculine" majors like mathematics, physical science, and engineering. This chilly climate extends to female graduate students, faculty members, and administrators as well (Flam 1991; "Michigan State" 1995).

These subtle and in many cases unconscious behaviors on the part of students, faculty, and administrators can, with time, become fused to form for women students a consistent, pervasive climate of devaluation, discouragement, and lowered expectations, in class and elsewhere on campus (Hall and Sandler 1984). Added to apparently pervasive, although often almost imperceptible, slights by campus authorities are all-too-frequent direct assaults on women's self-esteem. Comments that openly disparage women, their efforts, and their accomplishments; overt sexual harassment by faculty, administrators, or peers (Dziech and Weiner 1984; Hughes and Sandler 1986, 1988); and discrimination against women in the choice of faculty assistants, awards for undergraduate and graduate students, and promotion and tenure for faculty members have been documented at too many institutions. Added to these problems for women is overt sexual violence in the form of date or acquaintance rape (Hughes and Sandler 1987) and party or gang rape (Ehrhart and Sandler 1985), both apparently more prevalent on campus than commonly believed. Such actions further compromise our environment as a nurturing, developmental one, certainly for women, but also for men.

Although the climate may vary from institution to institution, the hidden or not-so-hidden message women too often receive from faculty, staff, and fellow students is that they are not on the same level as their male peers and are "outsiders" on campus (Hall and Sandler 1984, pp. 3–4).

Sexist attitudes persist on campus (Boyer 1990a). In one study, 40 percent of undergraduate women respondents indicated they had been sexually harassed on campus, and at Harvard, 34 percent of undergraduate women reported harassment from an institutional authority (Boyer 1990a). "Most shocking are the physical assaults against women, which were reported on nearly a third of the campuses . . . visited" (p. 34). At one university, 20 percent of the women studied said they had had "unwanted sexual intercourse."

Given what is often a clearly nonsupportive campus climate for women, many women come to devalue and doubt their own abilities and to reduce their expectations for their careers and lives. While the most obvious result is a loss to each student whose development is in this way retarded, there are also obvious costs to her institution, department, and future profession—and thus to society. Rather than abruptly halting an antidevelopmental process of diminishment often begun much earlier at home and school, in all too many cases our campuses clearly reinforce this damaging trend.

> *It seems clear that colleges do not serve to reduce many of the stereotypic differences between the sexes. . . . It would seem that these programs serve more to preserve, rather than to reduce, stereotypic differences between men and women in behavior, personality, aspirations, and achievement* (Astin 1977, p. 216).

Summarizing his major follow-up study 15 years later, Astin (1993) uses virtually identical words (p. 405). Reviewing research on the effects of student peer culture on women students, Baxter-Magolda (1993) asks, "What context allows the peer culture to have such a devastating effect on women's development during their undergraduate years?" (p. 372). And writing of women students in science, Tobias (1990) states her research suggests, at least for scientists, "the 'crisis' in science education is not yet their problem, but rather the nation's" (p. 12). We need to see as our problem the well-being, persistence, and success of each one of our women students.

Members of racial and ethnic minority groups on campus

"Perhaps more than any other institution in our society, it is the college that is crucially important to advancing prospects for black and Hispanic students" (Boyer 1987, p. 39). Yet the uncertainty, confusion, and anxiety many, if not most, students of majority groups feel in college can be substantially increased for students of racial and ethnic minority groups at primarily white institutions. What is the quality of the campus climate for students from minority groups?

In many cases, minority-group students bring with them to college inadequate academic preparation and poorly developed study skills and habits, and they can find it difficult to comprehend the often highly abstract content of their courses. On primarily majority-group campuses, many students from minority groups are often aware of their unconventional speech patterns and may fear saying something inappropriate when speaking in class, reducing their active participation (Saufley, Cowan, and Blake 1983). They may be shunned by majority-group students. They may feel guilty for consuming a disproportionately large share of their family's resources. And they may fear being thought academically inferior on campus. According to a University of Chicago survey, 53 percent of white Americans stated that African-Americans and members of other minority groups are less intelligent than they; 30 percent of African-American respondents agreed with the statement (Raymond 1991). Many of our students may themselves suffer from such a deadly misconception.

"Study after study reports the experiences of minority students from all backgrounds who encounter racism and overt or subtle forms of discrimination by other students or faculty" (Smith 1989, p. 22). *Campus Life: In Search of Community* expresses concern "about the racial tensions on campus, the lack of trust, the singular lack of success many colleges and universities have had in creating a climate in which minority students feel fully accepted on campus" (Boyer 1990a, p. 31). According to the report, two-thirds of the presidents at research and doctoral universities cited "racial tensions and hostilities" as problems on their campuses (Boyer 1990a). Of 3,119 students at eight Ivy League institutions, 73 percent of all respondents and 81 percent of African-Americans perceived racism as a problem on campus ("Ivy League" 1993). In the words of an African-American student at Columbia University, "Blacks . . . are admitted to Columbia, but they do not belong" (Bernstein 1990, p. 23).

Other instances are prevalent in the literature. At the University of Maryland–Baltimore County, for example, about one-fifth of minority-group students had suffered ethnoviolence (chiefly psychological in the form of verbal abuse) on campus, many repeatedly, one-third said their interpersonal relations had been "seriously affected," and an "overwhelming majority perceived themselves to be potential targets of discrimination" (Ehrlich 1988, p. 15). Jewish and Asian students had experienced similar amounts of ethnoviolence. At St. Cloud State University, 50 percent of minority-group and international students claimed to have heard *faculty members* make racist comments, and 46 percent had had ethnoviolence directed toward them in their residences on campus; 65 percent of the minority-group and international faculty had experienced disrespect from white students related to their race or nationality.

"The consistent theme of alienation experienced by students of nontraditional backgrounds in their campus environments is symptomatic of a deep underlying problem that has not been adequately addressed" (Smith 1989, p. 19). To what extent is it our responsibility to address this moral issue?

> *To the degree that issues of racism, sexism, homophobia, and the general presence of an alienating environment also affect performance, then lack of performance cannot be focused entirely on the student. All too often we have assumed the institution's perfection and students' incompetence* (Smith 1989, p. 64)

How do gifted minority-group students fare on campus? A decade-long longitudinal study of Illinois high school valedictorians and salutatorians explored in detail the experiences of eight African-American and Latina students (Arnold 1993). These gifted students also told of neglect, low expectations, discouragement, and demeaning behavior from faculty. As one put it, "They just go and lecture, they don't care" (p. 270). With "the predominantly white universities that the students attended [mirroring and replicating] larger oppressive structures in society" (p. 279), how did these students manage to succeed? "The top high school students of color make it through persistence, hard work, and almost unbelievable personal will" (p. 280), despite higher education's failing "even the 'best' African-American and Mexican-American students" (p. 280).

The degree to which African-American students "disidentify" with their institutions is a better predictor of their grades than even the quality of their educational preparation for college (Steele 1992). Seventy percent of African-American students in one study withdrew from four-year colleges, compared to 45 percent of whites, and African-

American—and white—students with SATs of 1200 to 1500 were just as likely to drop out of college as those with SATs of 800 (Steele 1992). An unsupportive campus climate is a major cause of minority-group students' withdrawal from college. "Evidence is growing that the poor quality of minority students' life on campus and their sense of isolation, alienation, and lack of support are more serious factors in attrition" (Smith 1989, p. 22) than their relatively poor preparation for academic work. Graduation rates of white students from New Jersey state colleges, for example, are about three times greater than those of African-American and Hispanic students, and about twice the rates of Asians (Goldberg 1993a). Similar comparative graduation rates for the state's community colleges are twice as great for whites as for Asians, four times as great for whites as for African-Americans, and seven times as great for whites as for Hispanics. We are far from effective in educating our minority-group students and enabling them to persist successfully to graduation. "It is . . . clear that the academic, social, and psychological worlds inhabited by most non-white students on predominantly white campuses are substantially different in almost every respect from those of their white peers" (Pascarella and Terenzini 1991, p. 644).

During the last decade, many institutions have established special retention programs whose avowed purpose is to help minority group students succeed. "The fact of the matter is that there have been few consistent successes, especially at predominantly white institutions" (Anderson n.d.). Two primary factors underpin the common failure of college retention programs to have their intended effect on nonwhite students: (1) our development of such programs on the basis of "Anglo-European notions about cognitive functioning, learning, and achievement"; and (2) the failure of these programs "to identify the cognitive assets and learning preferences of nonwhite students" (Anderson 1988, p. 3). Rather than adapting to our students, we demand that they adapt to us. The implications for minority students in the natural sciences and technology may illustrate the potential consequences of our inattention to these students' needs.

Given the acknowledged need for much greater representation of minority group members in scientific and technological professions, the campus climate has direct and

[Half] of minority-group and international students claimed to have heard faculty members make racist comments, and 46 percent had had ethnoviolence directed toward them.

specific effects for society we can no longer ignore. Many of these professions require graduate-level education.

The dynamics of graduate and professional education for minorities have as [their] most direct underpinning the counseling, guidance, and mentoring of minority undergraduates. For those minority students who do make it to undergraduate school, a major proportion of these individuals are somehow turned off to graduate education. One contributing factor is the lack of interest exhibited by many active Ph.D. researchers in the counseling, development, and long-term placement of these and other undergraduate science majors. Indeed, a . . . four-year study of biology undergraduate majors at Brown University indicated that less than 10 percent of these graduates matriculated into science graduate programs one year after graduation. . . . Given the historic changes in minority student enrollment in majority institutions since the late 1950s and early 1960s, majority four-year colleges and universities in the United States now enroll approximately 82 percent of all [African-American] undergraduates. HBCU [historically black college and university] graduates, however, represent 32 percent of all [African-Americans] earning science and engineering Ph.D.'s, 34 percent of physical science Ph.D.'s, 37 percent of math Ph.D.'s, and 33 percent of computer science Ph.D.'s. . . . A greater proportion of the minority science majors at HBCUs tend to go on to graduate programs versus their counterparts at majority institutions (Wyche and Frierson 1990, pp. 989–90).

Of the top 20 institutions granting bachelor's degrees to minority-group students who later earned Ph.D.'s from 1986 to 1990, 17, or 85 percent, were HBCUs (Stimpson 1992).

Of 6,320 African-Americans who earned doctorates in all fields from 1975 through 1980, 55 percent had earlier graduated from 87 HBCUs and 45 percent from 633 primarily white colleges and universities (Sudarkasa 1987). Eighty percent of African-American, Hispanic, and Native American college graduates receive their degrees from 20 percent of U.S. institutions, many of which have served predominantly minority group students (Deskins, cited in Richardson and Skinner 1991). The relative success of these institutions with minority-group students is somewhat ironic.

Minority-group students are concentrated in institutions that have the most limited resources (Richardson and Skinner 1991).

Despite the urgent need for minority faculty members, "the intolerably small pool of qualified minority applicants represents a shocking weakness, if not an indictment, of American education at all levels" (Boyer 1990b, p. 66). "For many minority students, particularly [African-American] students on predominantly white campuses, survival in a hostile environment is the preordinate goal and radically alters the usual standards of quality against which the student experience might be compared" (Kuh, Krehbiel, and MacKay 1988, p. 29). The reason that African-American and Hispanic students attend graduate school in low numbers is a result of their low rates of completing the bachelor's degree (Adelman 1990, p. 242). Given the special difficulty majority institutions experience in graduating African-American males, the finding that academically oriented men are at special risk for dropping out of college is of special interest (Brower 1992).

Conclusions

"Measures of cognitive development typically provide a report that reveals enormous gaps between minority and majority students. [And] trend analyses usually reveal little, if any, progress being made to eliminate the gaps" (Nettles 1991, p. 1). Minority students in particular bring with them to college two strongly positive characteristics that can make them unusually rewarding to work with (Saufley, Cowan, and Blake 1983). First, and "perhaps most important, minority-group students are generally characterized by strong commitment" to education or, perhaps at first, to helping their home community (p. 13). Second, "minority students are also generally characterized by an amazing perseverance. . . . If they are given a chance to see that they can succeed at the university, they exhibit a tenacious determination to work through or to beat the system" (pp. 13–14). Today, numerous resources are available to provide assistance in improving the college experience for minority students (Adams 1992; Border and Chism 1992; Cones, Noonan, and Janha 1983; Richardson, Matthews, and Finney 1992; Smith 1989; Wright 1987).

The research reviewed here shows clearly the unequal and antidevelopmental treatment we accord many of our students. Improving the climate and quality of community experienced by all students should dramatically improve their ability to succeed—and thus the quality of our outcomes.

ACADEMIC ADVISING: Guiding Development

Our students come from widely different family backgrounds and schools, with diverse values, goals, styles of learning, and levels of self-esteem and abilities. Few have a sophisticated understanding of higher education or skills in personal or career planning, and many have never been taught how to learn or been informed of the need to take an active role in their own learning. Large numbers are underprepared for the academic work we ask of them.

In college, students suddenly find themselves in a new, strange, and, for many, much more demanding and stressful environment than they have previously known. The quality of guidance they receive can markedly affect the degree to which they profit from their years at college. Their ability to understand their own development, clarify their personal values and goals, plan an appropriate developmental curriculum and other educational experiences, and feel emotionally secure, integrated, and at home on campus can all affect their degree of success, indeed, their very decision to remain in college. Academic advising by faculty provides a choice opportunity for close contact between students and faculty out of class, one that can have a major effect on students' values, goals, and behavior and significantly increase their satisfaction with college and thus persistence. Students who have no contact with faculty outside class experience "significantly lower growth in principled [ethical] reasoning" (McNeel 1994, p. 37). Racial tension is more likely on campuses "where there is a lack of concern for individual students" (Hurtado 1992, p. 562). High-quality academic advising unequivocally demonstrates our concern for each person throughout the college years and can provide the personal validation essential for students' success (Rendon 1994).

Entering students' expectations could confirm the need for close attention to advising, especially during the first year. The CIRP survey of first-year students in fall 1992 reveals that only 43.3 percent estimated the probability was "very good" they would make at least a B average; a mere 14.2 percent believed they would graduate with honors (Collison 1993, pp. A30–A31). Although many students enter college knowing little of themselves or of the world of work and many have substantial personal problems, few expect to seek vocational counseling (5.1 percent) or individual counseling (3.7 percent) (*Chronicle* 1991). Entering students need the personal challenge and reflection good advising provides to refine their personal values and goals. "Being well-off financially" was an essential or very important objective for 73 percent of student respondents in 1992. In fact, 69.8 percent of the students agreed that "the chief benefit of college is that it increases one's earning power." In contrast, only 45.6 percent had as an essential or very important objective "developing a meaningful philosophy of life." Students' social and political perspectives seemed at best narrow. Only 38.8 percent had as an essential or very important objective "keeping up to date with political affairs," a mere 20.1 percent "influencing the political structure." The need and opportunity for developmental advising in this democracy are great.

With regard to our guiding and counseling students, "we simply have to recognize that this is probably the most important kind of teaching we do and that these encounters are second in significance only to the daily life with other students" (Chickering 1969, p. 252). Academic advising is "a high calling" (Johnston, Shaman, and Zemsky 1987, p. 69), and "a college of quality has a year-round program of academic advising and personal counseling, structured to serve all undergraduates, including part-time and commuting students" (Boyer 1987, p. 289).

Developmental Advising: Keystone of Educational Quality

Effective high-quality advising today is developmental in design (Crookston 1972). Based on an ongoing relationship between student and adviser, developmental advising helps each student become more aware of his or her values, personal characteristics, and needs, and assists him or her in setting goals, making plans for postgraduate life and a career, and using opportunities for development effectively, thus solving problems and building self-esteem. Quality developmental advising can be conceived of as the hub of each student's experience on campus (Ender, Winston, and Miller 1982). Through a mentoring relationship with an adviser, a student can understand and plan his or her time in college. The adviser and student together can identify special developmental needs that interfere with learning and development, such as inadequate learning skills or learning disorders (Schmidt and Sprandel 1982), emotional concerns (Altmaier 1983; Hanfmann 1978; Whitman, Spendlove, and Clark 1986), social relationships, and health issues, and then determine resources available for dealing with them. Developmental advising is pivotal to the quality of an institution's educational process, for "academic advising can be conceived as the institution's quality control mechanism" (Winston, Grites, et al. 1984, p. 539). Developmental advising ensures the institution knows each student as an individual and understands and meets his or her needs. Rather than using summative assessment to weed out the unfit ("defect detection"), developmental advising functions as "defect prevention," ensuring that on graduation all students meet the criterion of "fitness for use."

Several studies demonstrate a positive relationship between academic advising and students' achievement, satisfaction with college, personal, social, and vocational development, and persistence on campus (Saunders and Ervin 1984). A positive association between self-esteem and academic performance suggests that, beyond improving their study skills, building students' self-esteem may be a good way of improving their academic success (Covington 1989). Developmental academic advising is an excellent way to foster sustained improvement in students' self-esteem and their study habits as well.

High-quality advising has a significant positive effect on students' persistence on campus by increasing their achievement and satisfaction and thus reducing their intent to withdraw (Pascarella and Terenzini 1991). A study of 947 institutions, for example, reveals that improved advising increased students' persistence on campus more than 25 percent (Ender, Winston, and Miller 1984). Better academic advising is therefore often recommended as a means of improving retention among students (Forrest 1985; Noel 1985; Saluri 1985). Over half of first-year students in one study who lacked significant involvement with an institutional authority, such as a teacher or adviser, failed to return to campus for a second year (Noel 1985). In another study, a sample of 1,033 students, 51.1 percent of all first-time, first-year students, at a large public, urban commuter university in the Midwest, rated the quality of the academic advising they had received (Metzner 1989). Fully one-third had received no advising at all, and, of those students, 35 percent were lost to the institution within one year of entry. Students who perceived their advising to be of good quality withdrew at a rate 25 percent less than those with poor advising and 40 percent less than those who had received no advising at all.*

How Good Is Our Advising?

Academic advising as it is generally now practiced in this country functions primarily as a means of dispensing information to students, such as requirements for registration and graduation, rather than serving as a powerful developmental tool to foster students' retention and success. "Advising in academic departments is viewed more as a clerical registration function than as a process in which the [adviser] intervenes at critical times" (Habley and Crockett 1988, p. 33).

Authorities on advising today recommend an intrusive approach that actively seeks out students and ensures quality advising for each one, but institutions tend not to be intrusive. A large number, perhaps even most, do not require their students to consult an adviser even for such weighty issues as declaring a major, unsatisfactory progress, and withdrawal from the college (Habley and Crockett 1988). We passively wait for our students to come to us.

Three hours per year is the minimum amount of time each student should spend with an adviser (Winston, Miller, et al. 1984), and "any college arguing that it cannot organize its personnel and budget to accomplish this modest proposal . . . is suspect as a viable educational institution" (p. 545). "Short, limited, and irregular interactions between [advisers and students] seldom have lasting impact" (Ender, Winston, and Miller 1984, p. 16), even though a third of nearly 20,000 students from 55 colleges in one study claimed usually to spend only 15 minutes when visiting their advisers during each of two or fewer visits a year (Noble 1988). For all respondent institutions in the same survey, the reported modal amount of faculty time spent advising was between 1 percent and 5 percent; a mere 3 percent of institutions reported more than 15 percent of

---

* See Saluri 1985 for a discussion of programs that have significantly improved retention by raising the quality of advising.

faculty time devoted to advising across all departments (Habley and Crockett 1988). In another national study, 55 percent of faculty spent four or fewer hours per week in contact of any sort with students outside the classroom (Finkelstein 1984).

Students' satisfaction with advising reflects our inattention to this key educational process. "According to several national surveys, undergraduates tend to be more dissatisfied with academic advising than with almost any other service they receive" (Astin 1987, p. 16), rating college advising programs "highly adequate" in 17 percent (academic advising), 9 percent (personal advising), and 7 percent (vocational advising) of cases in one survey (Boyer 1987). In a national study of the effects of college, only 44.1 percent of students said they were "satisfied" or "very satisfied" with advising on their campuses (Astin 1993).

The Necessity for Training

Most academic advising is conducted in academic departments. Overwhelmingly, it is the faculty who advise our students: 80 percent of all advising in one sample of 754 colleges and universities (Crockett and Levitz 1984). Regardless of who the advisers are, however, "training is one of the most important ingredients of an effective advising program" (Gordon 1984, p. 461). Yet faculty members are still ordinarily untrained for this important and complex work, approaching this responsibility unequipped with knowledge of student development and without the requisite skills in communication, counseling, decision making, or career planning.

Training for advisers is not mandatory in *any* department in 44.6 percent of institutions in one survey; it is mandatory in all departments in only 26.2 percent. In only 29.2 percent of the institutions with mandatory training (7.7 percent of all institutions) was this training said to be conducted systematically (Habley and Crockett 1988). Any training that does exist tends to focus on transmitting information to students: rules, policies, and procedures to follow. Training of some sort in such key skills as counseling, interviewing, and decision making is conducted in relatively few departments: 20.5 percent, 14.7 percent, and 11.4 percent, respectively. More surprising yet is the limited training provided for even the staffs of campus advising offices, where advising is often a full-time endeavor. Sixty percent of such offices provide no training whatever or do not mandate it.

Evaluation, Recognition, and Reward

The low esteem in which colleges and universities hold advising is indicated by the limited recognition accorded this complex and demanding task. Recognition and reward for advising in those few institutions where they exist at all are most often only "a minor consideration in the promotion and tenure process" (Habley and Crockett 1988, p. 41). When asked how they would rate their advising programs, college officials in one survey rated accountability, training, evaluation, and recognition and reward for work as an adviser least effective out of 11 stated characteristics (Habley and Crockett 1988).

> *The most significant methods by which advising can be improved are seen as both the least effective and least improved areas in the organization and administration of campus advising programs. Training, accountability, evaluation, and recognition/reward are the cornerstones of performance in every field or job. Yet those cornerstones continue to be stumbling blocks in most advising programs* (Habley and Crockett 1988, p. 68).

"This apparent lack of concern on the part of institutions with the effectiveness and outcomes of their advising programs is disappointing and difficult to understand" (Crockett and Levitz 1984, p. 44).

Conclusions

Not surprisingly, students perceive our apparent indifference toward our relationships with them. At the University of California, before the main incursion into colleges of the "new" students, 75 percent of freshmen and 63 percent of seniors stated they had no one on the faculty "whom they felt was particularly responsible to or for them" (Chickering 1969, p. 252). Thirty percent of seniors, looking back on their college experience, "felt that very few or no faculty members were really interested in students" (p. 252). And research provides scant evidence of change in the quality of advising over the 25-plus years since then.

Findings . . . depict a somewhat disappointing picture of the status of academic advising in American colleges and universities. The results, particularly when compared to those from earlier advising surveys [in 1979 and 1983], reveal little or no improvement . . . (Habley and Crockett 1988, p. 74).

Developmental academic advising became no more common in American colleges and universities during the 1980s than it was in the previous decade: It "is still more prominent in theory than it is in practice" (Habley and Crockett 1988, p. 67). "Academic advising is scandalously poor in higher education" (Johnston, Shaman, and Zemsky 1987, p. 69). Apparently the advising we offer our students in general continues the inadequate quality of the guidance most of them received in high school (Schmidt 1993). And concerns have been raised about the quality of advising at the graduate level (Mooney 1991).

"Faculty perceive that they provide much more beneficial advisement than students feel they receive. Students perceive a vast difference between what faculty advising should be and what it is" (Kramer and Spencer 1989, p. 105). Surprisingly, although 79 percent of presidents responding to a 1989 survey stated that poor academic advising was a problem on their campuses, only 14 percent believed it was a greater than moderate problem (Boyer 1990a). Apparently, students' and experts' perceptions of quality vary significantly from those of many faculty members and administrators.

"Greater efforts will have to be made to advise and counsel students if they are to actually complete the programs in which they enroll" (Solmon 1989, p. 36). Clearly, if colleges and universities are to produce the fair outcomes for all students society requires today, we will have to change our advising significantly.

Apparently, students' and experts' perceptions of quality vary significantly from those of many faculty members and administrators.

CAN TODAY'S STUDENTS LEARN? Achieving Success with High Standards for All

Given our students' common underpreparation for academic work and our striking lack of success in graduating many of them, some observers have asked whether today's diverse students, coming as they do from such disparate backgrounds, can reasonably be expected to succeed at a high level. Does widespread access to higher education by necessity preclude achievement of high-quality outcomes? Can these students learn?

Engaging the interest of our students and motivating them to the high quality of effort required for excellent achievement are no mean feats. Some faculty believe many students simply lack the intellectual equipment required to learn; achievement of a high school diploma may be the most to which they can realistically aspire. Research and experience elsewhere, however, suggest that understanding more fully the backgrounds and developmental and contextual reasons our students behave as they do can greatly enhance our ability to help them develop.

Professional opinion today views students' aptitudes as products not only of heredity but also of experience, not "a list of independent, fixed entities always in force . . . [but] exhibited *in consort* as resultant strengths or weaknesses *relative* to present and past conditions" (Snow 1986, p. 1037, emphasis in the original). The educational process must adapt to each individual if all are to succeed.

Specific and compelling evidence suggests we can be successful in fostering the development of virtually all our students to far higher levels than we have in the past. Using modern methods, some colleges and universities are now achieving striking results in retaining their students on campus and graduating them successfully. The research reviewed in this monograph strongly suggests that, by determinedly focusing on improving the quality of their educational processes, many institutions can achieve dramatic gains in student development.

Working with public elementary and secondary school students, who are in most cases far less rigorously selected and therefore much more heterogeneous and representative of Americans generally than are most college students, certain individual teachers and schools have, by dint of their enthusiasm, empathy, imagination, and technical professional skill, achieved startling results under improbable conditions. For example, Jaime Escalante, whose work has become well known nationally through the film *Stand and Deliver,* for years against daunting odds taught calculus in a Los Angeles barrio. These 98 percent Latino young people, believed by many unable to learn higher-level mathematics, consistently passed the ETS Advanced Placement Test in calculus at rates higher than students from all but a small number of far wealthier schools (Mathews 1992). These students went on to college in significant numbers, including to institutions of stature.

Henry Levin (1991) has developed accelerated schools where most students are at risk for failure, coming from impoverished, poorly educated, ethnic minority families (Wells 1989). By giving these students experiences typical of programs for the gifted and talented rather than remedial classes, Levin has dramatically improved their rate of learning.

The potential of schools and colleges today is suggested by a search for instructional methods that could increase productivity in teaching (Ellson 1986). This study uncovered 125 different methods that were at least twice as effective as more traditional methods used in experimental control groups on at least one index of productivity, such as effectiveness, cost, or instructional time.

Solving the Two-Sigma Problem
Benjamin S. Bloom and his doctoral students at the University of Chicago established that high school students tutored one-to-one, one-to-two, or one-to-three in various subjects achieved test scores averaging about two standard deviations or "sigmas" higher than similar students taught by conventional group instruction (Bloom 1984). In other words, the average tutored student performed better than 98 percent of the conventionally taught students. With tutoring, 90 percent of the students reached the level of performance of the top 20 percent of conventionally taught students. "The tutoring process demonstrates that *most of the students* do have the potential to reach this high level of learning" (p. 6, emphasis in the original). Compared with conventional group methods, however, tutoring is a very labor-intensive and thus expensive form of instruction.

Using mastery learning, a well-researched method of instruction (Block 1971; Bloom 1976; Guskey 1988; Kulik, Kulik, and Bangert-Drowns 1990; Levine and Associates

1985), the researchers consistently achieved a full one-sigma increase in assessed learning over conventional instruction; the average mastery student scored higher than 84 percent of those in the conventionally taught class. With mastery methods, 70 percent of the students achieved a level equal to only the top 20 percent of conventionally taught students. The researchers also discovered that the variation in amount of learning *among* students also changed dramatically, becoming much smaller in mastery groups. Taken together, these results demonstrate that *the higher the quality of instruction, the less relevant to achievement are the entering student's abilities.* Or, "the better the coaching, the less the correlation between height and success in basketball" (Baird 1985, p. 73).

In a search for those variables that have the strongest effects on learning, Walberg (1984) reviewed and summarized 3,000 empirical studies of students' learning in schools conducted during the previous 50 years. By manipulating certain of those variables, Bloom's group by 1984 was able to close fully the two-sigma gap between the outcomes produced by tutoring and conventional instruction with six different methods of group instruction. And optimizing all nine of the strongest variables Walberg identified should improve learning by 3.7 standard deviations or sigmas over current achievement produced by conventional methods (Walberg 1984, p. 24).

Bloom's group found that the higher the quality of instruction, the lower the correlations between students' assessed aptitude and their achievement. This correlation was .60 for the conventionally taught control groups in the studies. With mastery learning methods, the correlation dropped to .35 and with tutoring to .25 (Bloom 1984). In other words, improving the quality of instruction dramatically reduced the impact of students' abilities upon entry and enabled all of the students to learn at a high level. According to Bloom, the research is relevant to all levels of education, "including . . . college and even graduate and professional school" (p. 8).

Higher-order thinking
Dramatically improved learning is not limited to low-level facts and concepts alone. When comparing university students' learning from conventional instruction by lecture

with discussion groups using new materials and methods, "these and other approaches [make] it clear that most students *could* learn the higher mental processes if they became more central in the teaching-learning process" (Bloom 1984, p. 15, emphasis in the original). (Other research by the same group produced a 1.7-sigma increase in higher-order cognitive processes over conventional instruction.)

The potential for human development in college

Bloom's findings with ordinary students in schools are consistent with later studies by his group, of 120 Americans, each rated among the top 25 people in his or her field (Bloom 1985). In the later studies as well, in addition to motivation and effort, environmental factors were consistently essential to their success: chance opportunities and the very high standards (challenge) and guidance and encouragement (support) of teachers.

"Individual differences in school learning under very favorable conditions of schooling will approach a vanishing point . . . " (Bloom 1976, p. 6). "What any person in the world can learn, almost all persons can learn *if* provided with appropriate prior and current conditions of learning" (p. 7, emphasis in the original).

If these dramatic results can be achieved with ordinary students in schools, results with our often much more highly selected and therefore "able" college students can surely be as impressive.

> *We now have lots of research that shows that intelligence is essentially made up of learnable skills. This means we can teach intelligence! Students gain intelligence in college depending on what they study and how they learn. No longer can we dismiss students' aspirations as if they are in some kind of hopeless situation. . . . Rather, there is now evidence that we can work with students at all levels of ability* (McKeachie 1991, p. 226).

Success in Mathematics for Minority Students

On many campuses, undergraduate calculus courses are notorious for their low pass rates, and disadvantaged students with weak mathematics backgrounds are especially at risk in such courses. But a marked departure from traditional methods for working with students in academic diffi-

culty at the University of California–Berkeley that emphasized cooperative learning methods and very high standards rather than remediation achieved a high level of success with minority group calculus students (Treisman 1985).
Over a decade, more than 40 percent of African-American
nonprogram students regularly failed calculus each term
(grades of D+ or lower); of African-American students in
the program, however, over seven years only 3 percent
failed and repeated the course unsuccessfully. Less than a
quarter of nonprogram African-American students obtained
a grade of A or B in calculus, and their grade point averages in their mathematics courses were near the university's
cutoff for probationary status. More than half of the students in the program, however, received A's and B's; their
grade point averages in these courses were similar to the
overall class average. Most Berkeley students who withdraw from the university do so during their first two years.
Only 57 percent of nonprogram African-American students
persisted to their fourth semester, while 74 to 78 percent of
African-American students in the program, regardless of
their admission status, persisted to that point, the rate for
Berkeley students as a whole. After five years, only 41 percent of African-American students at Berkeley had graduated or still remained on campus, compared to 65 percent
for program completers (and 66 percent for the overall
campus). Ten percent of nonprogram African-American calculus students finished college in math-based majors, 44
percent of program completers.

The ability of minority group students to succeed in
mathematics is further underscored by experience at the
University of Texas–Austin. Under a similar program, 23
percent of the 500 mathematics majors were minority students, whereas 18 percent of all undergraduates were from
racial minorities (Selvin 1992). Twelve of 15 students in an
advanced Gaulois Theory course, or 80 percent, were
African-American or Latino.

A study of primarily Latino students in a similar cooperative learning program in basic calculus at California Polytechnic State University–Pomona reveals substantial correlation between program participation and achievement in
the course, achievement in successive calculus courses,
progress through the calculus sequence, retention in math,
science, and engineering majors, and persistence in college

(Bonsangue and Drew *n.d.*). For example, 42 percent of minority nonworkshop students withdrew from school over the six years after entry, compared to only 4 percent of the students who attended the workshop. Fully 23 percent of nonworkshop students required six semesters to complete the three-semester calculus sequence; only 5 percent of workshop participants required as long.

Graduate Professional Schools: Admission and Graduation for Minority Students

Xavier University of Louisiana is a small private institution with limited resources, 95 percent of whose 1,800 students are African-Americans from modest academic backgrounds. Xavier students have an average combined SAT score of 825, which "the Ivy League wouldn't touch" (Culotta 1992, p. 1217). Yet Xavier has become "a veritable factory for producing [African-American] graduates in science" (p. 1217). Whereas nationally the number of African-Americans entering science majors in college was dropping, at Xavier their numbers tripled, and half of all students major in science. Xavier has been first in the nation in African-Americans admitted to pharmacy schools and second in admission to medical schools; 86.3 percent of its 102 1988 graduates entering health professions were African-Americans ("PreHealth Highlights" 1988). Although the institution is very small, Xavier students were admitted to graduate programs in the health professions in significantly larger numbers than the much more highly selected minority group students from Harvard, Stanford, Johns Hopkins, and the University of California–Berkeley ("Information" 1992). For example, Harvard's fall 1985 entering class was both 20 percent minority and drawn from the top one-sixth of all applicants (Hodgkinson 1985). Xavier students earned graduate degrees at about the national rate for all students in these programs. Not surprisingly, the keys to success at Xavier include adaptation to students' needs, a strong introductory program in the development of abstract reasoning, extensive contact with faculty outside the classroom, strong social support, and a campus climate that encourages success (Carmichael et al. 1978; Culotta 1992).

Educational Effectiveness and Efficiency

If these methods work their dramatic effects with some of

the least well-prepared of our students, what might we accomplish with their more experienced peers? A preeminent indicator of our effectiveness as educators is the proportion of the students we admit whom we are able to graduate. The failure of their students to persist on campus—the ultimate lack of involvement—is a major concern for many institutions. Of all 210,739 first-year students at 431 two- and four-year institutions who responded to the 1991 ACE-UCLA CIRP survey, a mere 0.8 percent estimated they had a "very good" chance of dropping out permanently, 1 percent temporarily (*Chronicle* 1992). About 40 to 45 percent of all first-time college students do withdraw from college without graduating, however (Tinto 1985). For example, the rates of graduation after five years for students entering 10 New Jersey public four-year colleges and universities in 1983 ranged from 29 percent to 67 percent, with an institutional average of 42 percent (College Outcomes Evaluation Program 1990a). The range for students entering in 1984 at the 10 institutions was 26 percent to 65 percent, with an institutional average of 41 percent (College Outcomes Evaluation Program Council 1991). The average five-year graduation rate for minority students entering the 10 institutions in 1983 was 22.9 percent (College Outcomes Evaluation Program 1990a), in 1984, 24.2 percent (College Outcomes Evaluation Program Council 1991). Although some additional students will graduate from these institutions in succeeding years, their number is unlikely to be large. In more than a few institutions across the country, a majority of students who enter fail to graduate.

The losses incurred by unnecessary, inappropriate withdrawal from college are enormous to these students and their families, their institutions, which forfeit significant sums of money, the states, and the nation. Although the reasons for withdrawal are diverse, evidence suggests the quality of our educational processes and the climate we create on campus are primary factors affecting the decision whether to remain on campus or leave. Only a small minority of 10 to 15 percent of college withdrawals result from academic failure; in most cases, withdrawal has more to do with students' experiences in college than their characteristics on entry, particularly the degree to which a student is integrated into the life of the campus (Tinto 1987).

Of particular importance are those experiences [that] arise from the daily interactions between students and faculty outside the classroom. Other things being equal, the more frequent those interactions are, and the warmer and more rewarding they are seen to be by the students, the more likely is persistence—indeed, the more likely is social and intellectual development generally (Tinto 1987, p. 84).

Beyond the rates at which we are able to graduate our students, an important related concern is our ability to educate them efficiently, enabling them to complete their degrees in a timely manner and to move into society as fully productive members. Undergraduate students are taking longer and longer to graduate. The percentage of undergraduate students in regular four-year programs who take five years has doubled during the last 10 years (Kramer 1993). Only a third of the students at four-year institutions in Virginia graduate in four years ("Virginia" 1992). In 1992, the state colleges of New Jersey graduated 37 percent of their full-time, first-time, degree-seeking students in five years; the two-year community colleges graduated 15 percent of their equivalent cohort in three years (Goldberg 1993a). One recent study of 298 colleges and universities shows that, after six years, an average of only 54 percent of first-time, full-time, first-year students had graduated (Cage 1993). Another national study reveals that, of students entering four-year colleges and universities for the first time directly from high school, only 23 percent graduated in four years (16.5 percent in public institutions). After six years, the rate rose to 46 percent, still less than half (Porter 1990).

Students who are slow to finish can include among them many of our most academically able students. Studies by the Educational Testing Service have shown that only 51 percent of college students considered "high-ability" high school seniors who had scored in the top 25 percent on NAEP (National Assessment of Educational Progress) tests had graduated from college in seven years, a pattern that was stable through the 1970s and 1980s (Dodge 1991). As time passes, increasing frustration, alienation, and accumulating debt can discourage many students from continuing on campus, our institutional inefficiency leading them to withdraw.

Dropping out holds significant fiscal implications for us as well. "The fact that we get only half of our students through a baccalaureate degree in six years is a condemnation of higher education. If we were running an automobile plant, we would be out of business" (Reginald Wilson, cited in Cage 1993). Evidence suggests that, once we admit them, we are in many cases not providing the assistance students need.

Graduate programs suffer some of these same problems. The attrition rate of doctoral students, a decades-old concern ("Ph.D. under Attack" 1966) and deemed "disturbingly high" (Association 1990, p. 2), is estimated at 50 percent, frequently greater in some fields. The median time spent registered in graduate programs between the bachelor's and doctoral degrees in 1988 was 6.9 years (Association 1990). A study of a large and prestigious Ph.D. program at the University of California–Berkeley reveals the average time to degree was 9.6 years, about 25 percent of a graduate's 40-year career span, and only one-third of the students even completed a degree (Seymour 1992). These slow rates of learning and high rates of attrition have significant financial implications for our students and for society at large.

Only 51 percent of college students considered "high-ability" high school seniors had graduated from college in seven years.

Conclusions

Taken together, old-fashioned methods take a heavy toll in lost human potential and reduced learning productivity in colleges and universities. At the same time, the systematic use of methods validated by research holds promise for dramatically improving the value we are able to create for both our students and our supporters, and for society more broadly. If we would do what works and stop doing what does not, virtually all of our students could learn. The next section introduces a number of specific methods that have proven their worth in effecting high-quality learning.

IMPROVING QUALITY: The Need for a Sea Change

Our students' sojourn with us in higher education often resembles not so much a carefully crafted educational experience tailored to each person's developmental needs as one of fruit bouncing erratically on a conveyor in a mass packing facility. The student experience seems more frequently determined by academic tradition than research-based theory, our educational process more often based on expediency—the convenience of administrators and faculty—than our students' developmental needs. To produce high-quality results for our stakeholders requires the insights of research-based theory rather than what often seems to be an atheoretical or lay hypothetical approach to students and learning. In many cases, our students lack all but the most rudimentary academic advising—often they have received none at all—and they receive little assessment of their developmental levels or needs upon entry to college other than of basic verbal and mathematical skills. Thus, neither they nor their teachers have the crucial information both require to construct developmental plans and prescribe activities that can provide an appropriate response to their needs. For most students, academic activities apparently involve classes where they listen passively to authorities tell them facts; they seem to do relatively little learning on their own outside class, rarely work with other students or have contact with faculty outside class, infrequently reflect systematically about their own development, and consider college primarily as a station on the way to a better job and salary.

Even for culturally and educationally advantaged students, such experiences are ill suited to foster their development. Because of their previous status, however, these more privileged students may survive the system, even learn quite a bit, and certainly emerge with excellent grades. For their less advantaged peers, however, their experiences on campus can all too often be developmentally destructive. Unsure of what to expect in this new and foreign culture, frequently consumed by self-doubt, lacking adequate academic skills, and fearful of asserting their needs to authority, these students often find the college experience a frustrating and demoralizing path to failure—failure whose impact can last a lifetime.

The system of higher education in this country is often claimed to be the best in the world, and it may well be.

Our more than 3,600 institutions provide access to postsecondary schooling for a larger percentage of our people than do the colleges and universities of perhaps any other nation. Annually, other countries send 460,000 of their people here to attend our postsecondary institutions (Barbett et al. 1995). But, "what if, in light of what organizations *could* be, 'excellence' is actually 'mediocrity'?" (Senge 1990, p. 18, emphasis in the original). Judged by a standard more exacting than the current performance of colleges elsewhere, by the standard of human potential, by the standard of quality modern educational methods can produce, and by the standard of what society now requires, we fall far short. Our current standards no longer serve us well. Our institutions are, for the most part, mere shadows of what they could become as engines of human development.

The pattern of checkered quality and institutional ineffectiveness suggested by the studies reviewed in this monograph is fully consistent with serious concerns repeatedly raised in the long series of reports issued over the last decade by various government agencies and education organizations. These reports, prepared by panels of prominent academicians and other distinguished Americans, are sharply critical of colleges and universities. A number of books published during the same period further detail our perceived inability to educate our students (see, e.g., Bloom 1987; Huber 1992; Smith 1990; Sykes 1988; Von Blum 1986; Wilshire 1990). Other reports cited earlier are equally critical of our ineffectiveness in preparing both undergraduate and graduate students in specific disciplines and fields. Students' achievement is related to our own performance: "Development thrives in a richly interactive and personalized environment, a hothouse for intellectual growth. The potential for such growth remains largely untapped in most institutions of higher learning . . ." (Kurfiss 1988, p. 68).

Widespread agreement among observers suggests we are at a watershed in American higher education. The nation's social and economic future depends on a number of clearly identified and widely agreed-upon human qualities in its citizens, among them well-developed intellectual skills and values, the capacity to work well with others, and the desire for lifelong learning. Our research-based knowledge of how these human qualities can be developed is now sufficiently sophisticated for us to nurture development to a high level and on a truly wide scale. We cannot, however, accomplish this task using what are, in many cases, methods unchanged from the 1960s, 1950s, or even before.

Today, national and state leaders are calling for a significant restructuring of higher education analogous to the process now under way in the K–12 sector (Mingle 1993). Few knowledgeable observers believe isolated repairs made here and there—more add-on programs or tinkering with or fine-tuning the status quo—are likely to achieve the results required or to do so in a reasonable length of time. Society's needs require fundamental rethinking of how we in higher education work. Thus, at the 1992 annual meeting of the Education Commission of the States, the program "reflected the growing interest in radical approaches to solving higher education's problems" (Mercer 1992). A high-level task force has recommended a national council be established to develop standards for students' achievement in college and the means to assess achievement of those standards (Task Force on Assessing 1992).

We can modernize our educational processes and improve our capacity to produce learning in many important ways. A number of newer professional practices, if correctly applied (often in combination) and systematically and systemically managed, hold especially great promise for improving the quality and quantity of learning in our colleges and universities.

1. Clear Missions and Goals: Setting High Expectations, Focusing Effort, Reducing Waste

"If we don't know where we're going, we may end up someplace else." "Clarity of institutional purpose, communicated both through the curriculum and through the consistency with which the institution acts" (Peterson et al. 1986, p. 105), is "very important" in determining students' outcomes. "An effective college has a clear and vital mission. Administrators, faculty, and students share a vision of what the institution is seeking to accomplish" (Boyer 1987, p. 58). Moreover, "the moment we lose sight of the mission, we begin to stray, we waste resources" (Drucker 1990, p. 141).

Because of their broad language, mission statements need to be translated into more specific goals and objectives to be fully useful on an operational level (Gardiner 1989). Authorities today consider an essential foundation for all institutional activities—planning, implementation, and monitoring quality—a series of carefully stated outcomes describing clearly for everyone the results the institution and its programs intend to produce. These outcome goals and objectives guide the design of the curriculum, instruction, advising, and cocurricular activities, and the systematic assessment of the actual results these educational processes produce. If development is the aim of education, as Kohlberg and Mayer (1972) suggest:

> *The most important issue confronting educators and educational theorists is the choice of ends for the educational process. Without clear and rational educational goals, it becomes impossible to decide which educational programs achieve objectives of general import and which teach incidental facts and attitudes of dubious worth* (Kohlberg and Mayer 1972, p. 449).

Of course, both mission statements and goals must be used to be useful, and evidence suggests in all too many cases we are not now using them. "The American college or university is a prototypic organized anarchy. It does not know what it is doing. Its goals are either vague or in dispute" (Cohen and March 1974, p. 3). Many faculty members and others on campus do not understand their institution's objectives (Study Group 1984). "We found at most colleges in our study great difficulty, sometimes to the point of paralysis, in defining purposes and goals" (Boyer 1987, p. 59). The result of such confusion can be the adding on of programs and activities that could be peripheral to the institution's educational purpose, academic departments' controlling specialized pieces of what should be an integrated curriculum, and instruction occurring as uncoordinated, individual courses often the private preserves of individual professors. "Common goals are blurred" (p. 59), effort unfocused, resources wasted, and results mediocre. Successfully serving our diverse clients at a high level of quality will require us to take far more seriously than we in most cases now do the crafting and use of statements of our missions and intended outcomes.

"All leadership is goal-oriented [and] the failure to set goals is a sign of faltering leadership" (Burns 1978, p. 455). Through leadership and commitment—and more forceful pressure from their external stakeholders—our colleagues in the K–12 sector have outdistanced us in efforts to clarify intended results. Dozens of national and statewide efforts specify demanding outcome "standards" for all students, teachers, and institutions ("Struggling" 1995). "One is hard pressed to think of any organization that has sustained some measure of greatness in the absence of goals, values, and missions that become deeply shared throughout the organization" (Senge 1990, p. 9). Clarifying our educational missions, values, and goals for everyone is a first step we can take to move our institutions unequivocally toward high quality.

2. Knowledge of Results: Using Systematic Assessment To Create a Culture of Evidence

Equally as important as clearly defining the outcomes we intend to produce is assessing their actual achievement. Assessment is essential not only to guide the development of individual students but also to monitor and continuously improve the quality of programs, inform prospective students and their parents, and provide evidence of accountability to those who pay our way. Nevertheless, "it is rare that an institution evaluates its impact on individual students across a coherent spectrum of institutional objectives" (Korn 1986, p. 5). In most cases, we simply do not know how our students are developing or how effective we are. Even today, we often fly blind.

Given the inadequacy of grades as indicators of students' learning, "the consequent lack of data about [students'] performance and a college's leaves the stakeholders in higher education . . . with little information about the learning outcomes of a single college or system of colleges" (Turnbull 1985, p. 24). Baccalaureate-level results are not the only ones shrouded in mystery. A widely publicized report on quality in basic medical education states, "The effectiveness of an educational program should be measured by how well its students perform later in their careers. Most institutions of higher education employ short-term measures, if any, to determine whether or not their education goals are accomplished" (Panel 1984, p. 31). "Outsiders find this peculiar, given academia's thirst for data and knowledge" (Keller 1983, p. 131)—not to mention our virtually universal trained expertise in research.

In the absence of timely and reliable information produced by effective assessment and evaluation, how can we be sure of what is happening in our institutions? An additional consequence of our failure to assess results regularly could be our own misperception of reality. Thirty-seven percent of faculty respondents to one survey said their institutions did an "excellent" job in undergraduate general education, and another 38 percent selected "better than adequate"; only 6 percent believed their institutions did a job that was "less than adequate," 1 percent "poor" (Boyer 1989).

Monitoring results continuously and at every point will have to become an important focus for us if we are to improve the quality of our work as required. Moreover, assessment will have to apprise us not only of the *outcomes* we produce, but also of *inputs*—the specific characteristics of our incoming students—and the quality of our educational *processes* (Adelman 1988, 1989; Anderson et al. 1975; *Assessment Update;* Astin 1991; Banta 1988, 1993; Banta et al. 1995; Dressell 1976; Erwin 1991; Halpern 1987; Hanson 1982, 1989; Light, Singer, and Willett 1990; Mentkowski et al. 1991). (For assessment in courses, see p. 65.)

3. Coherent Curricula: Integrating Development
As the overarching, integrated framework for students' development, the curriculum and its purpose, design, and function are fundamental to educational quality. "The curriculum, too, if properly designed, should intellectually integrate the campus. In a *purposeful* community, learning is pervasive" (Boyer 1990a, p. 16, emphasis in the original). The studies reviewed earlier strongly suggest many institutions may need to rethink their curricula. "Traditional curricula and course structures are generally insensitive to the needs, interests, and abilities of the individual student, unaffected by the changing needs of society, and inefficient in their use of available talents and resources" (Diamond 1989, p. 188). A necessary starting point for curricular design or redesign, as for any other program, is to define clearly the specific outcomes the curriculum is expected to produce and then to assess continuously in a valid and reli-

able fashion both the actual results produced and the quality of the curricular processes that produced them. To produce high-quality results consistently, curricula must be actively *managed*.

Use psychological theory at every point

Goals and objectives for curricular outcomes, instructional processes, the cocurriculum, academic advising, and assessment should all systematically incorporate what we now know about our students' psychological development, such as their capacity for abstraction, epistemology, moral development, ego development (Knefelkamp, Parker, and Widick 1978; Kronholm 1996; Loevinger 1976; Weathersby 1981), capacity for intimacy (Douvan 1981), interpersonal social skills (Torbert 1981), and identity (Chickering and Reisser 1993). *Students should be helped to understand the implications of this research and learn to apply it metacognitively in their own lives.*

If the preeminent outcome we value is students' cognitive development, the curriculum should at all points focus on producing this result. Thorough step-by-step training specifically designed to develop critical thinking skills and dispositions, and the ability for and habit of metacognition should be planned throughout the curriculum and should provide abundant practice with timely corrective feedback in diverse contexts (Brookfield 1987; Cromwell 1986; Facione 1990; Facione, Sanchez, and Facione 1993; Halonen 1986; Kurfiss 1988; Meyers 1986; Paul 1995; Stice 1987). We should consciously be developing, in a word, wisdom (Sternberg 1990).

> *Cognitive development, although central to our enterprise, is . . . not enough. To the extent that cognition develops apart from affective development, it is likely to result in a distorted, fragmented conception of reality where one is wholly unaware of one's projections. Psychopathology is the likely result. . . . An educational system that fosters the development of cognitive processes at the expense of that of the whole, integrated person fails in its mission if the goal is, in part, to nurture people capable of contributing to the betterment of society and, indeed, all of life* (Kramer and Bacelar 1994, p. 39).

A Japanese religious sect, among its other antisocial, destructive, and criminal activities, produced and released in a crowded Tokyo subway the deadly military chemical agent sarin, killing and injuring many people. A number of Japanese university faculty members linked the attraction of the sect for graduates of some of Japan's most prestigious universities to the quality of these universities' curricula (WuDunn 1995). These teachers attributed their students' inability to resist charismatic, authoritarian ideology to their institutions' emphasis on memorizing rather than thinking. "It reflects a profound crisis in the educational system," said one. Students "are absorbing ever greater amounts of information, but they don't acquire the ability to make value judgments on basic human values like responsibility for human life or respect for freedom of the individual" (p. A6).

Here, in the United States, a young man is thought to have used the knowledge he gained as a chemical engineering major at Rutgers University to bomb the World Trade Center for a righteous cause, in the process killing six people, injuring over a thousand, and causing many millions of dollars of damage. These true believers (Hoffer 1951) are, of course, extreme examples. But how much reassurance can we draw from the research reviewed in this monograph concerning the critical thinking skills and dispositions of the rest of our graduates and their ability to pick their way reliably through the minefields of potentially destructive social, political, and religious blather surrounding them?

Fundamental humane and democratic values characteristic of well-developed people should be specifically developed across the curriculum (Collins 1983; Earley, Mentkowski, and Schafer 1980; McBee 1980; Morrill 1980; Valuing 1987; White 1981). At every point, we should build our students' general and academic self-esteem (California 1990; Covington 1985, 1989; Covington and Beery 1976). Students should be specifically taught to understand their own emotional dynamics, particularly the interaction between their levels of self-esteem and hostile responses, and apply this understanding skillfully in their personal decision making and interactions with others (Altemeyer 1988; Layden 1977; Saul 1976).

Use available curricular resources

A wide variety of curricular formats are available that can serve our institutions' diverse missions and students' needs. To achieve a high-quality curriculum, colleges reviewing their curricula must seek specific guidance in the professional literature on curricular design (see, e.g., Chickering et al. 1977; Conrad and Pratt 1986; Diamond 1989; Fincher 1986; Gaff 1983, 1991; Gaff et al. 1980; Levine 1978; Project on Liberal Learning 1991; Project on Redefining 1985; Stark 1989; Toma and Stark 1995; Toombs and Tierney 1991; Wood and Davis 1978; Zemsky 1989).

4. Research-Based Methods of Instruction: Doing What Works

A curriculum can only be as strong as its constituent courses. The design, implementation, and assessment of courses require newer, more modern professional methods than we generally now use, methods that are known empirically to respond effectively to students' diverse levels of development and styles of learning (see, e.g., Claxton and Murrell 1987; Keirsey and Bates 1978; Kolb 1981; McKeachie 1994; McKeachie et al. 1990; Myers and McCaulley 1985; Myers and Myers 1980; Provost and Anchors 1987; Schroeder 1993).

The untoward effects of large size on organizational effectiveness (see, e.g., Chickering 1969; Chickering and Reisser 1993; McKeachie et al. 1990; Sale 1980) means we need to make the large small. Every method described in this subsection can be used to reduce the effect of large size, thereby individualizing mass instruction.

Systematically designed instruction

Systematic design provides an overarching framework for the many components of instruction. It can help a teacher specify important developmental outcomes that should be achieved, analyze the learning tasks students must perform to reach those outcomes, identify the resources required for this learning, structure activities for the course, and assess the results achieved (Briggs 1977; Davis and Alexander 1977b; Davis, Alexander, and Yelon 1974; Diamond 1989; Gagné and Briggs 1974; Hannum and Briggs 1982; Kemp 1977; Rothwell and Kazanas 1992; Russell and Johanningsmeier 1981). Systematic design provides an effective means

A young man is thought to have used the knowledge he gained as a chemical engineering major to bomb the World Trade Center.

for organizing the components of instruction of all types: for all outcomes, students, instructors, and programs. Although most teachers in higher education are unaware of systematic design, this now-standard professional convention should become widely used in colleges and universities.

Students' active involvement in learning

Systematic design is the framework for planning instruction. But what methods of learning can produce the diverse and abstract higher-order cognitive outcomes society demands, involve students in sustained, intensive work with one another, develop a challenging and supportive classroom climate that builds self-esteem, specifically teach interpersonal and team skills, develop the capacity and desire for lifelong learning, and, in large institutions, personalize mass instruction? Clearly, our one-size-fits-all educational tool, the traditional lecture, cannot produce these results.

Diverse forms of individualized instruction that respond to students' widely divergent styles and rates of learning consistently produce greater learning of content than passive listening only (Pascarella and Terenzini 1991). "How, then, does one reconcile . . . [students'] heterogeneity with the homogeneity of most institutions in their . . . curricular content and structure, course content and sequences, [and] instructional methods?" (p. 645). Today, newer, empirically based methods of instruction await widespread use in higher education. Some of these methods of individualizing and personalizing mass instruction permit even a lecture with large numbers of students to include substantial interaction among students and between students and teachers.

We need to ensure our students are actively involved in learning at every point, both inside and outside the classroom and in both academic and nonacademic, cocurricular activities. Ninety-one percent of college and university presidents in a Carnegie Foundation study said an "important" need exists for more collaborative learning among students as a means of improving campus life; 33 percent said this need is "very important" (Boyer 1990a).

The use of active learning may limit the amount of content we can cover in a course, but the research reviewed earlier shows that much, if not most, of the conceptual material we now cover is poorly learned and soon forgotten. Under traditional instruction, students will have covered more but learned less in the sense of meaningfully retaining and integrating knowledge (Kurfiss 1983). We need to be more selective in choosing the outcomes we value most. Describing its new science-as-a-liberal-art curriculum, the American Association for the Advancement of Science states, "The traditional survey course and concern about 'coverage' have no place in the curriculum described here" (Project on Liberal Education 1990, p. xviii). Workshop Physics at Dickinson College has reduced course content by 30 percent (Tobias 1992). A plan now being implemented in British universities to improve the competencies of physics graduates will cut "the content of physics degrees by at least two-thirds. 'If we aimed to teach less, we could teach far better'" ("English Physics" 1990). Disciplining ourselves to prune away forgettable and forgotten content and focus on the most important knowledge, skills, and values can lead to learning so deeply embedded it cannot easily be lost.

Mastery learning: Reaching high expectations

Rather than accepting most students' low-quality learning semester after semester, mastery learning emphasizes high-quality achievement on the part of all students (Block 1971; Bloom 1976; Guskey 1988; Kulik, Kulik, and Bangert-Drowns 1990; Levine and Associates 1985). Mastery learning eliminates time as the independent variable in learning and replaces it with mastery of specific, preidentified knowledge and skills, allowing variable amounts of time according to the needs of individual learners and thus removing a major barrier to success. The focus of mastery learning is on results, not time spent.

Integrated systems of instruction

Powerful instructional systems that specifically use the results of empirical research on learning have been developed to achieve higher education's important aims. The superiority of these systems to conventional instruction is supported by numerous studies. These overarching instructional frameworks systemically link together principles of good educational practice.

Personalized System of Instruction. PSI, or the Keller plan, is characterized by clearly defined objectives, dependence on the written word, students' active involvement in learning at every point, self-pacing to accommodate widely differing rates of learning, insistence on mastery of a subject, use of student "proctors" or peer tutors, frequent contact between students, and timely and nonpunitive assessment and feedback (Guskey 1988; Keller 1968; Keller and Sherman 1974; Reboy and Semb 1991; Ruskin 1976). In a PSI course, the instructor serves as a manager of learning rather than primarily as a transmitter of information through lectures. The instructor specifies the outcomes of the course through learning objectives, sets the standards of mastery, and evaluates, selects, and develops instructional materials. PSI depends on the written word. All students are assumed capable of high achievement, and mastery is required of all. They are given considerable responsibility for their own learning as well as freedom to achieve the course objectives at their own rate and methods, and at times and in places of their own choice. Students progress through the course in a carefully predetermined sequence, achieving the objectives of each unit before being permitted to proceed to the next. Students who do not achieve "mastery" on a unit test restudy until they can demonstrate their understanding and skills at that level on additional tests.

More advanced students (proctors), in a ratio of about one proctor to 10 students, help students learn by administering, scoring, and recording tests and discussing course material with them. They also provide valuable feedback to the instructor on all aspects of students' progress and course functioning.

PSI courses can include textbooks, laboratory work, discussions, and other traditional methods. Lectures, however, are few in number, short, of relatively minor significance, optional for students, and reserved primarily for motivational purposes rather then the transmission of information.

Cooperative learning. "The best thing colleges could do for students in coming years would be to train them how to engage in group efforts productively" (Light 1990, p. 71). "Few students, if any, have these skills when they arrive at college. Fewer still ever get formal training in them" (p. 71). The complex of methods collectively known as "cooperative learning" (CL) is a highly flexible and variable group of instructional procedures that can involve students actively in learning, provide extensive contact between and among students, specifically teach interpersonal and team skills, help students learn personal responsibility to others, and be used to achieve almost any desired cognitive, affective, or motor learning outcome in any discipline (Bouton and Garth 1983; Cooper et al. 1990; Johnson, Johnson, and Smith 1991a, 1991b; Kagan 1989; Michaelsen 1992; Millis 1991; Winston et al. 1988). CL has been used widely at all levels of schooling and has substantial empirical support for its effectiveness. The methods used in CL can be linked to form a coordinated instructional system or used with both traditional methods or other research-based methods, such as group problem solving with Guided Design (Wales and Stager 1977; White and Coscarelli 1986). Widespread, effective use of CL methods throughout higher education could lead to major gains in the development of students of almost every kind.

The use of CL has dramatically improved class attendance—with absenteeism dropping from 50 percent to 1 percent in one study—and has had strong positive effects on students' self-esteem, relations among members of different races, and cooperativeness in other situations (Bonwell and Eison 1991). CL could have especially powerful effects in achieving the major paradigm shifts that characterize development of abstract thinking, epistemology, and principled ethical reasoning. These types of development may be better facilitated by interaction among peers, who in most cases are closer to each other in developmental level than faculty. CL can also significantly increase contact of various sorts between students and faculty.

Learning communities
Across the country teachers and students are developing communities that are involved in collaborative learning in courses, programs, academic departments, and residence halls (Gabelnick et al. 1990; Schroeder 1994; Wilcox and Ebbs 1992), perhaps most notably through the Washington Center for Improving the Quality of Undergraduate Education (Washington 1994). Such learning communities bring everyone involved together in a joint quest for learning. A psychological climate can be developed that brings together students different in experience, ethnicity, religion,

and other characteristics and permits them to learn from each other intensively and cooperatively. Learning communities can help integrate fragmented curricula, build social and team skills, reduce students' boredom and attrition from courses and institutions, and validate the worth of each as a person and learner.

5. Campus Climate: Beginning in the Classroom

Most students have their most sustained contact with official representatives of their institutions in the classroom. Although development and management of a campus climate requires many specific actions, the classroom—the individual teacher—is central: "It is in the classroom where community begins. . ." (Boyer 1990a, p. 16). Although important for all students, community on campus is especially critical for the "new" students: women, minority-group students, older students, and commuters.

> *It's in the classroom where social and intellectual bonding is most likely to occur. For commuter students this is the primary point of campus contact. . . . The classroom can be an oasis of social and emotional support in the often hectic lives of older students* (Boyer 1990a, p. 53).

Cooperative learning and learning communities are powerful methods for structuring just this sort of supportive, validating learning environment in virtually every course. Well-designed instruction can set the psychological tone across the entire curriculum and campus.

6. Learning to Learn: Strategies that Work

The hours students reported studying per week, in Astin's 1993 study, were significantly correlated with over two-thirds of his 82 student outcome variables, including virtually all academic outcomes. Hours spent in class per week were correlated with far fewer outcomes. Students who use effective learning strategies tend to be retained on campus; those who do not tend to withdraw. The effort put forth by students is possibly the most important factor in their development. According to the research reviewed earlier, most students do not study nearly enough for effective learning in college. Students learn what they study, and it is important that they understand just how much they need to study. But effort from students is not enough; quality of effort is what counts.

Today, much is known about how students learn (see, e.g., Schmeck 1988; Weinstein 1988b). Most students do not learn effective study methods by themselves or use them to good effect (McKeachie et al. 1990). Many students routinely use methods for learning that are well known not to work, such as repeatedly rereading their textbooks; as long ago as 1917, this method was shown to be far inferior to reciting the material being learned (Gates, cited by Brethower 1977). Students need to be directly taught specific methods of learning and metacognition (McKeachie et al. 1990). Research shows formal instruction in effective learning strategies can help students achieve significantly greater learning (Dansereau 1985; Davies 1983; McKeachie et al. 1990; Weinstein 1988a), yet despite urgings for us to teach our students how to be skilled and avid lifelong learners, able to improve their own intelligence, very few students have ever been taught how to learn, either in high school or in college. Of 745 Rutgers University undergraduates surveyed informally, for example, only 14.1 percent claimed ever to have been taught how to study. By withholding this essential information from our students, we are in many cases foreclosing them from success and from the pleasure of learning in college and perhaps throughout their lives. The attendant toll for society is enormous.

If we are to enable our students to be effective learners both in college and beyond, to engage in deep rather than "surface" learning ("Deep Learning" 1993), we should systematically ensure that every person becomes skilled at learning. This one act on our part could alone dramatically improve students'—and therefore our own—learning productivity while transforming the college experience for many thousands of students. Using tools like the LASSI, E-LASSI (Weinstein, Palmer, and Schulte 1987), and MSLQ (Pintrich and Johnson 1990; Pintrich et al. 1991) to assess learning skills can help systematically diagnose the learning skills students need to develop. Other resources can help us teach them how to learn effectively, enjoy learning, and be successful at it (Johnson et al. 1991; Sherman 1985; Weinstein 1988a, 1988b; Weinstein and Mayer 1986; Weinstein and Underwood 1985).

7. Developmental Academic Advising: Building Supportive Relationships

Academic and personal guidance, advising, and counseling appropriate to each person throughout his or her college years are well established as vitally important for students' development and institutions' educational success. Equally well known is the generally poor quality—or even complete lack—of academic advising on most campuses. The resulting confusion and developmental loss for students, frustration and disappointment for faculty and staff, and financial loss to colleges and universities because of students' attrition are significant. And despite the well-established central importance for development of contact between students and faculty outside class, Pascarella and Terenzini (1991) concluded from their review of research that interaction between students and faculty in many institutions is generally limited to "formalized, somewhat structured situations, such as the lecture, laboratory, or discussion section" (p. 393).

The concept of developmental academic advising is an overarching, research-supported concept that systematically links various advising and counseling efforts now typically disjunct and scattered across campus (Brown and DeCoster 1982; Crookston 1972; Gordon 1992, 1994; King 1993; Winston, Ender, and Miller 1982; Winston, Miller, et al. 1984). Responding to the needs of each student, developmental academic advising provides thorough assessment of a student's characteristics and feedback, guidance, and mentoring from trained advisers throughout college.

Rather than being a frill peripheral to the real educational enterprise of classroom teaching and a drain on more important work, high-quality academic advising can be one of the most prudent investments an institution can make, particularly in a time of fiscal austerity. "Probably the single most important move an institution can make to increase persistence to graduation is to ensure that students receive the guidance they need at the beginning of the journey through college to graduation" (Forrest 1985, p. 74). And high-quality developmental advising need not require a major increase in fiscal resources (Hines 1984). Even for public institutions, where tuition is relatively low, "if effective academic advising is associated with higher retention rates, the tuition revenue alone will compensate for the institution's investment in academic advising as a separate and distinct budget item" (p. 340). The cost of quality is zero.

Conclusions
This section has focused on only a handful of basic actions we can and should take to transform our institutions and achieve the very large gains in students' learning and development society requires. We can do many more things to improve the quality of our results, and the resources cited throughout this monograph can point the way.

We need to act with dispatch. Higher education often takes twice as long to adopt innovations as industry (Siegfried, Getz, and Anderson 1995). Society cannot wait for us; we need to act now.

This review of the research on student development in colleges and universities has revealed numerous substantive problems in our educational processes. Twelve years of efforts to reform and restructure the schools, efforts far more vigorous, comprehensive, and sustained than those so far applied to higher education, have led to success only in a limited number of schools and districts ("From Risk" 1993). How can we in higher education act in a more effective and timely way to improve the quality of postsecondary education?

We need a new way of leading and managing our enterprise.

Managing for Quality

Just as research has clarified the process of student development itself, it has illuminated the functioning of our complex academic organizations, and methods exist today for managing our educational work systematically and systemically. We have been using the relatively laissez-faire methods of the past, however, which have often lacked clear goals and objectives; regular monitoring of entering students' characteristics, outcomes produced, or educational processes used; and systematic coordination and links among units. These methods have permitted educational activities—curricula, instruction, advising, assessment, general education, the disciplinary majors—each to run along on its own track. As has been so clearly shown by the research surveyed in this monograph, our educational processes are all too often incoherent and fragmented; efforts are unfocused and thus fail to achieve the synergy required to produce the complex, high-quality developmental results we want and society requires. We need a new way of leading and managing our enterprise.

Continuous Quality Improvement is a powerful synthetic method that can integrate these efforts systematically and comprehensively, consistently focusing on the quality of both processes and results (Crosby 1979; Deming 1986; Juran 1988, 1989; Walton 1986). Where it has been used, quality improvement has often led to dramatic increases in morale, more efficient use of resources, and higher-quality results. The widespread application of the philosophy and methods of quality improvement in Japan after World War II is credited with transforming that nation's war-weakened industry into the highly effective international economic powerhouse of today.

Principles and methods of quality improvement are now being successfully adapted to the needs and culture of colleges and universities (Chaffee and Sherr 1992; Cornesky and Associates 1990; Cornesky and McCool 1992; Cornesky et al. 1991; Harris, Hillenmeyer, and Foran 1989; Marchese 1991b, 1993; North Dakota *n.d.;* Seymour 1991, 1992; Seymour and Collett 1991; Sherr and Teeter 1991). Quality improvement focuses everyone's attention—faculty members, administrators, staff, students, trustees—on improving quality at every point; everyone is involved. A continuous, never-ending effort is made to improve the quality of *outcomes* by improving the quality of the educational *process* at every point along the way by identifying, understanding, and eliminating problems that reduce quality.

Using Research to Improve Quality
The professional literature in higher education
In a very real sense, ours is an amateur industry. Although our primary mission is almost always education, we ourselves have traditionally been well trained for neither classroom nor administrative office. What is perhaps even more surprising, however, is our common unwillingness to employ in our own affairs those appreciable skills we do possess, those of scholarship and research. As long as two decades ago, Chickering (1974) noted that "the results of social science research are seldom seriously taken into account by educational decision makers" (p. xii). More recently, the NIE Study Group concurred: "Colleges, community colleges, and universities rarely seek and apply this knowledge in shaping their educational policies and practices" (Study Group 1984, p. 17). Others ask "why the evidence of systematic social science research is rarely brought to bear on actual decisions about educational planning or goal attainment" (Winter, McClelland, and Stewart 1981, p. ix). Quality processes that produce quality results will require us not only to produce research but also to use it. Institutions that apply research succeed with all their students; those that ignore research can help relatively few. "We educators may do well to think more explicitly and unsentimentally about our business and try to found it on the emerging consensus of scientific evidence" (Walberg 1984, p. 20); it is time for research to inform and guide educational policy and planning.

Research on assessment: Understanding our educational processes and developing a culture of evidence

U.S. colleges and universities have increased tremendously in complexity since World War II. The huge influx of students, their increasing diversity, the growing number and technical complexity of our disciplines and thus the diversity of departments and programs and of their faculty and staff—all have profoundly changed the nature of our institutions. We need to match this organizational reality with newer, more effective, and more productive methods that can help us ensure high-quality educational processes and high-quality results throughout our institutions. But "conventional wisdom concerning what constitutes 'high-quality education' will not be appropriate for most institutions in the 1990s" (Bergquist and Armstrong 1986, p. xiv).

Quality improvement emphasizes clearly defined outcomes and institutional research—using continuous assessment to provide everyone with crucial evidence about what is happening in the institution. *Input assessment* provides information about important characteristics of entering students, both individually and as a group, such as their knowledge, abstract and critical thinking skills, learning styles, and levels of epistemological development. *Process assessment* continuously monitors the educational process: how programs—orientation, curricula, instruction, advising—are functioning. *Outcome assessment* shows what results are being produced. Faculty-conducted classroom assessment is a natural part of this effort.

Traditionally, we have depended for our judgments of quality on quantitative measures of our resources or inputs, such as the SAT or ACT scores of entering students, number of volumes in the library, percentage of faculty members who hold doctorates, and size of physical plant and endowment. Although these types of information are important, they paint a far from complete picture of institutional quality. None tell us how effective we are in using these resources to produce results—the desired outcomes— and *it is the results that count.*

The 1980s brought a national refocusing of attention on results: a college or university's *intended* results as described by its stated outcome goals and objectives and the *actual* results produced by the institution's educational processes. Ironically, because most of us have only limited information on the results of our work by which to judge our true quality, many institutions have come to depend on the opinions of writers for popular magazines, "quantified gossip" as it has been called, to judge their quality compared to other institutions—in reputation (an input), not results (outcomes).

Of course, specifying and assessing outcomes does not tell the whole story. Necessary as it is, assessment of outcomes can tell us only *what* our results are and *how much* of them we have reached. It cannot tell us *why* we have reached them. We cannot identify the educational processes that caused the outcomes or determine whether we ourselves are even responsible for the results. Perhaps, for example, our students possessed the same characteristics when they entered, or the outcomes are products of biological maturation or off-campus experiences.

In other words, in addition to knowing both the resources or inputs provided to an institution and its outcomes, we need to devote considerable attention to understanding its educational processes. We need to identify clearly the characteristics theory suggests typify effective processes—the experiences our students must have if we are to help them achieve important outcomes. Then we need to assess educational processes to learn the extent to which they possess these essential characteristics.

> *The central focus in defining and achieving "high quality" must be on the educational process[, which] requires serious attention to be given to what actually happens to promote (and inhibit) the cognitive and affective development of the individual student through the educational program* (Bergquist and Armstrong 1986, p. xiv).

We need to invest time and energy in applying powerful research methods and findings to the design and management of our own educational activities. We will now need to use this valuable information and what is today considered by experts to be accepted professional practice in a much more deliberate and systematic way if we are to achieve the complex developmental outcomes we desire for our students and for the well-being of society.

Adequate Resources: The Cost of Waste

Our institutions may seem deceptively orderly and businesslike on the surface. Students are admitted, classes are taught, and commencement ceremonies stir emotions. As we have seen when we examine our educational processes and results with the more powerful lens of research-based principles of modern professional education and management, however, another, less satisfying image of academe too often emerges. The research reviewed in this monograph presents an all-too-consistent picture of an enterprise that has not kept pace with developments in education and management. Like Rip van Winkle of Sleepy Hollow, we have allowed the developments of the last two decades in our profession to pass us by. As a result, the effectiveness of our colleges and universities in achieving the results society urgently needs and the efficiency with which they expend their resources are both generally far lower than they can and should be.

Every student who withdraws from college unnecessarily because of dissatisfaction or avoidable failure induces costs beyond those of dreams delayed or development retarded. The average cost to students of a degree at a public four-year college is more than $40,000 (Goldberg 1993b). Loss of this income to the institution is significant, but other financial losses accrue as well: (1) annual income lost in tuition, room, board, bookstore sales, incidental food, and purchases by visitors to campus, all multiplied by, say, three years, as most withdrawals occur during the first year; (2) lost gifts from alumni, multiplied by 50 years; and (3) the cost of replacing these students with new ones (with the average recruitment cost for a single student, according to the Admissions Marketing Group, ranging from about $1,700 to as much as $2,400, covering the admission staff's time, publications, videos, postage, telephone calls, and travel) (Seymour 1992). With many institutions losing one-half or more of their students before graduation, a 5 percent increase in persistence could "[recapture] $750,000 in lost revenue. Figures like that command attention" (Marchese, cited by Noel et al. 1985, p. 456).

We need to be much more concerned than we now are about the losses resulting from the attrition of students, or "scrap."

And how does the institution respond? With quiet indiffer-
ence. In fact, as long as the aggregate numbers hold up—
enough newcomers to replace the ones who left—the loss
usually goes virtually unnoticed. No one takes the time to
calculate the cost of scrap. No one seems to care (Seymour
1992, p. 139).

With finances in such short supply, we need to calculate
and we need to care. Clearly, we can be far more effective
and efficient. Beyond the practical matters of quality results
and, for some institutions, survival itself, clear ethical issues
are involved: our treatment of our student clients and our
stewardship of our supporters' resources. We need to be
considerate and responsible; we need to become aware of
our students.

Although perhaps more obvious than others, unnecessary
withdrawal is just one source of waste on campus. Unin-
volved, unmotivated students, ineffective and inefficient
curricula and instruction, and mediocre advising all lead to
additional significant costs beyond withdrawal: taking the
wrong courses and learning the wrong things, repeating
courses unnecessarily ("rework"), and that ocean of mediocre learning signified by ubiquitous C and D—but "pass-
ing"—grades. Each inefficiency can be thought of as having
a concrete dollar value now and in the future to both students and institutions, and each is a form of waste.

Business organizations can waste fully 15 to 20 percent
of sales income by "doing things wrong . . . without even
trying," as "a result of not doing things right the first time"
(Crosby 1979, p. 15). Quality experts assert the cost of
waste in manufacturing organizations can be 25 to 30 percent of income and as high as 40 percent in service organizations like colleges and universities (Cornesky et al. 1991,
pp. 13, 35; Seymour 1993b). With only about 50 percent of
all students who intend to earn degrees graduating (Study
Group 1984) and the greater than 50 percent rate of students' withdrawal in many institutions, the real waste of
resources is substantial from doing things wrong and having to redo them—or simply discarding the results. In our
concern with fiscal solvency, we have allowed "educational
solvency . . . to drift" (Cross 1986, p. 10). Beyond its obvious central importance to our mission, educational solvency
also has enormous fiscal implications.

A well-run business organization "can get by with [a cost of] less than 2.5 percent of sales" (Crosby 1979, p. 15), which, rather than being wasted, is invested in preventing waste and monitoring to ensure high quality. The American Society for Training and Development has estimated that, each year, businesses must expend no less than 2 percent of their payroll on professional development training to be competitive internationally (Howard *n.d.*). Some well-managed companies spend as much as 5 or 6 percent of salaries on training. Baldrige National Quality Award winner Motorola calculates a 30-to-1 return on training expenditures (Marchese 1993). What would we learn about our colleges and universities, and what would be the effect on quality, if we were to invest 2 to 2.5 percent of our education-related budgets, a small fraction of our waste, on assessment and training and then use the results of this research deliberately and systematically to improve quality and productivity by doing things right the first time?

W. Edwards Deming, a long-time professor at New York University and centrally influential in Japan's postwar economic resurgence, noted that we need to monitor quality:

> *If anybody needs quality control, it's the service industries, including universities. College presidents, like most executives, fail to see that improving quality is their main business. We're in a new economic era. Quality is the key to higher productivity, because approximately 20 percent of the cost of things, from automobiles to college educations, is a charge for waste* (Deming, cited in Keller 1983, p. 136).

Our Standards: Setting High Expectations for Ourselves

If we are to achieve high-quality outcomes, we need to have high expectations, not only for our students but also for ourselves, and we must be willing to change. "It's not the case that American higher education lacks all standards. The problem is that the standards we deploy are often not notably high, evenly applied, or much discussed; they are various, idiosyncratic, and private—to outsiders they look like cheese" (Marchese 1991a, p. 4). The expectations others now have for us—clearly defined goals for outcomes and regular assessment of results, the maintenance of high public standards, the continuous use of research to improve our educational processes—"contravene a century's way of doing things in American universities" (Marchese 1991a, p. 4).

Consider the academic culture that characterizes many institutions. The culture of the academic department, where students and faculty interact, is often observed to be hostile to students and learning. Based on interviews with 300 faculty members at 20 diverse colleges and universities, researchers observed widespread isolation of faculty from their colleagues, a "veneer of civility," lack of common purpose and effort to solve educational problems, and primary emphasis on disciplinary research coupled with neglect of teaching with respect to serious evaluation, salary, and promotions (Massey, Wilger, and Colbeck 1994).

Blaming our students (our paying clients) for not knowing or caring or studying, blaming the schools (our suppliers) for sending them to us in what we often believe is an undereducated condition, and blaming our sponsors (also our customers) for not giving us more resources cannot become excuses to justify inaction on our part. Lack of clear mission, vision, values, goals, and knowledge of results, and low standards and untrained faculty and staff are all our own responsibilities. Our students' level of involvement or quality of effort may ultimately be most important in producing results, but

> . . . one should not conclude that what the college does is of minor influence. . . . It is the college—the administration as well as the professors—that sets the intellectual standards, the quality of performance it expects from students, and exemplifies its values by the quality of facilities it provides (Pace 1984, p. 97).

Concluding their massive review of research on the development of students in college, Pascarella and Terenzini (1991), call for a "shift in the decision-making orientation" of administrators toward "learning-centered management . . . that consistently and systematically" focuses on the consequences of decisions on students' development (p. 656). "Modern colleges and especially universities seem far better structured to process large numbers of students efficiently than to maximize [their] learning" (p. 646). We need a new standard of quality, one based on the quality of our results in producing student development. Pascarella and Terenzini found few durable differences among institutions as a whole in the cognitive, psychosocial, or economic outcomes they produced. Despite large differences in size, selectivity, resources, prestige, type of governance, or curricular emphasis, large differences in outcomes disappeared once students' characteristics upon entry were accounted for.

> *These findings . . . support [the] argument that many current notions of institutional quality may be misleading, particularly those based on resources (library holdings, endowment, faculty degrees, and so on), simpleminded outcomes (such as the quality of an institution's graduates unadjusted for their precollege characteristics), or reputation* (Pascarella and Terenzini 1991, p. 637).

We often claim very high quality in our public relations materials, but the research reviewed here suggests we often tolerate a far less exacting performance. Today, quality in organizations is often defined as meeting or exceeding customers' needs. Such a standard invites dramatic changes in the way we manage our affairs and promises equally dramatic improvement in the results we produce.

Being Clear about Purpose: What Business Are We In?
Effective organizations understand their missions—their purposes—clearly. Yet many of us are confused about our institutions' missions. What is our business and what business *should* we be in? "Teaching is in fact the business of the business. Teaching is the task that distinguishes colleges and universities, along with primary and secondary schools, from all other service agencies" (Pew 1989, p. 2). Judging by the evidence reviewed in this monograph, however, we are not attending nearly closely enough to our central mission, our students' development: who our students are and what their needs are, what research has shown us about how students develop, what good professional practice is today and how closely our own educational processes approximate those practices, what we want our results to be and what they actually are.

Prominent management authority Peter Drucker notes, "Most managements, if they ask the question at all, ask 'what is our business?' when the company is in trouble. Of course, then it *must* be asked" (Drucker 1974, p. 86, emphasis in the original). Many commentators today suggest that higher education in this country is in trouble. Perhaps we should ask what business we are in and what business we *should* be in. Doing so can have great potential value: "Then asking the question may, indeed, have spectacular results and may even reverse what appears irreversible decline" (p. 86).

Who Owns These Problems? Management's Role of Leadership

If the findings of research on students' development in college and the considered views of numerous authorities and study groups who have found us wanting are actively used, these critiques can play a key role in improving the quality of our work. "Institutional change and improvement are motivated more by knowledge of problems than by knowledge of successes: *Negative feedback is more conducive to advancement than is positive feedback*" (Cameron 1984, p. 71, emphasis added). Although looking back across the research reviewed in this monograph is somewhat discouraging, each area of difficulty can with equal justification be viewed as an area of opportunity: an opportunity to significantly improve quality.

Accomplishing missions, setting goals, maintaining standards, monitoring quality of process and results, managing the organizational culture, rewarding effective work, and providing staff development are all responsibilities of management. These complex issues and tasks must be deliberately *managed* to ensure they are executed effectively, both individually and collectively. In higher education, some of these functions and elements are responsibilities primarily of administrators and faculty. Ultimately, however, the president as chief executive officer must take responsibility for accomplishing the mission at a high level of quality.

Leadership, communication, and cooperative teamwork

An improvement in quality begins with vigorous and sustained leadership—a relentless "championship" of quality—

from the president. Leadership for quality is based on personal integrity, clear moral values, and a strong effort to build community. It is characterized by open communication throughout the institution—sharing of information and power, cooperation rather than competition among people and departments, teamwork rather than isolation, vigorous identification and removal of barriers to pride in workmanship, the elimination of fear, and accordance of respect and consideration to everyone (Bennis 1989; Birnbaum 1992; Bogue 1994; Burns 1978; Deming 1986; Guskin and Bassis 1985; McLaughlin and Riesman 1990). Administrators, faculty members, nonacademic staff, and students all become partners rather than isolates or adversaries.

Leadership for quality is based on personal integrity, clear moral values, and a strong effort to build community.

The "85-15 rule"

Experience in organizations of many types has demonstrated that most of the problems discussed in this monograph are beyond the control of individual members of the faculty or staff; they reside in the organizational system—the academic department, the college, the university as a whole. As such, these problems "belong" to management rather than faculty and staff members as individuals. An enormous 85 percent or even more of potentially waste-generating institutional problems are of this sort (Cornesky et al. 1991; Crosby 1979; Deming 1986; Seymour 1992). "The 85-15 rule . . . states that 85 percent of what goes wrong lies within the system, and only 15 percent lies with the individual" (Seymour 1992, pp. 85–86). Managers own systems; they themselves must first provide the leadership and commitment to quality if the needed change in quality is to occur. "Since we assume that administrators control 85 to 90 percent of the processes and systems, we are convinced that if they seriously commit to quality, they can influence faculty and students to do likewise" (Cornesky et al. 1991, p. 56). Quality management of this sort will require the best-trained manager-leaders as well as the best-trained faculty and staff.

The management of the nonbusiness, public-service institutions will indeed be a growing concern from now on. Their management may well become the central management problem—simply because the lack of management of the public-service institution is such a glaring weakness,

whether municipal water department or public university
(Drucker 1974, p. 8).

Collectively, colleges and universities "constitute one of the largest industries in the nation but are among the least businesslike and well-managed of all organizations" (Keller 1983, p. 5). If we are to meet the needs of our many clients—students, parents, employers, state, and nation—we will have to be considerably more attentive to managing our affairs than we have been, more businesslike in the best, most positive sense.

Professional Development: Prerequisite of Quality

Quality improvement strongly emphasizes professional training and education of faculty and staff; everyone is thoroughly trained for his or her work. As the work or conditions of the work change, high-quality, effective professional development training and retraining are provided automatically and continuously. Perhaps this training aspect of quality is most relevant here. The studies reviewed earlier suggest we in the academy can dramatically improve students' development by adopting newer, more empirically grounded and effective educational methods. But every one of the several powerful, modern methods recommended here, such as systematic instructional design, cooperative learning, and developmental academic advising, requires for its effective use the mastery of a body of professional knowledge and the development of new and complex skills. More complex methods are required to produce today's more complex outcomes. The telling of knowledge—lectures—known to instructors is inadequate. Used unskillfully, however, the new methods cannot perform effectively. Developing effective statements of intended outcomes, designing valid and reliable assessments of actual outcomes for both courses and curricula, leading discussions, advising, and managing complex instructional systems are all intellectual, social, emotional, and moral challenges that require considerable professional knowledge and skill. A significant improvement in the quality of higher education will require a major investment in the development of institutions' human resources.

Management Development: Enhancing Leadership

Existing research-based professional methods in both education and management can enable us to create unparalleled high-quality learning on campus. While "we know enough to revolutionize education if the knowledge were applied to the improvement of education" (Brethower 1977, p. 18), the problem is that, on the whole, we in academe are unfamiliar with these methods; we have in most cases studied neither education nor management. A number of barriers impede our institutions' success. Among our pressing needs are articulation of clearer missions and visions of the future, the definition of outcomes, and comprehensive assessment throughout the institution. Effecting these changes and producing results will first require more effective leadership at all levels and deliberate management of key organizational processes. "Leadership is accountable for results" (Drucker 1990, p. 47), and leadership is the responsibility of management (Deming 1986).

Two cultures on campus?

To what extent do academic managers communicate with and understand their subordinates? Most of the presidents in one study "portrayed themselves as listeners who were open to influence. But the perceptions of their constituents were often quite different" (Birnbaum 1992, p. 176). The campus environment administrators perceive as rational and orderly is one in which the faculty believe they must "scheme" and "compete" to acquire necessary resources (Neumann 1992). A study of 23,302 faculty members and administrators at 47 universities found a striking gap in perception between academic administrators and faculty with respect to the proper balance between teaching and research (Gray, Froh, and Diamond 1992). Although administrators as a group strongly favored an emphasis on teaching, their faculty perceived unit heads, deans, and central administrators as favoring research over teaching. Another national survey found consistent and striking gaps between the perceptions of 454 presidents and other administrators and 2,730 members of their own faculties in characteristics valued in faculty members and degree of faculty influence in their departments (Blackburn and Lawrence *n.d.*). Although the faculty agreed administrators valued research skills, beyond this point their "responses seem a bit cynical: the valued faculty member . . . may be an 'operator' who may not be an excellent teacher. . . . Faculty feel relatively impotent in their ability to influence certain kinds of decisions and to control their work environment" (p. 14). "Surprisingly high levels of job stress" exist in academe (Seldin 1987, p. 13). In one study, 62 percent of 2,000 faculty at 17 colleges claimed "severe" or "moderate" stress associated with their work, and in another, 1,900 faculty at 80 public and independent universities claimed 60 percent of daily stress was job related (Seldin 1987).

Among other common causes cited for faculty burnout, now "one of the most pressing problems facing academe" (Armour et al. 1987, p. 4), are perceived lack of control over their work, inadequate psychic rewards for their efforts, lack of community on campus, and lack of creative leadership in their institutions. The quality of the institutional psychological climate is the key to developing maximum vitality and productivity among faculty, particularly senior faculty.

Some suggest that two cultures exist on campus, administrative and faculty, and that such different perceptions of the climate on campus are unlikely to improve the quality of the faculty's performance (Blackburn and Lawrence *n.d.*). The same research also reveals faculty's considerable lack of trust that administrators will act in good faith to better their institutions and a belief that resources are inequitably distributed within the institution. (Administrators share the latter belief, although to a lesser extent.)

A further concern relates to administrators' understanding of the core student development processes they manage. For example, administrators "believe that competition improves students' learning" (Blackburn and Lawrence *n.d.*, p. 14), a misconception inconsistent with research and expert opinion. Most of these managers had had experience as faculty and presumably were trained in ways similar to other faculty, although 30 percent of them claimed their highest degree was in education.

The need for training
Other indicators also suggest we need to improve our leadership and management of education. About two-fifths (39 percent) of respondents to one survey of faculty disagreed

that their institutions were managed effectively (Boyer 1989). In addition, 36 percent rated their administration as excellent or good, 64 percent as fair or poor. Fully 69 percent stated that the administration of their institution was autocratic—30 percent very autocratic—and 44 percent found their jobs to be a source of considerable personal strain. In another survey of faculty at 392 institutions, only 11.9 percent of respondents said their administrations were open about their policies (*Chronicle* 1994). Everyone needs to know skilled, devoted work in support of the institution's central mission of students' development is appreciated and rewarded, yet a paltry 9.8 percent of respondents believed faculty were rewarded for being good teachers on their campuses. Today, just as faculty require a high level of professional knowledge and skill for facilitating students' development, so too do those who lead and manage our complex institutions require the highest-quality training for this demanding work.

Among the barriers to effective management in colleges and universities is our lack of training for complex and important tasks beyond our disciplines (Kells 1988). Well trained in their disciplinary specialties, faculty are frequently

> . . . *asked to perform in other areas for which they have little or no training. They are exceptionally good examples of "Peter Principled" professionals. . . . The good biologist may become a good teacher or researcher, but he/she may not be able to run a department or an agency if little or no training is provided for the job"* (Kells 1988, p. 6, emphasis in the original).

The picture of disorganized—even anarchic or chaotic—organizations that often emerges from the research on colleges and universities reviewed here surely reflects the level of our knowledge and management skills.

Those among us who hold management responsibilities, whether faculty, staff members, or administrators, require professional knowledge and skill for tasks like working with missions, strategy, and goals and objectives, and assessing achievement. They also need to understand student development, modern educational practices, and professional development for staff. They must be able to deal effectively with ever-changing organizational complexity and have the knowledge and skills for understanding people and building effective relationships among them. Managers need to provide leadership by inspiring a shared vision that can energize and win commitment from everyone, develop a supportive climate of unwavering integrity and respect for all, build trust, and develop effective teams.

Despite their crucial role in ensuring quality, however, managers in higher education, like the faculty, are at best unevenly trained for their work. "I know of no institution in our society that does a poorer job of educating its own employees than higher education" (management professor Lawrence Sherr, cited in Seymour 1992, p. 104). Of 377 senior academic administrators, 47 percent of whom were chancellors, vice presidents, or provosts, only two-fifths claimed to have taken formal college courses in management (Gallagher 1991). Half said they had attended workshops on management. If such experiences are not followed by practice and critical feedback to develop skills, however, they are unlikely to lead to long-term changes in professional behavior or to have an impact on participants' organizations (Levinson-Rose and Menges 1981). Many of the major reports of the last decade critical of higher education have stressed the need for far broader and more rigorous programs of faculty and instructional development than we now have. We need to do as much for those among us who manage education.

The academic department chair

Academic departments constitute the core of a college or university. The department "is regarded, quite properly, as the primary agent for maintaining and improving the quality and productivity of undergraduate education" (Consortium for Policy Research in Education, cited in Goldberg 1993a, p. 16). The academic department chair therefore plays a key, frontline leadership role in ensuring high-quality educational processes and outcomes. Like other members of the faculty, however, department chairs are rarely trained for their complex and demanding tasks. They often lack the essential knowledge and skills they need concerning organizations, education, and people to perform their roles effectively. For example, of over 4,000 academic department chairs, only about one-quarter reported being "very successful" or "successful" in motivating poor teachers or alienated or burned out tenured members of the faculty to be more effective.*

Detailed interviews with new faculty and administrators in one research university found a striking gap between department chairs' perceptions of the quality of support they provided for their new professors and the perceptions of the faculty themselves (Whitt 1991). The chairs used adjectives like "exciting," "challenging," and "nonthreatening" to describe the faculty experience in their departments; the faculty used "confusion, anxiety, isolation, and lack of support" (p. 193). We need to do better, and help is available (see, e.g., Bennett and Figuli 1990; Booth 1982; Lucas 1989, 1994; McDade 1987; Tucker 1992).

Faculty Development: Foundation for Student Development

The range of knowledge and skills required of us today if we are to educate all our students is substantial. The modern philosophy of quality improvement emphasizes thorough professional development for everybody in preparation for each role they will assume and continuous high-quality training throughout their careers. How well do we now prepare the professoriat for its complex and demanding educational work?

Large universities produce almost all new members of the professoriat. Seventy-five percent or more of the graduate students in some disciplines intend to teach in higher education (Diamond and Wilbur 1990), and these graduate students often serve as teaching assistants while they study. Research conducted during the last decade on universities' efforts to prepare their graduate students to teach shows consistently that these programs (1) are ordinarily voluntary (Weimer, Svinicki, and Bauer 1989); (2) reach a minority of graduate student teachers (Bowman, Loynachan, and Schafer 1986; Chism 1991; Diamond and Wilbur 1990; Fink 1985; Ford 1991; Stanley and Chism 1991); (3) are usually limited to a few workshop sessions rather than constituting a systematic, sustained, and demanding professional curriculum (Chism 1991; Ford 1991; Parrett 1987);

*Ann F. Lucas 1993, personal communication.

and (4) in most cases, provide little or no supervision either by experts in learning and teaching or senior members of the disciplinary faculty (Chism 1991; Diamond and Wilbur 1990; Ford 1991; McQuade 1989). In some cases, senior faculty actively discourage their students from participating in this training (Diamond and Wilbur 1990). According to former Stanford University President Donald Kennedy, faculty development efforts "encounter quiet opposition in many departmental locations, where graduate students are told that teaching doesn't really matter—at least not in comparison with research" (Kennedy 1995, p. 13). When formal courses are available to novice teachers, what do they learn? The primary instructional method taught is the lecture (Parrett 1987).

When graduate students finally earn their degrees and assume their first faculty positions, many of them never having taught or having taught but without any significant training as educators, rather than the careful nurturing they now require from their institutions and new senior faculty colleagues, they are more likely than not to find themselves abandoned, left to their own devices as educators (Boice 1991a, 1992; Fink 1984; Sands, Parson, and Duane 1991; Whitt 1991). Once again, some are actively discouraged by their superiors from participating in training that might take time away from their research (Boice 1991a). Not surprisingly, these new teachers more often than not lecture "facts-and-principles style" (Boice 1991a, p. 168) and are unable "to stimulate students to high intellectual effort" (Fink 1985, p. 144). Only 5 to 9 percent of one group of new professors were effective, comfortable with their students, and enjoying their work (Boice 1991b).

The numbers of other types of part-time teachers, often moonlighters with other, full-time careers off campus, jumped from 23 percent of all instructors in 1966 to 41 percent in 1980 (Study Group 1984). Today, about half of all teachers in New Jersey public colleges and universities are part-timers (Goldberg 1993c). These instructors taught about one-third of all course sections in the state. Part-timers generally receive even less training and supervision as educators than graduate TAs (Arden 1995; Gappa and Leslie 1993).

Much is made of the radical changes technology will allegedly bring to the "delivery" of education (Dolence and

Norris 1995; Green and Gilbert 1995). Although the Internet, sophisticated multimedia instructional software, and other developments will certainly greatly benefit students' learning, the faculty must still understand student development, instructional design, assessment, and all the other modern impedimenta of the profession if they are to use technological innovations to good effect in fostering their students' development.

The single-minded emphasis on research that dominates universities and distracts from the faculty's professional development is often justified by the strong salutary impact faculty research is alleged to have on the quality of undergraduate education. A meta-analysis of 29 studies that examined a possible relationship between the quality of faculty research and the quality of their teaching, however, found the former made a less than 2 percent contribution to the latter under the most favorable analytic assumptions (Feldman 1987)—an altogether unremarkable finding in light of the research reviewed in this monograph (see also Webster 1985). The knowledge, skills, values, and dispositions that underpin creation of knowledge in a specialized subdiscipline are usually very different from those required for competence in nurturing human development.

Clearly, our casual approach to developing and sustaining our new colleagues—and renewing and upgrading the skills of the senior faculty—must be directly responsible for much of the low-quality student experience portrayed by research and the low-quality educational results many of our societal stakeholders decry. Significant improvement in the quality of our educational processes and outcomes awaits dramatic improvement in the quantity and quality of the professional knowledge and skill development we achieve with each member of our faculties.

We need to move beyond one-shot, flash-in-the-pan workshops on this or that toward systemic and systematic professional development. The last two decades have witnessed the growth in professional methods for faculty development that now permit widespread, effective preparation of the college and university faculty for their work as educators of all students (see, e.g., Bergquist and Phillips 1975, 1977, 1981; Brookfield 1986, 1987; Brown and Atkins 1987; Chism 1987; Diamond 1989; Eble and McKeachie 1985; Fuhrmann and Grasha 1983; Gaff 1975; Katz and

Meta-analysis of 29 studies found the quality of research made a less than 2 percent contribution to the quality of teaching.

Henry 1988; Lewis 1988, 1993; Lindquist 1978; McKeachie 1994; Menges and Mathis 1988; Menges and Svinicki 1991; Nyquist et al. 1991; Povlacs-Lunde and Healy 1991; Prichard and Sawyer 1994; Quinlan 1991; Richlin 1993; Svinicki 1990; Wadsworth 1988; Weimer 1990; Wright and O'Neil 1994).

Current efforts to reform K–12 education emphasize retraining for teachers and principals. "Massive professional development" (Price 1993, p. 32) of school teachers is needed if national educational reform is to be successful. How much more needed is a continuous, never-ending program of high-quality faculty development in higher education, where traditionally most of us have had no formal training whatsoever for these complex roles. In our case, we have the additional task of helping the current faculty develop that base of professional knowledge and skills they now require.

Increasingly knowing only a narrow slice of a research specialty, new faculty may have only a rudimentary grasp of their wider disciplines and have spent little time reflecting on their philosophical grounding, historical development, and social implications—important contextual foundations for any teacher. After assuming their first faculty position, in many cases isolated even from colleagues within their own academic departments, these professors are ill-prepared to nurture the broad intellectual, emotional, and social development required by their students and society. Trained only in the technical subtleties of literary, historical, or scientific research and in many cases cloistered in libraries or laboratories for years during their graduate training, they may never have read and reflected on the great classics of American liberal education (Bell 1966; Committee on the Objectives 1945; Hutchins 1936; Newman 1959; Van Doren 1943) and the history of the American college and university, studied the research illuminating their students' developmental psychology, learned the theory and practice of modern developmental academic advising, read the influential contemporary critical reports on higher education, or studied and practiced under supervision the design and implementation of modern instruction. Cast adrift in the profession without chart or oar by their graduate school mentors and new colleagues and lacking the perspective, personal philosophy, and basic educational

skills requisite for professional competence, new faculty
sink or swim in the classroom and advising conference to
the enormous detriment of their students and society.

Conclusions

Using the professional literature as a guide, we have discovered in each of four core areas crucial to our students'
development many opportunities to significantly improve
the quality of our educational processes and thus the outcomes we produce. Understanding the processes as a global,
systemic whole and skillfully managing them together are
essential to the organizational success of each. Every person needs to have the knowledge, skills, and climate required to perform his or her role at a high level. Management's leadership role is foundation to the entire enterprise:
achieving widespread commitment to the vision, inducing
enthusiasm for high standards, maintaining a consistent
focus on students' needs, developing teamwork, and
engendering willingness to challenge old assumptions,
comfortable habits, and familiar methods.

An overarching framework for examining quality in an
institution, subunit, or system of institutions is provided by
the education criteria for the Malcolm Baldrige National
Quality Award ("Education Pilot Criteria" 1995). Combining
the rigorous, professional standards of the criteria with the
specific research-based education concepts and principles
reviewed in this monograph can provide powerful guidance for every institution. Used correctly, together they bid
fair to produce the dramatic improvements in student learning promised by the title of this monograph.

A CALL TO ACTION: A New Kind of Community

Today, we in higher education in this country face an opportunity unmatched in human history. We are being asked to educate all the people and to educate them to a very high level. They are coming to us in greater numbers and diversity than ever before. For the first time, we have the opportunity to creatively link these vast human resources with our new knowledge of human and organizational development and thus to lead the way to a far more developed, mature, and humane society than the world has ever known. More fundamental to societal success than the broad learning our students should acquire in diverse fields of knowledge, however, is their cognitive, ethical, emotional, and social development as human beings. We need to help them move beyond their relatively simple, concrete, and self-centered orientation to one that is more complex, abstract, and prosocial. Recognition is now widespread that higher education must change, and, as in other sectors of society, repeated and insistent calls have been made for a significant, even radical, reinvention, redefinition, and restructuring of our industry (see, e.g., Guskin 1994a, 1994b; Heydinger 1994; "It's Time" 1993; Osborne and Gaebler 1992; "Twice Imagined" 1995). If we use our new research-based knowledge to construct curricula and courses that engage our students' imaginations and activate their energies in achieving important outcomes—that purposefully and consistently involve them in active, social, cooperative modes of learning—and if we effectively use new developmental styles of advising, our students will surely rise to heretofore unknown levels of accomplishment. The impact on our states and on society more widely, not to mention our institutions, could be dramatic.

Research, theory, and their skilled application are now essential to high-quality education, but they are not enough; quality has still another dimension. We need to create on campus a climate that inspires and supports high-quality effort and respect from everyone: students, teachers, leaders alike. We need to create a pervasively moral culture, a culture of integrity and of service to our clients. We need "a much richer, more complex and paradoxical understanding of what happens when we teach and learn" (Parker J. Palmer, cited in Edgerton 1992, p. 6). Subjective and objective, personal and professional, emotional and intellectual "intertwine, and you can't get people to think well without attention to the feelings that block—and animate—good thinking" (p. 6). We need to interact with students and with each other in a deeply human way. "A modern college or university should be a place where every individual feels affirmed and where every activity of the community is humane. Caring is the key" (Boyer 1990a, p. 47).

We need to model for both our students and society well-managed and effective organizations: organizations that support people who are striving to develop, organizations whose behavior is richly developmental and humane. Yet we have seen that many students and staff often perceive our campuses as hostile and alienating. "The truth is that academic community has been destroyed. Universities and many colleges, even small ones, are places where faculty do the main business of their craft alone[, isolated] from one another and from the purposes of their institutions" (Gamson 1993, p. 4). The quality of our community is key to the quality of our results. A barrier to our success is our common inexperience in working cooperatively together (Kells 1988).

> *Cooperation is relatively low. . . . Members are . . . inexperienced at working together to solve problems. . . . Solving complex tasks—the kind we find all the time at places like colleges and universities—requires flexibility, trust, warmth, and risk-taking, which are often in short supply in these organizations. . . . [For these and other reasons,] most groups or committees at postsecondary . . . institutions function very badly* (Kells 1988, pp. 5–6).

Across the country people are reaching out to each other to build community (Etzioni 1993); we should lead the way.

"A pervasive belief system exists in many colleges and universities that questions the importance of values, emotions, and personal growth and places a premium on cognitive rationality and intellectual development" (Kuh, Krehbiel, and MacKay 1988, p. 9). As we strive for objectivity, our social values and behavior have become competitive and individualistic, our own learning and teaching impersonal and anticommunal, and we model this world view for our students (Palmer 1987). We should create campus communities in our departments and courses

where natural conflict over ideas can be used creatively
for understanding.

> *There is very little conflict in American classrooms, and*
> *the reason is that the soft virtues of community are lack-*
> *ing there. . . . What prevents conflicts in our classrooms is*
> *fear . . . in the hearts of teachers as well as students. It is*
> *fear of exposure, of appearing ignorant, of being ridiculed*
> (Palmer 1987, p. 25).

Ninety-eight percent of chief student affairs officers in one
survey believed that "greater effort to build a stronger overall sense of community" was "very important" or "somewhat important" to improving campus life (Boyer 1990a).

An analysis of metaphors used in interviews with 83
administrators, faculty members, and department secretaries
at a large urban state university found that 65 percent of
the "metaphors expressed some intense emotive ventilation,
. . . 75 percent . . . were negative . . . 20 percent were positive" (Deshler 1985, p. 22). Many of the metaphors, "an
emotional barometer of campus culture" (p. 23), expressed
hostility, aggression, combativeness. The author suggests
these negative metaphors may reveal:

> *. . . underlying positive values that are perceived as being*
> *frustrated. . . . When viewed this way, one can detect a*
> *hunger for appreciation and recognition, professional*
> *survival, a sense of community or shared fate, empathy*
> *and compassion for others, active participation in gover-*
> *nance, and academic responsibility. . . . One can hear*
> *the cry for increased appreciation, recognition, dignity,*
> *and status on the part of faculty members. . . . A desire for*
> *solidarity, unity, collaboration, reconciliation, and inter-*
> *dependence can be inferred from many of the metaphors.*
> *. . . [These metaphors] reflect a longing for increased com-*
> *munity and shared fate], and they] can be interpreted as*
> *a reflection of empathy or compassion toward others*
> (Deshler 1985, pp. 23–24).

In visits to numerous campuses across the country,
Parker J. Palmer has observed "'the pain of disconnection,'
a sense on the part of faculty of being detached from stu-

dents, from colleagues, from their own intellectual vocation and the passion that originally animated it" (cited in Edgerton 1992, pp. 3–4). Not only new faculty feel isolated, lonely, cut off from community; many of the rest of us do as well.

A concerted plan to construct and maintain a cooperative, considerate, caring, and moral developmental climate, in classrooms and elsewhere on campus, will be necessary to support this vision. For many of us, this new climate of community will require significant changes in the way we conduct our affairs. We will need to have an inspiring vision of the campus we want to create, and, beginning with strong leadership from the top, we will need to involve everyone in making this vision a reality. We need to develop a culture of uncompromising service to everyone, inside and outside our institutions' walls. Each of us will have to develop the professional tools—the new knowledge, skills, and sensitivities—that can enable us to transform our vision into actuality. Continuous professional development for everyone will be an essential underpinning for the entire endeavor as we seek together to improve our quality everywhere and forever. We also need to develop a collegiality on campus in which we take the risk of being vulnerable to each other, to expose our selves, and to allow for others' weaknesses as humans (Bennett 1991). We need to care more about each other; we need to be connected to each other in a much more human way.

Our colleges and universities are among the most influential institutions in America *and therefore the world.* "There are few institutions in our society, with the exception of the family, that have a more powerful impact on individual lives and the society as a whole" (Gamson 1991, p. 52). Our graduates fill the ranks of leadership in every sector: government, the military, business and industry, nonprofit service organizations, and education, at home and around the world. The changes we can evoke in our students through our own renewal and the changes we can evoke in society through them are virtually limitless.

The perceptions of increasing class division and antisocial behavior in society, a coarsening of civic discourse, and the threat of authoritarianism have produced a concern to increase prosocial behavior and significantly enhance community everywhere (Etzioni 1993). Society looks to us for leadership.

Central to dealing with these social challenges is the development of the dispositions and skills of critical thinking, master tool for all manner of self-motivated development and personal change and, when coupled with principled ethical reasoning, a powerful reparative and developmental force in society. We need to develop a nation of self-aware, enthusiastic, and skilled critical thinkers.

Society needs us as never before. It needs better trained school teachers and principals. It needs technologically skilled and ethical professionals in all fields, leaders and managers, competent and humane citizens—men and women of wisdom—who can interact effectively with others in the workplace and the community. Developing them is our job. The nation also needs us to help it to come together in community, to respect others who are different, to resolve conflict creatively and nonviolently, to heal its divisions. The future of our democratic traditions depends on a more mature community that can solve its many problems in respectful, nonviolent ways. In addition to teaching in our courses specifically how to do these things, we ourselves need to show how to live together peaceably and respectfully.

We know how to do these things better than ever before. Many of us believe it is time to act, to seize the moment. We can develop new relationships with our students and with each other. We can develop and articulate a vision for what society can be. And we can organize our affairs so that we are able to lead the way to the future manifestation of the vision, a nation that is a true community, a learning society, *a pervasively developmental culture*. This exciting prospect can energize us all—staff, students, supporters—in a grand cooperative venture to create our future.

REFERENCES

The Educational Resources Information Center (ERIC) Clearinghouse
on Higher Education abstracts and indexes the current literature on
higher education for inclusion in ERIC's data base and announce-
ment in ERIC's monthly bibliographic journal, *Resources in Education* (RIE). Most of these publications are available through the
ERIC Document Reproduction Service (EDRS). For publications cited
in this bibliography that are available from EDRS, ordering number
and price code are included. Readers who wish to order a publication should write to the ERIC Document Reproduction Service,
7420 Fullerton Rd., Suite 110, Springfield, Virginia 22153-2852.
(Phone orders with VISA or MasterCard are taken at 800/227-ERIC
or 703/823-0500.) When ordering, please specify the document (ED)
number. Documents are available as noted in microfiche (MF) and
paper copy (PC). If you have the price code ready when you call
EDRS, an exact price can be quoted. The last page of the latest issue
of *Resources in Education* also has the current cost, listed by code.

AAHE Education Trust. 1994. *Thinking K–16* 1(1): 1–15.

"AAHE's New Agenda on School/College Collaboration." 1993.
AAHE Bulletin 45(9): 10–13.

Adams, M., ed. 1992. *Promoting Diversity in College Classrooms:
Innovative Responses for the Curriculum, Faculty, and Institutions.*
New Directions for Teaching and Learning No. 52. San Francisco:
Jossey-Bass.

ADAPT. 1978. *Multidisciplinary Piagetian-Based Programs for
College Freshmen: ADAPT, DOORS, SOAR, STAR, the Cognitive
Program, the Fourth R.* Lincoln: Univ. of Nebraska.

Adelman, C. 1990. *A College Course Map. Taxonomy and Transcript
Data: Based on the Postsecondary Records, 1972–1984, of the High
School Class of 1972.* Washington, D.C.: U.S. Dept. of Education.
ED 326 153. 260 pp. MF–01; PC–11.

———. 1994. *Lessons of a Generation: Education and Work in the
Lives of the High School Class of 1972.* San Francisco: Jossey-Bass.

———, ed. 1988. *Performance and Judgment: Essays on Principles
and Practice in the Assessment of College Student Learning.*
Washing-ton, D.C.: U.S. Dept. of Education, Office of Educational
Research and Improvement. ED 299 888. 328 pp. MF–01; PC–14.

———, ed. 1989. *Signs and Traces: Model Indicators of College
Student Learning in the Disciplines.* Washington, D.C.: U.S. Dept.
of Education, Office of Educational Research and Improvement.
ED 318 310. 195 pp. MF–01; PC–08.

Aerospace Education Foundation. 1989. *America's Next Crisis: The
Shortfall in Technical Manpower.* Arlington, Va.: Author.

"Alliance for Learning: Enlisting Higher Education in the Quest for
Better Schools." 13 April 1994. *Education Week* (Special Report).

Altemeyer, Bob. 1988. *Enemies of Freedom: Understanding Right-*

Wing Authoritarianism. San Francisco: Jossey-Bass.

Altmaier, E.M., ed. 1983. *Helping Students Manage Stress.* New Directions for Student Services No. 21. San Francisco: Jossey-Bass.

Altman, L.K. 14 November 1989. "Physicians Endorse More Humanities for Premed Students." *New York Times.*

America 2000. 1991. Washington, D.C.: U.S. Dept. of Education.

American Economics Association. 1990. "Economics." In *Liberal Learning and the Arts and Sciences Major.* Vol. 2. *Reports from the Fields.* Washington, D.C.: Association of American Colleges, Project on Liberal Learning, Study-in-Depth, and the Arts and Sciences Major.

American Institute of Biological Sciences. 1990. "Biology." In *Liberal Learning and the Arts and Sciences Major.* Vol. 2. *Reports from the Fields.* Washington, D.C.: Association of American Colleges, Project on Liberal Learning, Study-in-Depth, and the Arts and Sciences Major.

Anderson, J.A. *n.d.* "College Survival. Retaining the High-Risk Minority Student: Idealism vs. Realism." Unpublished manuscript. Indiana, Pa.: Indiana Univ., Dept. of Psychology.

———. 1988. "Cognitive Styles and Multicultural Populations." *Journal of Teacher Education* 39(1): 2–9.

Anderson, S.G., S. Ball, R.T. Murphy, and Associates. 1975. *Encyclopedia of Educational Evaluation.* San Francisco: Jossey-Bass.

Angelo, T.A., and K.P. Cross. 1993. *Classroom Assessment Techniques: A Handbook for College Teachers.* San Francisco: Jossey-Bass.

Arden, E. 21 July 1995. "Ending the Loneliness and Isolation of Adjunct Professors." *Chronicle of Higher Education:* A44.

Armour, R.A., R.S. Caffarella, B.S. Fuhrmann, and J.F. Wergin. 1987. "Academic Burnout: Faculty Responsibility and Institutional Climate." In *Coping with Faculty Stress,* edited by P. Seldin. New Directions for Teaching and Learning No. 29. San Francisco: Jossey-Bass.

Arnold, K.D. 1993. "The Fulfillment of Promise: Minority Valedictorians and Salutatorians." *Review of Higher Education* 16(3): 257–83.

Assessment Update (bimonthly newsletter). San Francisco: Jossey-Bass.

Association of American Universities. 1990. *Institutional Policies to Improve Doctoral Education.* Washington, D.C.: Author.

Astin, A.W. 1977. *Four Critical Years.* San Francisco: Jossey-Bass.

———. July 1984. "Student Involvement: A Developmental Theory for Higher Education." *Journal of College Student Personnel* 25: 297–308.

———. 1985. *Achieving Educational Excellence.* San Francisco: Jossey-

Bass.

———. 1987. "Competition or Cooperation? Teaching Teamwork as a Basic Skill." *Change* 19(5): 12–19.

———. 1991. *Assessment for Excellence: The Philosophy and Practice of Assessment and Evaluation in Higher Education.* New York: ACE/Macmillan.

———. 1993. *What Matters in College?* Four Critical Years *Revisited.* San Francisco: Jossey-Bass.

Bainbridge, W.S. 1978. "Chariots of the Gullible." *Skeptical Inquirer* 3(2): 33–48.

Baird, L.L. 1985. "Do Grades and Tests Predict Adult Accomplishment?" *Research in Higher Education* 23(1): 3–85.

Baker, J., Jr. 1989. *And the Cheat Goes On: An Exposé on How Students Are Cheating in School.* Salem, Ore.: Forum Press International.

Balderston, F.E. 1974. *Managing Today's University.* San Francisco: Jossey-Bass.

Banta, T.W. 1988. *Implementing Outcomes Assessment: Promise and Perils.* New Directions for Institutional Research No. 49. San Francisco: Jossey-Bass.

———. 1993. *Making a Difference: Outcomes of a Decade of Assessment in Higher Education.* San Francisco: Jossey-Bass.

Banta, T.W., J.P. Lund, K.E. Black, and F.W. Oblander. 1995. *Assessment in Practice: Putting Principles to Work on College Campuses.* San Francisco: Jossey-Bass.

Barbett, S.F., J.L. Hollins, R.A. Korb, and F.B. Morgan. 1995. *Enrollment in Higher Education: Fall 1984 through Fall 1993.* NCES 95-238. Washington, D.C.: U. S. Dept. of Education, Office of Educational Research and Improvement.

Barnes, C.P. 1983. "Questioning in College Classrooms." In *Studies of College Teaching: Experimental Results, Theoretical Interpretations, and New Perspectives,* edited by C.L. Ellner and C.P. Barnes. Lexington, Mass.: Lexington Books.

Baron, J. 1985. "What Kinds of Intelligence Components Are Fundamental?" In *Thinking and Learning Skills.* Vol. 2. *Research and Open Questions,* edited by S.F. Chipman and J.W. Segal. Hillsdale, N.J.: Erlbaum.

Barton, P.E., and A. Lapointe. 1995. *Learning by Degrees: Indicators of Performance in Higher Education.* Princeton, N.J.: Educational Testing Service, Policy Information Center.

Battersby, J.L. 1973. *Typical Folly: Evaluating Student Performance in Higher Education.* Washington, D.C.: National Council of Teachers of English.

Baxter-Magolda, M.B. 1990a. "Gender Differences in Epistemological Development." *Journal of College Student Development* 31: 555–61.

————. 1990b. "The Impact of the Freshman Year on Epistemological Development: Gender Differences." *Review of Higher Education* 13(3): 259–84.

————. 1992a. *Knowing and Reasoning in College: Gender-Related Patterns in Students' Intellectual Development*. San Francisco: Jossey-Bass.

————. 1992b. "Students' Epistemologies and Academic Experiences: Implications for Pedagogy." *Review of Higher Education* 15(3): 265–87.

————. 1993. "Relational Views of Self, Relationship, and Knowledge: Pathways to Marginalization?" *Review of Higher Education* 16(3): 371–84.

Baxter-Magolda, M.B., and W.D. Porterfield. 1985. "A New Approach to Assess Intellectual Development on the Perry Scheme." *Journal of College Student Personnel* 26(4): 343–50.

Bean, J. 1980. "Dropouts and Turnover: The Synthesis and Test of a Causal Model of Student Attrition." *Research in Higher Education* 12: 155–87.

Bebeau, M. 1994. "Influencing the Moral Dimensions of Dental Practice." In *Moral Development in the Professions: Psychology and Applied Ethics,* edited by J.R. Rest and D. Narváez. Hillsdale, N.J.: Erlbaum.

Belenky, M.F., B.M. Clinchy, N.R. Goldberger, and J.M. Tarule. 1986. *Women's Ways of Knowing: The Development of Self, Voice, and Mind*. New York: Basic Books.

Bell, D. 1966. *The Reforming of General Education: The Columbia College Experience in Its National Setting*. Garden City, N.Y.: Doubleday.

Bennett, J.B. 1991. "Collegiality as 'Getting Along.'" *AAHE Bulletin* 44(2): 7–10.

Bennett, J.B., and D.J. Figuli, eds. 1990. *Enhancing Departmental Leadership: The Roles of the Chairperson*. New York: ACE/ Macmillan.

Bennett, W.J. 1984. *To Reclaim a Legacy: A Report on the Humanities in Higher Education.* Washington, D.C.: National Endowment for the Humanities. ED 247 880. 63 pp. MF–01; PC–03.

Bennis, W. 1989. *Why Leaders Can't Lead: The Unconscious Conspiracy Continues*. San Francisco: Jossey-Bass.

Bergquist, W.H., and J.L. Armstrong. 1986. *Planning Effectively for Educational Quality*. San Francisco: Jossey-Bass.

Bergquist, W.H., and S.R. Phillips. 1975. *A Handbook for Faculty Development*. Vol. 1. Washington, D.C.: Council of Independent Colleges.

————. 1977. *A Handbook for Faculty Development*. Vol. 2. Washington, D.C.: Council of Independent Colleges.

———. 1981. *A Handbook for Faculty Development*. Vol. 3. Washington, D.C.: Council of Independent Colleges.

Bernstein, A. 1990. "Sex, Race, and Diversity Tapes: Students on Campus." *Change* 22(2): 18–23.

Bernstein, A., and J. Cock. 15 June 1994. "A Troubling Picture of Gender Equity." *Chronicle of Higher Education:* B1–B3.

Bernstein, R. 26 May 1988. "Black and White on Campus: Learning Tolerance, not Love, and Separately." *New York Times.*

"Better History Teaching Called for in Report." 22 November 1992. *Chronicle of Higher Education:* A2.

"Big Gaps Found in College Students' Grasp of Current Affairs." 18 April 1993. *New York Times.*

Binet, A. 1909. *Les Idées Modernes sur les Enfants.* Paris: Ernest Flamarion.

Birnbaum, R. 1992. *How Academic Leadership Works: Understanding Success and Failure in the College Presidency.* San Francisco: Jossey-Bass.

Blackburn, R.T., and J.H. Lawrence. *n.d.* "Same Institution, Different Perceptions: Faculty and Administrators Report on the Work Environment." Ann Arbor: Univ. of Michigan, National Center for Research to Improve Postsecondary Teaching and Learning.

Blackburn, R.T., G.R. Pellino, A. Boberg, and C. O'Connell. 1980. "Are Instructional Improvement Programs Off Target?" *Current Issues in Higher Education* 2(1): 32–48.

Block, J.H., ed. 1971. *Mastery Learning: Theory and Practice.* New York: Holt, Rinehart & Winston.

Bloland, P.A., L.C. Stamatakos, and R.R. Rogers. 1994. "Reform in Student Affairs: A Critique of Student Development." Greensboro, N.C.: ERIC Counseling and Student Services Clearinghouse.

Bloom, A. 1987. *The Closing of the American Mind.* New York: Simon & Schuster.

Bloom, B.S. 1976. *Human Characteristics and School Learning.* New York: McGraw-Hill.

———. 1984. "The Search for Methods of Group Instruction as Effective as One-to-One Tutoring." *Educational Leadership* 41(8): 4–17.

———. 1985. *Developing Talent in Young People.* New York: Ballantine Books.

Bloom, B.S., ed. 1956. *Taxonomy of Educational Objectives.* Vol. 1. *Cognitive Domain.* New York: Longman.

Bloom, B.S., J.T. Hastings, and G.F. Madaus. 1971. *Handbook on Formative and Summative Evaluation of Student Learning.* New York: McGraw-Hill.

Blum, D.E. 1 July 1992. "MIT Head Calls for 'Transformation' of Engineering Education, Hits Accreditors." *Chronicle of Higher*

Education: A13.

Bogue, E.G. 1994. *Leadership by Design: Strengthening Integrity in Higher Education.* San Francisco: Jossey-Bass.

Boice, R. 1991a. "New Faculty as Teachers." *Journal of Higher Education* 62(2): 150–73.

———. 1991b. "Quick Starters: New Faculty Who Succeed." In *Effective Practices for Improving Teaching,* edited by M. Theall and J. Franklin. New Directions for Teaching and Learning No. 48. San Francisco: Jossey-Bass.

———. 1992. *The New Faculty Member.* San Francisco: Jossey-Bass.

Bonsangue, M.V., and D.E. Drew. *n.d.* "Long-Term Effectiveness of the Calculus Workshop Model." Unpublished manuscript.

Bonwell, C.C., and J.A. Eison. 1991. *Active Learning: Creating Excitement in the Classroom.* ASHE-ERIC Higher Education Report No. 1. Washington, D.C.: George Washington Univ., School of Education and Human Development. ED 336 049. 121 pp. MF–01; PC–05.

Booth, D.B. 1982. *The Department Chair: Professional Development and Role Conflict.* AAHE-ERIC Higher Education Report No. 10. Washington, D.C.: American Association for Higher Education. ED 226 689. 60 pp. MF–01; PC–03.

Border, L.L.B., and N.V.N. Chism, eds. 1992. *Teaching for Diversity.* New Directions for Teaching and Learning No. 49. San Francisco: Jossey-Bass.

Bouton, C., and R.Y. Garth, eds. 1983. *Learning in Groups.* New Directions for Teaching and Learning No. 14. San Francisco: Jossey-Bass.

Bowen, H.R. 1977. *Investment in Learning: The Individual and Social Value of American Higher Education.* San Francisco: Jossey-Bass.

———. 1980. "Outcomes Assessment: A New Era in Accreditation." Proceedings of the 93rd Annual Convention of the Middle States Association of Colleges and Schools, December 1979, Philadelphia, Pennsylvania. Philadelphia: Middle States Association of Colleges and Schools.

Bowen, H.R., and J.H. Schuster. 1986. *American Professors: A National Resource Imperiled.* New York: Oxford Univ. Press.

Bowman, R.A., T.E. Loynachan, and J.W. Schafer. 1986. "Attitudes of Agronomy Teachers on Preparation for Teaching." *Journal of Agronomic Education* 15(2): 96–100.

Boyer, E.L. 1987. *College: The Undergraduate Experience in America.* New York: Harper & Row.

———. 1989. *The Condition of the Professoriate: Attitudes and Trends, 1989.* Princeton, N.J.: Carnegie Foundation for the Advancement of Teaching. ED 312 963. 162 pp. MF–01; PC not available EDRS.

———. 1990a. "Campus Life: In Search of Community." Princeton, N.J.: Carnegie Foundation for the Advancement of Teaching. ED 319 276. 16 pp. MF–01; PC–01.

———. 1990b. *Scholarship Reconsidered: Priorities of the Professoriate.* Princeton, N.J.: Carnegie Foundation for the Advancement of Teaching. ED 326 149. 151 pp. MF–01; PC not available EDRS.

Bredemeier, B.L., and D.L.L. Shields. 1994. "Applied Ethics and Moral Reasoning in Sport." In *Moral Development in the Professions: Psychology and Applied Ethics,* edited by J.R. Rest and D. Narváez. Hillsdale, N.J.: Erlbaum.

Brethower, D.M. 1977. "Recent Research in Learning Behavior: Some Implications for College Teaching." In *Teaching in Higher Education,* edited by S. Scholl and F.S. Inglis. Columbus: Ohio Board of Regents.

Briggs, L.J., ed. 1977. *Instructional Design: Principles and Applications.* Englewood Cliffs, N.J.: Educational Technology Publications.

Brittingham, B.E. 1988. "Undergraduate Students' Use of Time: A Classroom Investigation." *To Improve the Academy* 7: 45–52.

Brookfield, S.D. 1986. *Understanding and Facilitating Adult Learning.* San Francisco: Jossey-Bass.

———. 1987. *Developing Critical Thinkers: Challenging Adults to Explore Alternative Ways of Thinking and Acting.* San Francisco: Jossey-Bass.

Brophy, J. 1986. "Teacher Influences on Student Achievement." *American Psychologist* 4(10): 1069–77.

Brower, A.M. 1992. "The 'Second Half' of Student Integration: The Effects of Life Task Predominance on Student Retention." *Journal of Higher Education* 63(4): 441–62.

Brown, G., and M. Atkins. 1987. *Effective Teaching in Higher Education.* New York: Methuen.

Brown, R.D., and D.A. DeCoster, eds. 1982. *Mentoring-Transcript Systems for Promoting Student Growth.* New Directions for Student Services No. 19. San Francisco: Jossey-Bass.

Burns, J.M. 1978. *Leadership.* New York: Harper & Row.

Burrows, G.N. 20 June 1990. "The Body of Medical Knowledge Required Today Far Exceeds What Students Can Learn in 4 Years." *Chronicle of Higher Education:* B1+.

Cabrera, A.F., M.B. Castañeda, A. Nora, and D. Hengstler. 1992. "The Convergence between Two Theories of College Persistence." *Journal of Higher Education* 63(2): 143–64.

Cabrera, A.F., A. Nora, and M.B. Castañeda. 1993. "College Persistence: Structural Equations Modeling Test of an Integrated Model of Student Retention." *Journal of Higher Education* 64(2): 123–39.

Cage, M.C. 26 May 1993. "Graduation Rates of American Indians and

Blacks Improve, Lag behind Others'." *Chronicle of Higher Education:* A29.

———. 26 January 1994. "Beyond the B.A." *Chronicle of Higher Education:* A29–A31.

California Task Force to Promote Self-Esteem and Personal and Social Responsibility. 1990. "Toward a State of Esteem." Sacramento: California State Dept. of Education.

Cameron, K.S. 1984. "Assessing Institutional Ineffectiveness: A Strategy for Improvement." In *Determining the Effectiveness of Campus Services,* edited by R.A. Scott. New Directions for Institutional Research No. 41. San Francisco: Jossey-Bass.

Candy, P.C., and R.G. Crebert. 1991. "Ivory Tower to Concrete Jungle: The Difficult Transition from the Academy to the Workplace as Learning Environments." *Journal of Higher Education* 62(5): 570–92.

Carey, L.M. 1988. *Measuring and Evaluating School Learning.* Boston: Allyn & Bacon.

Carmichael, J.W., Jr., J. Hunter, H. Hassell, L.W. Jones, M.A. Ryan, and H. Vincent. 1978. "Project SOAR (Stress on Analytical Reasoning)." In *ADAPT: Multidisciplinary Piagetian-Based Programs for College Freshmen.* Lincoln: Univ. of Nebraska.

Carnevale, A.P., L.J. Gainer, and A.S. Meltzer. 1990. *Workplace Basics: The Essential Skills Employers Want.* San Francisco: Jossey-Bass.

Cashin, W.E. 1987. "Improving Essay Tests." IDEA Paper No. 17. Manhattan: Kansas State Univ., Center for Faculty Evaluation and Development.

Ceci, S.J. 1990. *On Intelligence . . . More or Less.* Englewood Cliffs. N.J.: Prentice-Hall.

Chaffee, E.E., and L.A. Sherr. 1992. *Quality: Transforming Postsecondary Education.* ASHE-ERIC Higher Education Report No. 3. Washington, D.C.: George Washington Univ., School of Education and Human Development. ED 351 922. 145 pp. MF–01; PC–06.

"Challenge: To Acknowledge the Role of Work-Related Behavioral Skills and Attitudes as Both a Cause of and Remedy for the Skills Gap." 1995. *EQW Issues* No. 9.

Cheney, L.V. 1990. *Tyrannical Machines: A Report on Educational Practices Gone Wrong and Our Best Hopes for Setting Them Right.* Washington, D.C.: National Endowment for the Humanities.

Chickering, A.W. 1969. *Education and Identity.* San Francisco: Jossey-Bass.

———. 1974. *Commuting versus Resident Students: Overcoming the Educational Inequities of Living off Campus.* San Francisco: Jossey-Bass.

Chickering, A.W., and Associates. 1981. *The Modern American College.* San Francisco: Jossey-Bass.

Chickering, A.W., and Z.F. Gamson. 1987. "Seven Principles for Good Practice in Undergraduate Education." *Wingspread Journal* 9 (Insert 2): 1–4.

———. 1991. *Applying the Seven Principles for Good Practice in Undergraduate Education.* New Directions for Teaching and Learning No. 47. San Francisco: Jossey-Bass.

Chickering, A.W., D. Halliburton, W.H. Bergquist, and J. Lindquist. 1977. *Developing the College Curriculum: A Handbook for Faculty and Administrators.* Washington, D.C.: Council for the Advancement of Small Colleges.

Chickering, A.W., and R.J. Havighurst. 1981. "The Life Cycle." In *The Modern American College,* edited by A.W. Chickering and Associates. San Francisco: Jossey-Bass.

Chickering, A.W., and L. Reisser. 1993. *Education and Identity.* San Francisco: Jossey-Bass.

Chism, N.V. 1991. "Supervisors and TAs on the Teaching Help They Give and Receive." In *Preparing the Professoriate of Tomorrow to Teach: Selected Readings in TA Training,* edited by J.D. Nyquist, R.D. Abbott, D.H. Wulff, and J. Sprague. Dubuque, Ia.: Kendall/Hunt.

———, ed. 1987. "Institutional Responsibilities and Responses in the Employment and Education of Teaching Assistants. Readings from a National Conference." Columbus: Ohio State Univ., Center for Teaching Excellence.

Chronicle of Higher Education. 28 August 1991. "Almanac" 38(1): 28.

———. 26 August 1992. "Almanac" 39(1): 13.

———. 1 September 1994. "Almanac" 41(1): 34.

——— 17 February 1995a, "Notebook": A37.

——— 23 June 1995b. "Notebook": A27.

———. 4 August 1995c. "Notebook": A27.

Claxton, C.S., and P.H. Murrell. 1987. *Learning Styles: Implications for Improving Educational Practices.* ASHE-ERIC Higher Education Report No. 4. Washington, D.C.: Association for the Study of Higher Education. ED 293 478. 116 pp. MF–01; PC–05.

Clegg, V.L., and W.E. Cashin. 1986. "Improving Multiple-Choice Tests." IDEA Paper No. 16. Manhattan: Kansas State Univ., Center for Faculty Evaluation and Development.

Clement, J. 1981. "Solving Problems with Formulas: Some Limitations." *Engineering Education* 72(2): 152–62.

Clinchy, B. 1989. "On Critical Thinking and Connected Knowing." *Liberal Education* 75(5): 14–19.

Cohen, M.D., and J.G. March. 1974. *Leadership and Ambiguity: The American College President.* New York: McGraw-Hill.

Cohen, P.A. 1984. "College Grades and Adult Achievement: A Research Synthesis." *Research in Higher Education* 20(3): 281–93.

Colby, A., and L. Kohlberg. 1987. *The Measurement of Moral Judg-*

ment. Vol. 1. *Theoretical Foundations and Research Validation.*
Cambridge: Cambridge Univ. Press.

Cole, C.C., Jr. 1982. *Improving Instruction: Issues and Alternatives for Higher Education.* AAHE-ERIC Higher Education Research Report No. 4. Washington, D.C.: American Association for Higher Education. ED 222 159. 75 pp. MF–01; PC–03.

College Outcomes Evaluation Program. 1990a. *Assessing Higher Education's Outcomes: An Annual Report on Outcomes and Assessment Activities at Public Colleges and Universities in New Jersey.* Trenton: New Jersey Dept. of Higher Education.

————. 1990b. "Report to the Board of Higher Education on the First Administration of the General Intellectual Skills (GIS) Assessment." Trenton: New Jersey Dept. of Higher Education.

College Outcomes Evaluation Program Council. 1991. "A Report on Access, Retention, Transfer, and Graduation at New Jersey's Public Colleges and Universities." Trenton: New Jersey Dept. of Higher Education.

Collins, M.J. 1983. *Teaching Values and Ethics in College.* New Directions for Teaching and Learning No. 13. San Francisco: Jossey-Bass.

Collison, M. N-K. 13 January 1993. "Survey Finds Many Freshmen Hope to Further Racial Understanding." *Chronicle of Higher Education:* A29–A32.

Commission on Admission to Graduate Management Education. 1990. "Leadership for a Changing World: The Future Role of Graduate Management Education." Los Angeles: Graduate Management Admission Council.

Commission for Educational Quality. 1994. *Changing States: Higher Education and the Public Good.* Atlanta: Southern Regional Education Board. ED 366 280. 55 pp. MF–01; PC–03.

Commission on Higher Education and the Adult Learner. 1984. "Adult Learners: Key to the Nation's Future." Columbia, Md.: Author.

Commission on Minority Participation in Education and American Life. 1988. *One-Third of a Nation.* Washington, D.C.: American Council on Education/Education Commission of the States.

Committee on Education. 1984. "Science as a Way of Knowing." Vol. 1. *American Zoologist* 24: 421–534.

————. 1985. "Science as a Way of Knowing." Vol. 2. *American Zoologist* 25: 377–641.

————. 1986. "Science as a Way of Knowing." Vol. 3. *American Zoologist* 26: 569–918.

————. 1987. "Science as a Way of Knowing." Vol. 4. *American Zoologist* 27: 411–732.

————. 1988. "Science as a Way of Knowing." Vol. 5. *American*

Zoologist 28: 441–808.

———. 1989. "Science as a Way of Knowing." Vol. 6. *American Zoologist* 29: 481–817.

———. 1990. "Science as a Way of Knowing." Vol. 7. *American Zoologist* 30: 403–505+.

Committee on the Objectives of a General Education in a Free Society. 1945. "General Education in a Free Society: Report of the Harvard Committee." Cambridge, Mass.: Harvard Univ. Press.

Cones, J.H., III, J.F. Noonan, and D. Janha, eds. 1983. *Teaching Minority Students*. New Directions for Teaching and Learning No. 16. San Francisco: Jossey-Bass.

Conrad, C.F., and A.M. Pratt. 1986. "Research on Academic Programs: An Inquiry into an Emerging Field." In *Higher Education: Handbook on Theory and Practice,* edited by John C. Smart. New York: Agathon.

Cooper, J., S. Prescott, L. Cook, L. Smith, R. Mueck, and J. Cuseo. 1990. "Cooperative Learning and College Instruction: Effective Use of Student Learning Teams." Long Beach: California State Univ. Foundation.

Cornesky, R.A., and Associates. 1990. *W. Edwards Deming: Improving Quality in Colleges and Universities*. Madison, Wis.: Magna.

Cornesky, R., and S. McCool. 1992. *Total Quality Improvement Guide for Institutions of Higher Education*. Madison, Wis.: Magna.

Cornesky, R., S. McCool, L. Byrnes, and R. Weber. 1991. *Implementing Total Quality Management in Higher Education*. Madison, Wis.: Magna. ED 343 535. 154 pp. MF–01; PC–06.

Covington, M.V. 1985. "Strategic Thinking and the Fear of Failure." In *Thinking and Learning Skills*. Vol. 1. *Relating Instruction to Research,* edited by J.W. Segal, S.F. Chipman, and R. Glaser. Hillsdale, N.J.: Erlbaum.

———. 1989. "Self-Esteem and Failure in School: Analysis and Policy Implications." In *The Social Importance of Self-Esteem,* edited by A.M. Mecca, N.J. Smelser, and J. Vasconcellos. Berkeley: Univ. of California Press.

Covington, M.V., and R.G. Beery. 1976. *Self-Worth and School Learning*. New York: Holt, Rinehart & Winston.

Crawford, A.B. 1930. "Rubber Micrometers." *School and Society* 32(816): 233–40.

Crockett, D.S., and R.S. Levitz. 1984. "Current Advising Practices in Colleges and Universities." In *Developmental Academic Advising,* edited by R.B. Winston, Jr., T.K. Miller, S.C. Ender, T.J. Grites, and Associates. San Francisco: Jossey-Bass.

Cromwell, L.S., ed. 1986. *Teaching Critical Thinking in the Arts and Humanities*. Milwaukee: Alverno Productions.

Cronbach, L.J. 1984. *Essentials of Psychological Testing*. New York:

Harper & Row.

Crookston, B.B. January 1972. "A Developmental View of Academic Advising as Teaching." *Journal of College Student Personnel* 13: 12–17.

Crosby, P.B. 1979. *Quality Is Free: The Art of Making Quality Certain.* New York: New American Library.

Cross, K.P. 1971. *Beyond the Open Door: New Students to Higher Education.* San Francisco: Jossey-Bass.

———. 1976. *Accent on Learning.* San Francisco: Jossey-Bass.

———. 1986. "A Proposal to Improve Teaching: What 'Taking Teaching Seriously' Should Mean." *AAHE Bulletin* 39(1): 9–15.

Culotta, E. 13 November 1992. "A Trio of Teaching Successes." *Science* 258: 1217.

Dansereau, D.F. 1985. "Learning Strategy Research." In *Thinking and Learning Skills.* Vol. 1. *Relating Instruction to Research,* edited by J.W. Segal, S.F. Chipman, and R. Glaser. Hillsdale, N.J.: Erlbaum.

Darling-Hammond, L., and L. Hudson. 1990. "Precollege Science and Mathematics Teachers: Supply, Demand, and Quality." *Review of Research in Education* 16: 223–64.

Davies, L.J. 1983. "Teaching University Students How to Learn." *Improving College and University Teaching* 31: 160–65.

Davis, R.H., and L.T. Alexander. 1977a. "The Lecture Method." Guides for the Improvement of Instruction in Higher Education No. 5. East Lansing: Michigan State Univ.

———. 1977b. "The Systematic Design of Instruction." Guides for the Improvement of Instruction in Higher Education No. 12. East Lansing: Michigan State Univ.

Davis, R.H., L.T. Alexander, and S.C. Yelon. 1974. *Learning System Design: An Approach to Improving Instruction.* New York: McGraw-Hill.

Davis, R.H., J.P. Fry, and L.T. Alexander. 1977. "The Discussion Method." Guides for the Improvement of Instruction in Higher Education No. 6. East Lansing: Michigan State Univ.

Davis, T., and P.H. Murrell. 1993. *Turning Teaching into Learning: The Role of Student Responsibility in the Collegiate Experience.* ASHE-ERIC Higher Education Report 8. Washington, D.C.: George Washington Univ. ED 372 703. 122 pp. MF–01; PC–05.

"Deep Learning, Surface Learning." 1993. *AAHE Bulletin* 45(8): 10–13.

Delworth, W., G. Hanson, and Associates. 1989. *Student Services: A Handbook for the Profession.* San Francisco: Jossey-Bass.

"Demand for College-Educated Workers May Outstrip Supply in 1990s." 3 January 1990. *Chronicle of Higher Education:* A2.

Deming, W.E. 1986. "Out of the Crisis." Cambridge, Mass.: MIT Center for Advanced Engineering Design.

Deshler, D. 1985. "Metaphors and Values in Higher Education." *Academe* 71(6): 22–28.

Diamond R.M. 1989. *Designing and Improving Courses and Curricula in Higher Education: A Systematic Approach*. San Francisco: Jossey-Bass.

Diamond, R.M., and F.P. Wilbur. 1990. "Developing Teaching Skills during Graduate Education." *To Improve the Academy* 9: 199–216.

Dodge, S. 20 November 1991. "Poorer Preparation for College Found in 25-Year Study of Freshmen." *Chronicle of Higher Education:* A37.

"Does the Harrison Case Reveal Sexism in Math?" 28 June 1991. *Science* 252: 1781–83.

"Does Research Fraud Have Its Origins in Student Cheating?" 30 November 1988. *Chronicle of Higher Education:* A31.

Dolence, M.G., and D.M. Norris. 1995. *Transforming Higher Education: A Vision for Learning in the 21st Century*. Ann Arbor, Mich.: Society for College and University Planning.

Douvan, E. 1981. "Capacity for Intimacy." In *The Modern American College,* edited by A.W. Chickering and Associates. San Francisco: Jossey-Bass.

Dressell, P.L. Winter 1957. "Facts and Fancy in Assigning Grades." *Basic College Quarterly:* 6–12.

———. 1976. *Handbook of Academic Evaluation*. San Francisco: Jossey-Bass.

Drucker, P.F. 1974. *Management: Tasks, Responsibilities, Practices*. New York: Harper & Row.

———. 1990. *Managing the Nonprofit Organization: Practices and Principles*. New York: Harper (Collins).

Duckett, L.R., and M.B. Ryden. 1994. "Education for Ethical Nursing Practice." In *Moral Development in the Professions: Psychology and Applied Ethics,* edited by J.R. Rest and D. Narváez. Hillsdale, N.J.: Erlbaum.

Dunlop, D.L., and F. Fazio. 1976. "Piagetian Theory and Abstract Preferences of College Science Students." *Journal of College Science Teaching* 5: 297–300.

Duster, T. 25 September 1991. "Understanding Self-Segregation on Campus." *Chronicle of Higher Education:* B1–B2.

Dziech, B.W., and L. Weiner. 1984. *The Lecherous Professor: Sexual Harassment on Campus*. Boston: Beacon Press.

Earley, M., M. Mentkowski, and J. Schafer. 1980. "Valuing at Alverno: The Valuing Process in Liberal Education." Milwaukee: Alverno Productions.

Eble, K.E., and W.J. McKeachie. 1985. *Improving Undergraduate Education through Faculty Development*. San Francisco: Jossey-Bass.

Edgerton, R. 1992. "Community and Commitment in Higher Education." *AAHE Bulletin* 45(1): 3–7.

"Education Pilot Criteria." 1995. Malcolm Baldrige National Quality Award Program. Gaithersburg, Md.: U.S. Dept. of Commerce, National Institute of Standards and Technology.

Ehrhart, J.K., and B.R. Sandler. November 1985. "Campus Gang Rape: Party Games?" Washington, D.C.: Association of American Colleges.

Ehrlich, H.J. August 1988. "Campus Ethnoviolence and the Policy Options." A Report to the New Jersey Dept. of Higher Education, Office of Educational Policy. Baltimore: National Institute against Racism and Prejudice.

Ellner, C.L., and C.P. Barnes, eds. 1983. *Studies of College Teaching: Experimental Results, Theoretical Interpretations, and New Perspectives.* Lexington, Mass.: D.C. Heath.

Ellson, D.G. 1986. *Improving the Productivity of Teaching: 125 Exhibits.* Bloomington, Ind.: Phi Delta Kappa Center on Evaluation, Development, and Research.

Ender, S.C., R.B. Winston, Jr., and T.K. Miller. 1982. "Academic Advising as Student Development." In *Developmental Approaches to Academic Advising,* edited by R.B. Winston, Jr., S.C. Ender, and T.K. Miller. New Directions for Student Services No. 17. San Francisco: Jossey-Bass.

———. 1984. "Academic Advising Reconsidered." In *Developmental Academic Advising,* edited by R.B. Winston, Jr., T.K. Miller, S.C. Ender, T.J. Grites, and Associates. San Francisco: Jossey-Bass.

"English Physics Hits the Fat Farm." 6 July 1990. *Science* 249: 21.

Erwin, T.D. 1991. *Assessing Student Learning and Development.* San Francisco: Jossey-Bass.

Etzioni, A. 1993. *The Spirit of Community: Rights, Responsibilities, and the Communitarian Agenda.* New York: Crown.

Evangelauf, J. 10 May 1989. "Accounting Educators Plan to Update Curriculum, Debate Tighter Entrance Requirements for CPAs." *Chronicle of Higher Education:* A31–A32.

———. 9 May 1990. "Education Research Seen in Ferment; Retention Studies Called Too Narrow." *Chronicle of Higher Education:* A18.

Evans, E.D., P.K. Dodson, and D.T. Bailey. 1981. "Assessment of Psychology Instructors' Perceptions and Use of Textbook Test-Item Manuals for Measuring Student Achievement." *Teaching of Psychology* 8(2): 88–90.

Eve, R.A., and F.B. Harrold. 1986. "Creationism, Cult Archeology, and Other Pseudoscientific Beliefs: A Study of College Students." *Youth and Society* 117(4): 396–421.

Ewell, P.T. 1991. "Assessment and Public Accountability: Back to the

Future." *Change* 23(6): 12–17.

Facione, P.A. 1990. *Critical Thinking: A Statement of Expert Consensus for Purposes of Educational Assessment and Instruction. Research Findings and Recommendations.* Newark, Del.: American Philosophical Association. ED 315 423. 112 pp. MF–01; PC–05.

Facione, P.A., C.A. Sanchez, and N.C. Facione. 1993. "Are College Students Disposed to Think?" Paper presented at a meeting of the AAHE Assessment Forum, June, Chicago, Illinois. ED 368 311. 18 pp. MF–01; PC–01.

Feder, K.L. 1986. "The Challenges of Pseudoscience." *Journal of College Science Teaching* 15: 180–86.

———. 1987. "Cult Archeology and Creationism: A Coordinated Research Project." In *Cult Archeology and Creationism: Understanding Pseudoscientific Beliefs about the Past,* edited by F.B. Harrold and R.A. Eve. Iowa City: Univ. of Iowa Press.

Feldman, K.A. 1987. "Research Productivity and Scholarly Accomplishment of College Teachers as Related to Their Instructional Effectiveness: A Review and Exploration." *Research in Higher Education* 26(3): 227–98.

Feldman, K.A., and T.M. Newcomb. 1969. *The Impact of College on Students.* 2 vol. San Francisco: Jossey-Bass.

Field, M.J., ed. 1995. *Dental Education at the Crossroads: Challenges and Change.* Washington, D.C.: National Academy Press.

Fife, J.D. 1991. "Foreword." In *Meeting the Mandate: Renewing the College and Departmental Curriculum,* by W. Toombs and W. Tierney. ASHE-ERIC Higher Education Report No. 6. Washington, D.C.: George Washington Univ., School of Education and Human Development. ED 345 603. 124 pp. MF–01; PC–05.

Fincher, C. 1986. "Trends and Issues in Curricular Development." In *Higher Education: Handbook of Theory and Research,* edited by J.C. Smart. Vol. 2. New York: Agathon.

Fink, L.D. 1984. "First Year on the Faculty: Being There." *Journal of Geography in Higher Education* 8(1): 11–25.

———. 1985. "First Year on the Faculty: The Quality of Their Teaching." *Journal of Geography in Higher Education* 9(2): 129–45.

Finkelstein, M.J. 1984. *The American Academic Profession: A Synthesis of Social Scientific Inquiry since World War II.* Columbus: Ohio State Univ. Press.

Fischer, C.G., and G.E. Grant. 1983. "Intellectual Levels in College Classrooms." In *Studies of College Teaching: Experimental Results, Theoretical Interpretations, and New Perspectives,* edited by C.L. Ellner and C.P. Barnes. Lexington, Mass.: D.C. Heath.

Flam, F. 21 June 1991. "Still a 'Chilly Climate' for Women?" *Science* 252: 1604–6.

Ford, W.S.Z. 1991. "An Interdepartmental, Research-Based Assessment of Training Needs for Teaching Assistants." Paper presented at the Third National Conference on the Training and Employment of Teaching Assistants. November, Austin, Texas.

Forrest, A. 1985. "Creating Conditions for Student and Institutional Success." In *Increasing Student Retention,* edited by L. Noel, R. Levitz, D. Saluri, and Associates. San Francisco: Jossey-Bass.

Foster, P.J. 1983. "Verbal Participation and Outcomes in Medical Education: A Study of Third-Year Clinical Discussion Groups." In *Studies of College Teaching: Experimental Results, Theoretical Interpretations, and New Perspectives,* edited by C.L. Ellner and C.P. Barnes. Lexington, Mass.: D.C. Heath.

Fried, J., ed. 1981. *Education for Student Development.* New Directions for Student Services No. 15. San Francisco: Jossey-Bass.

"From Risk to Renewal: Stymied by Barriers to Fixing the Schools, Reformers Seek Pathway to True and Lasting Change." 10 February 1993. *Education Week* (Special Supplement): 1–18.

Fuerst, P.A. 1984. "University Student Understanding of Evolutionary Biology's Place in the Creation/Evolution Controversy." *Ohio Journal of Science* 84(5): 218–28.

Fuhrmann, B.S., and A.F. Grasha. 1983. *A Practical Handbook for College Teachers.* Boston: Little, Brown.

Gabelnick, F., J. MacGregor, R. Matthews, and B.L. Smith. 1990. *Learning Communities: Building Connections among Disciplines, Students, and Faculty.* New Directions for Teaching and Learning No. 41. San Francisco: Jossey-Bass.

Gaff, J.G. 1975. *Toward Faculty Renewal.* San Francisco: Jossey-Bass.
———. 1983. *General Education Today: A Critical Analysis of Controversies, Practices, and Reforms.* San Francisco: Jossey-Bass.
———. 1991. *New Life for the College Curriculum: Assessing Achievements and Furthering Progress in the Reform of General Education.* San Francisco: Jossey-Bass.

Gaff, J.G., J. Lindquist, K. Mohrman, C.H. Reynolds, and R. Yount, eds. 1980. *General Education: Issues and Resources.* Project on General Education Models, Society for Values in Higher Education. Washington, D.C.: Association of American Colleges.

Gagné, R.M., and L.J. Briggs. 1974. *Principles of Instructional Design.* New York: Holt, Rinehart & Winston.

Gallagher, D.R. 1991. "A Study of the Preparation of College and University Academic Administrators in the United States." Unpublished manuscript. Glassboro, N.J.: Glassboro State College, Communication Dept.

Gallagher, J.J. 1989. "Research on Secondary School Science Teachers' Practices, Knowledge, and Beliefs: A Basis for Restructuring." In *Looking into Windows: Qualitative Research in Science Education,* edited by M.L. Matyas, K. Tobin, and B.J. Fraser. Washington, D.C.: American Association for the Advancement of Science.

Gamson, Z.F. 1991. "Why Is College So Influential? The Continuing Search for Answers." *Change* 23(6): 50–53.

———. 1993. "The Destruction and Re-creation of Academic Community: A Personal View." *Association for the Study of Higher Education Newsletter* 6(2): 4–7.

Gappa, J.M., and D.W. Leslie. 1993. *The Invisible Faculty: Improving the Status of Part-Timers in Higher Education.* San Francisco: Jossey-Bass.

Gardiner, L.F. 1989. *Planning for Assessment: Mission Statements, Goals, and Objectives.* Trenton: New Jersey Dept. of Higher Education. Available from author.

Gardner, H. 1985. *Frames of Mind: The Theory of Multiple Intelligences.* New York: Basic Books.

———. 1991. *The Unschooled Mind: How Children Think and How Schools Should Teach.* New York: Basic Books.

Gilligan, C. 1977. "In a Different Voice: Women's Conceptions of Self and of Morality." *Harvard Educational Review* 47(4): 481–517.

———. 1981. "Moral Development." In *The Modern American College,* edited by A.W. Chickering and Associates. San Francisco: Jossey-Bass.

———. 1982. *In a Different Voice: Psychological Theory and Women's Development.* Cambridge, Mass.: Harvard Univ. Press.

Gold, A.R. 20 April 1988. "President of Harvard Urges More Instruction on Ethics." *New York Times.*

Goldberg, E.D. January 1993a. "Chancellor's Report to the Board of Higher Education." Trenton: New Jersey Dept. of Higher Education.

———. April 1993b. "Special Chancellor's Report to the Board of Higher Education." Trenton: New Jersey Dept. of Higher Education.

———. October 1993c. "Special Chancellor's Report to the Board of Higher Education." Trenton: New Jersey Dept. of Higher Education.

Gordon, V.N. 1984. "Training Professional and Paraprofessional Advisors." In *Developmental Academic Advising,* edited by R.B. Winston, Jr., T.K. Miller, S.C. Ender, T.J. Grites, and Associates. San Francisco: Jossey-Bass.

———. 1992. *Handbook on Academic Advising.* Westport, Conn.: Greenwood Press.

———. 1994. *Academic Advising: An Annotated Bibliography.* Westport, Conn.: Greenwood Press.

Gose, B. 14 April 1995. "Many Freshmen Become Binge Drinkers during First Semester, Study Finds." *Chronicle of Higher Education:* A39.

Gray, P.J., R.C. Froh, and R.M. Diamond. 1991. "Myths and Realities." *AAHE Bulletin* 44(4): 4–5.

———. 1992. "A National Study of Research Universities on the Balance between Research and Undergraduate Teaching." Syracuse, N.Y.: Syracuse Univ., Center for Instructional Development. ED 350 967. 23 pp. MF–01; PC–01.

Gray, T. Spring 1984. "University Course Reduces Belief in Paranormal." *Skeptical Inquirer* 8: 247–51.

———. 1987. "Educational Experience and Belief in Paranormal Phenomena." In *Cult Archeology and Creationism: Understanding Pseudoscientific Beliefs about the Past,* edited by F.B. Harrold and R.A. Eve. Iowa City: Univ. of Iowa Press.

Green, K.C., and S.W. Gilbert. 1995. "Great Expectations: Content, Communications, Productivity, and the Role of Information Technology in Higher Education." *Change* 27(2): 8–18.

Green, M.F., ed. 1989. *Minorities on Campus: A Handbook for Enhancing Diversity.* Washington, D.C.: American Council on Education.

Griffiths, D.H. 1973. "The Study of the Cognitive Development of Science Students in Introductory Level Courses." Doctoral dissertation, Rutgers Univ.

Guskey, T.R. 1988. *Improving Student Learning in College Classrooms.* Springfield, Ill.: Charles C Thomas.

Guskin, A.E. 1994a. "Reducing Student Costs and Enhancing Student Learning: The University Challenge of the 1990s." Part 1. "Restructuring the Administration." *Change* 26(4): 22–29.

———. 1994b. "Reducing Student Costs and Enhancing Student Learning: The University Challenge of the 1990s." Part 2. "Restructuring the Role of Faculty." *Change* 26(5): 16–25.

Guskin, A.E., and M.A. Bassis. 1985. "Leadership Styles and Institutional Renewal." In *Leadership and Institutional Renewal,* edited by R.M. Davis. New Directions for Higher Education No. 49. San Francisco: Jossey-Bass.

Gustav, A. 1969. "Retention of Course Material after Varying Intervals of Time." *Psychological Reports* 25: 727–30.

Habley, W.R. 1988. "Introduction and Overview." In *The Status and Future of Academic Advising: Problems and Promise,* edited by W.H. Habley. ACT National Center for the Advancement of Educational Priorities.

Habley, W.R., and D.S. Crockett. 1988. "The Third ACT National Survey of Academic Advising." In *The Status and Future of Academic Advising: Problems and Promise,* edited by W.H. Habley. ACT National Center for the Advancement of Educational Priorities.

"Half of Waterloo Students Say They Considered Suicide." 1 May

1985. *Chronicle of Higher Education:* 35.

Hall, R.M., and B.R. Sandler. 1982. "The Classroom Climate: A Chilly One for Women?" Washington, D.C.: Association of American Colleges.

————. 1984. "Out of the Classroom: A Chilly Campus Climate for Women?" Washington, D.C.: Association of American Colleges. ED 254 125. 22 pp. MF–01; PC–01.

Halonen, J.S., ed. 1986. *Teaching Critical Thinking in Psychology.* Milwaukee: Alverno Productions.

Halpern, D.F., ed. 1987. *Student Outcomes Assessment: What Institutions Stand to Gain.* New Directions for Higher Education No. 59. San Francisco: Jossey-Bass.

Hanfmann, E. 1978. *Effective Therapy for College Students.* San Francisco: Jossey-Bass.

Hanna, G.S., and W.E. Cashin. 1987. "Matching Instructional Objectives, Subject Matter, Tests, and Score Interpretations." IDEA Paper No. 18. Manhattan: Kansas State Univ., Center for Faculty Evaluation and Development. ED 298 152. 7 pp. MF–01; PC–01.

Hannum, W.H., and L.J. Briggs. January 1982. "How Does Instructional Systems Design Differ from Traditional Instruction?" *Educational Technology* 22: 9–14.

Hanson, G.R. September 1989. *The Assessment of Student Development Outcomes: A Review and Critique of Assessment Instruments.* Trenton: New Jersey Dept. of Higher Education, College Outcomes Evaluation Program.

————, ed. 1982. *Measuring Student Development.* New Directions for Student Services No. 20. San Francisco: Jossey-Bass.

Hardy-Brown, K. 1981. "Formal Operations and the Issue of Generalizability: The Analysis of Poetry by College Students." In *Social Development in Youth: Structure and Content,* edited by J.A. Meacham and N.R. Santilli. Basel: Karger.

Harris, J., S. Hillenmeyer, and J.V. Foran. 1989. "Quality Assurance for Private Career Schools." Washington, D.C.: Association of Independent Colleges and Schools.

Harrold, F.B., and R.A. Eve. Fall 1986. "Noah's Ark and Ancient Astronauts: Pseudoscientific Beliefs about the Past among a Sample of College Students." *Skeptical Inquirer* 11: 61–75.

————. 1987. "Patterns of Creationist Belief among College Students." In *Cult Archeology and Creationism: Understanding Pseudoscientific Beliefs about the Past,* edited by F.B. Harrold and R.A. Eve. Iowa City: Univ. of Iowa Press.

Hartnett, R.T., and B.C. Schroder. August 1987. "The Validity of Undergraduate Grades." New Brunswick, N.J.: Rutgers Univ., Educational Policy Studies.

Haskins, C.H. 1957. *The Rise of Universities.* Ithaca, N.Y.: Cornell

Univ. Press.

Heath, D.H. 1968. *Growing Up in College*. San Francisco: Jossey-Bass.

Heller, S. 11 October 1989. "More Than Half of Students in Survey Flunk History and Literature Test." *Chronicle of Higher Education:* A15.

Helm, H., and J.D. Novak, eds. 1983. *Proceedings of the International Seminar Misconceptions in Science and Mathematics.* Cornell University, June, Ithaca, New York.

Heydinger, R.B. 1994. "A Reinvented Model for Higher Education." *On the Horizon* 3(1): 1–2+.

Hines, E.R. 1984. "Delivery Systems and the Institutional Context." In *Developmental Academic Advising,* edited by R.B. Winston, Jr., T.K. Miller, S.C. Ender, T.J. Grites, and Associates. San Francisco: Jossey-Bass.

Hodgkinson, H.L. 1985. "All One System: Demographics of Education, Kindergarten through Graduate School." Washington, D.C.: Institute for Educational Leadership. ED 261 101. 22 pp. MF–01; PC not available EDRS.

Hoffer, E. 1951. *The True Believer: Thoughts on the Nature of Mass Movements*. New York: Harper & Row.

Holmes Group 1995. *Tomorrow's Schools of Education*. East Lansing, Mich.: Author.

Hood, A.B., and C. Arceneaux. 1990. *Key Resources on Student Services: A Guide to the Field and Its Literature*. San Francisco: Jossey-Bass.

"Hours Students Spent Each Week in Various Activities." 14 January 1987. *Chronicle of Higher Education:* 38.

Howard, A. *n.d.* "The Economy: Long-Term Economic Trends and Their Implications for Higher Education." In *The Academy and the Economy: Working Papers for the Advisory Council on General Education*. Trenton: New Jersey Dept. of Higher Education.

Huber, R.M. 1992. "How Professors Play the Cat Guarding the Cream." Lanham, Md.: George Mason Univ. Press.

Hudak, M.A., and D.E. Anderson. 1990. "Formal Operations and Learning Style Predict Student Success in Statistics and Computer Science Courses." *Teaching of Psychology* 17(4): 231–34.

Hudson, L. 1987. "East Is East and West Is West? A Regional Comparison of Cult Belief Patterns." In *Cult Archeology and Creationism: Understanding Pseudoscientific Beliefs about the Past,* edited by F.B. Harrold and R.A. Eve. Iowa City: Univ. of Iowa Press.

Hughes, J.O., and B.R. Sandler. 1986. "In Case of Sexual Harassment: A Guide for Women Students." Washington, D.C.: Association of American Colleges. ED 268 920. 9 pp. MF–01; PC–01.

———. 1987. "'Friends' Raping Friends: Could It Happen to You?" Washington, D.C.: Association of American Colleges.

———. 1988. "Peer Harassment: Hassles for Women on Campus." Washington, D.C.: Association of American Colleges. ED 299 925. 16 pp. MF–01; PC–01.

Hurtado, S. 1992. "The Campus Racial Climate: Contexts of Conflict." *Journal of Higher Education* 63(5): 539–69.

Hurtado, S., A.W. Astin, and E.L. Dey. 1991. "Varieties of General Education Programs: An Empirically Based Taxonomy." *Journal of General Education* 40(1): 133–62.

Hutchings, P., T. Marchese, and B. Wright. 1991. *Using Assessment to Strengthen General Education*. Washington, D.C.: American Association for Higher Education.

Hutchins, R.M. 1936. *The Higher Learning in America*. New Haven, Conn.: Yale Univ. Press.

"Information for High School Students Interested in Medicine or Dentistry: Probability of Success." 1992. New Orleans: Xavier Univ. of Louisiana.

Inhelder, B., and J. Piaget. 1958. *The Growth of Logical Thinking from Childhood to Adolescence*, translated by A. Parsons and S. Milgram. New York: Basic Books.

Irvine Group. 1990. "Renewing Undergraduate Education: Recommendations from the Irvine Group." Irvine, Cal.: Author.

"It's Time to Reinvent Higher Education." 1993. *On the Horizon* 1(5): 1–2+.

"Ivy League African-Americans Dissatisfied with Schools, Says New Poll." 4 April 1993. Washington, D.C.: Luntz-Weber.

Jacobs, L.C., and C.I. Chase. 1992. *Developing and Using Tests Effectively: A Guide for Faculty*. San Francisco: Jossey-Bass.

Jacoby, B. 1989. *The Student-as-Commuter: Developing a Comprehensive Institutional Response*. ASHE-ERIC Higher Education Report No. 7. Washington, D.C.: George Washington Univ., School of Education and Human Development. ED 319 298. 118 pp. MF–01; PC–05.

Johnson, D.W., and R.T. Johnson. 1989. *Cooperation and Competition: Theory and Research*. Edina, Minn.: Interaction Book Co.

Johnson, D.W., R.T. Johnson, and K.A. Smith. 1991a. *Active Learning: Cooperation in the College Classroom*. Edina, Minn.: Interaction Book Co.

———. 1991b. *Cooperative Learning: Increasing College Faculty Instructional Productivity*. ASHE-ERIC Higher Education Report No. 4. Washington, D.C.: George Washington Univ., School of Education and Human Development. ED 343 465. 168 pp. MF–01; PC–07.

Johnson, G.R. 1986. "A Cognitive Interaction Analysis System." College Station, Tex.: Author.

———. 1987a. "Changing the Verbal Behavior of Teachers." *Journal of Staff, Program, and Organization Development* 5(4): 155–58.

——. 1987b. "An Eclectic Systematic Instruction Model for Exposi-
tory Instruction." *Journal of Staff, Program, and Organization
Development* 5(3): 91–99.

Johnson, G.R., J.A. Eison, R. Abbott, G.T. Meiss, K. Moran, J.A.
Morgan, T.L. Pasternak, E. Zaremba, and W.J. McKeachie. 1991.
"Teaching Tips for Users of the Motivated Strategies for Learning
Questionnaire (MSLQ)." Technical Report No. 91-B-005. Ann
Arbor: Univ. of Michigan, National Center for Research to Improve
Postsecondary Teaching and Learning.

Johnston, J.S., Jr., S. Shaman, and R. Zemsky. 1987. *Unfinished
Design: The Humanities and Social Sciences in Undergraduate
Engineering Education*. Washington, D.C.: Association of
American Colleges. ED 299 900. 83 pp. MF–01; PC not avail-
able EDRS.

Johnstone, D.B. April 1993. "Learning Productivity: A New Imperative for American Higher Education." Studies in Public Higher
Education No. 3. Albany: SUNY, Office of the Chancellor.

Jones, E.A., and J.R. Ratcliff. 1990. "Is a Core Curriculum Best for
Everybody? The Effect of Different Patterns of Coursework on the
General Education of High- and Low-Ability Students." Paper presented at an annual meeting of the American Educational Research Association, April, Boston, Massachusetts.

Juran, J.M. 1988. *Juran on Planning for Quality*. New York: Free
Press.

——. 1989. *Juran on Leadership for Quality: An Executive
Handbook*. New York: Free Press.

Kagan, S. 1989. *Cooperative Learning Resources for Teachers*. San
Juan Capistrano, Cal.: Resources for Teachers.

Karplus, R., A.E. Lawson, W. Woolman, M. Appel, R. Bernoff, A.
Howe, J.J. Rusch, and F. Sullivan. 1977. *Science Teaching and the
Development of Reasoning: Biology*. Berkeley: Univ. of California.

Katz, J., and M. Henry. 1988. *Turning Professors into Teachers: A
New Approach to Faculty Development and Student Learning*. New
York: ACE/Macmillan.

Keirsey, D., and M. Bates. 1978. *Please Understand Me: Character
and Temperament Types*. Del Mar, Cal.: Prometheus Nemesis
Books.

Keller, F.S. 1968. "Good-bye, Teacher. . . . " *Journal of Applied
Behavior Analysis* 1: 78–89.

Keller, F.S., and J.B. Sherman. 1974. *PSI: The Keller Plan Handbook*.
Menlo Park, Cal.: Benjamin.

Keller, G. 1983. *Academic Strategy: The Management Revolution in
American Higher Education*. Baltimore: Johns Hopkins Univ.
Press.

Kells, H.R. 1988. *Self-Study Processes: A Guide for Postsecondary and Similar Service-Oriented Institutions and Programs.* New York: ACE/Macmillan.

Kemp, J.E. 1977. *Instructional Design: A Plan for Unit and Course Development.* Belmont, Cal.: Fearon.

Kennedy, D. 1995. "Another Century's End, Another Revolution for Higher Education." *Change* 27(3): 9–15.

King, M.C. 1993. *Academic Advising: Organizing and Delivering Services for Student Success.* New Directions for Community Colleges No. 82. San Francisco: Jossey-Bass.

King, P.M. 1978. "William Perry's Theory of Intellectual and Ethical Development." In *Applying New Developmental Findings,* edited by L. Knefelkamp, C. Widick, and C.A. Parker. New Directions for Student Services No. 4. San Francisco: Jossey-Bass.

King, P.M., and K.S. Kitchener. 1994. *Developing Reflective Judgment: Understanding and Promoting Intellectual Growth and Critical Thinking in Adolescents and Adults.* San Francisco: Jossey-Bass.

Kirschenbaum, H., S.B. Simon, and R. Napier. 1971. *Wad-ja-get? The Grading Game in American Education.* New York: Hart.

Knefelkamp, L., C.A. Parker, and C. Widick. 1978. "Jane Loevinger's Milestones of Development." In *Applying New Developmental Findings,* edited by L. Knefelkamp, C. Widick, and C.A. Parker. New Directions for Student Services No. 4. San Francisco: Jossey-Bass.

Knefelkamp, L., and R. Slepitza. 1978. "A Cognitive-Developmental Model of Career Development: An Adaptation of the Perry Scheme." In *Encouraging Development in College Students,* edited by C.A. Parker. Minneapolis: Univ. of Minnesota Press.

Knefelkamp, L., C. Widick, and C.A. Parker, eds. 1978. *Applying New Developmental Findings.* New Directions for Student Services No. 4. San Francisco: Jossey-Bass.

Kohlberg, L. 1981. *The Philosophy of Moral Development: Moral Stages and the Idea of Justice.* San Francisco: Harper & Row.

Kohlberg, L., D.R. Boyd, and C. Levine. 1990. "The Return of Stage 6: Its Principle and Moral Point of View." In *The Moral Domain: Essays in the Ongoing Discussion between Philosophy and the Social Sciences,* edited by T.E. Wren. Cambridge, Mass.: MIT Press.

Kohlberg, L., C. Levine, and A. Hewer. 1983. *Moral Stages: A Current Formulation and a Response to Critics.* Basel: Karger.

Kohlberg, L., and R. Mayer. 1972. "Development as the Aim of Education." *Harvard Educational Review* 42(4): 449–96.

Kohn, A. 1992. *No Contest: The Case against Competition.* Boston: Houghton Mifflin.

———. 1993. *Punished by Rewards: The Trouble with Gold Stars,*

Incentive Plans, A's, Praise, and Other Bribes. Boston: Houghton Mifflin.

Kolb, D.A. 1981. "Learning Styles and Disciplinary Differences." In *The Modern American College,* edited by A.W. Chickering and Associates. San Francisco: Jossey-Bass.

Kolbert, E. 23 March 1989. "Nearly 10% of Law Partners Fail to File New York Taxes." *New York Times.*

Kolodiy, G. 1975. "The Cognitive Development of High School and College Science Students." *Journal of College Science Teaching* 5(1): 20–22.

Korn, H.A. 1986. "Psychological Models Explaining the Impact of College on Students." Ann Arbor, Mich.: National Center for Research to Improve Postsecondary Teaching and Learning. ED 287 440. 24 pp. MF–01; PC–01.

Kramer, D.A., and W.T. Bacelar. 1994. "The Educated Adult in Today's World: Wisdom and the Mature Learner." In *Interdisciplinary Handbook of Adult Lifespan Learning,* edited by J.D. Sinnott. Westport, Conn.: Greenwood Press.

Kramer, G.L., and R.W. Spencer. 1989. "Academic Advising." In *The Freshman Year Experience: Helping Students Survive and Succeed in College,* edited by M.L. Upcraft, J.N. Gardner, and Associates. San Francisco: Jossey-Bass.

Kramer, M. 1993. "Lengthening of Time-to-Degree: The High Cost of Dithering." *Change* 25(3): 5–7.

Kronholm, M.M. 1996. "The Impact of Developmental Instruction on Reflective Judgment." *Review of Higher Education* 19(2): 199–225.

Kuh, G.D. 1981. *Indices of Quality in the Undergraduate Experience.* AAHE-ERIC Research Report No. 4. Washington, D.C.: American Association for Higher Education.

Kuh, G.D., L.E. Krehbiel, and K. MacKay. 1988. "Personal Development and the College Student Experience: A Review of the Literature." Report to the College Outcomes Evaluation Program, New Jersey Dept. of Higher Education. Bloomington: Indiana Univ., School of Education, Dept. of Leadership and Policy Studies.

Kuhn, D., J. Langer, L. Kohlberg, and N. Haan. 1977. "The Development of Formal Operations." *Genetic Psychology Monographs* 95: 97–188.

Kulik, C-L. C., J.A. Kulik, and R.L. Bangert-Drowns. 1990. "Effectiveness of Mastery Learning Programs: A Meta-analysis." *Review of Educational Research* 60(2): 265–99.

Kurfiss, J. May 1983. "Intellectual, Psychosocial, and Moral Development in College: Four Major Theories." Ogden, Utah: Weber State College.

————. 1988. *Critical Thinking: Theory, Research, Practice, and Possi-bilities.* ASHE-ERIC Higher Education Report No. 2.

Washington, D.C.: Association for the Study of Higher Education. ED 304 041. 164 pp. MF–01; PC–07.

Lambert, C. May/June 1993. "Desperately Seeking Summa." *Harvard Magazine*: 36–40.

Lawson, A.E. 1988. "A Better Way to Teach Biology." *American Biology Teacher* 50(5): 266–78.

Lawton, M. 10 April 1991. "More Than a Third of Teens Surveyed Say They Have Contemplated Suicide." *Education Week*: 5.

Layden, M. 1977. *Escaping the Hostility Trap.* Englewood Cliffs, N.J.: Prentice-Hall.

"Learning Slope." 1991. Pew Higher Education Research Program *Policy Perspectives* 4(1): 1A–8A.

Lederman, D. 9 March 1994. "Weapons on Campus?" *Chronicle of Higher Education*: A33–A34.

Lenning, O.T. 1977. *Previous Attempts to Structure Educational Outcomes and Outcome-Related Concepts: A Compilation and Review of the Literature.* Boulder, Colo.: National Center for Higher Education Management Systems. ED 272 109. 266 pp. MF–01; PC–11.

Lerner, B. 1989. "Intelligence and Law." In *Intelligence: Measurement, Theory, and Public Policy,* edited by R.L. Linn. Urbana: Univ. of Illinois.

Levin, H.M. 1991. *Learning from Accelerated Schools.* Philadelphia: Pew Higher Education Research Program.

Levine, A. 1978. *Handbook on Undergraduate Curriculum.* San Francisco: Jossey-Bass.

Levine, D.U., and Associates. 1985. *Improving Student Achievement through Mastery Learning Programs.* San Francisco: Jossey-Bass.

Levinson-Rose, J., and R.J. Menges. 1981. "Improving College Teaching: A Critical Review of Research." *Review of Educational Research* 51(3): 403–34.

Lewis, K.G. 1984. "What Really Happens in Large University Classes?" Paper presented at a meeting of the American Educational Research Association, April, New Orleans, Louisiana.

———. 1986. "Using an Objective Observation System to Diagnose Teaching Problems." *Journal of Staff, Program, and Organization Development* 4(4): 81–90.

———. 1988. *Face to Face: A Sourcebook of Individual Consultation Techniques for Faculty/Instructional Developers.* Stillwater, Okla.: New Forums Press.

———, ed. 1993. *The TA Experience: Preparing for Multiple Roles.* Stillwater, Okla.: New Forums Press.

Lewis, K.G., and G.R. Johnson. 1986. "Programmed Workbook for Developing Coded Skills Using Johnson's Cognitive Interaction Analysis System (CIAS)."

Light, R.J. 1990. *The Harvard Assessment Seminars: Explorations with Students and Faculty about Teaching, Learning, and Student Life.* First Report. Cambridge, Mass.: Harvard Univ., Graduate School of Education.

————. 1992. *The Harvard Assessment Seminars: Explorations with Students and Faculty about Teaching, Learning, and Student Life.* Second Report. Cambridge, Mass.: Harvard Univ., Graduate School of Education.

Light, R.J., J.D. Singer, and J.B. Willett. 1990. *By Design: Planning Research on Higher Education.* Cambridge, Mass.: Harvard Univ. Press.

Lindquist, J., ed. 1978. *Designing Teaching Improvement Programs.* Berkeley, Cal.: Pacific Soundings Press.

Linn, R.L., ed. 1989. *Intelligence: Measurement, Theory, and Public Policy.* Urbana: Univ. of Illinois.

Lively, K. 21 July 1993. "Disappointments in School Reform Laid to Training." *Chronicle of Higher Education:* A22.

Locke, E.A., and G.P. Latham. 1984. *Goal Setting: A Motivational Technique That Works!* Englewood Cliffs, N.J.: Prentice-Hall.

————. 1990. *A Theory of Goal Setting and Task Performance.* Englewood Cliffs, N.J.: Prentice-Hall.

Loevinger, J. 1976. *Ego Development.* San Francisco: Jossey-Bass.

Lucas, A.F. 1994. *Strengthening Departmental Leadership: A Team-Building Guide for Chairs in Colleges and Universities.* San Francisco: Jossey-Bass.

————, ed. 1989. *The Department Chairperson's Role in Enhancing College Teaching.* New Directions for Teaching and Learning No. 37. San Francisco: Jossey-Bass.

McBee, M.L. 1980. *Rethinking College Responsibilities for Values.* New Directions for Teaching and Learning No. 31. San Francisco: Jossey-Bass.

McCabe, D.L. 1992. "The Influence of Situational Ethics on Cheating among College Students." *Sociological Inquiry* 62(3): 365–74.

McDade, S.A. 1987. *Higher Education Leadership: Enhancing Skills through Professional Development Programs.* ASHE-ERIC Higher Education Report No. 5. Washington, D.C.: Association for the Study of Higher Education. ED 293 479. 138 pp. MF–01; PC–06.

MacGregor, J. 1987. "Intellectual Development of Students in Learning Community Programs, 1986–1987." Occasional Paper No. 1. Olympia, Wash.: Washington Center for Undergraduate Education.

McKeachie, W.J. 1986. *Teaching Tips: A Guidebook for the Beginning College Teacher.* Lexington, Mass.: D.C. Heath.

————. 1991. "Learning, Teaching, and Learning from Teaching." In *Preparing the Professoriate of Tomorrow to Teach: Selected Readings in TA Training,* edited by J.D. Nyquist, R.D. Abbott, D.H.

Wulff, and J. Sprague. Dubuque, Ia.: Kendall/Hunt.

———. 1994. *Teaching Tips: Strategies, Research, and Theory for College and University Teachers.* Lexington, Mass.: D.C. Heath.

McKeachie, W.J., P.R. Pintrich, Y-G. Lin, D.A.F. Smith, and R. Sharma. 1990. *Teaching and Learning in the College Classroom: A Review of the Research Literature.* Ann Arbor, Mich.: National Center for Research to Improve Postsecondary Teaching and Learning.

McKinnon, J.W., and J.W. Renner. 1971. "Are Colleges Concerned with Intellectual Development?" *American Journal of Physics* 39: 1047–52.

McLaughlin, J.B., and D. Riesman. 1990. *Choosing a College President: Opportunities and Constraints.* Princeton, N.J.: Carnegie Foundation for the Advancement of Teaching. ED 334 878. 403 pp. MF–01; PC–17.

McLeish, J. 1968. *The Lecture Method.* Cambridge, Eng.: Cambridge Institute of Education.

McNeel, S.P. 1994. "College Teaching and Student Moral Development." In *Moral Development in the Professions: Psychology and Applied Ethics,* edited by J.R. Rest and D. Narváez. Hillsdale, N.J.: Erlbaum.

McQuade, D. 1989. "The Teaching Assistantship as Preparation for an Academic Career." Paper presented at the American Association for Higher Education National Conference on Higher Education, April, San Francisco, California.

Malizio, A.G. 1995. *National Postsecondary Student Aid Study: Estimates of Student Financial Aid, 1992–93.* Washington, D.C.: U.S. Dept. of Education, Office of Educational Research and Improvement.

Maramark, S., and M.B. Maline. 1993. "Academic Dishonesty among College Students." Washington, D.C.: U. S. Dept. of Education, Office of Educational Research and Improvement. ED 360 903. 17 pp. MF–01; PC–01.

Marchese, T. 1991a. "Standards and Us." *Change* 12(6): 4.

———. 1991b. "TQM Reaches the Academy." *AAHE Bulletin* 44(3): 3–9.

———. 1993. "TQM: A Time for Ideas." *Change* 25(3): 10–13.

Marshall, M.S. 1968. *Teaching without Grades.* Corvallis: Oregon State Univ. Press.

Marshall, R. 1989. "The Education Crisis and the Future of Our Economy." Occasional Paper. New York: Carnegie Corporation.

Massey, W.F., A.K. Wilger, and C. Colbeck. 1994. "Overcoming 'Hollowed' Collegiality: Departmental Cultures and Teaching Quality." *Change* 26(4): 11–20.

"Math Students Needed." 20 April 1990. *Science* 248: 306.

Mathews, J. 20 July 1992. "Escalante Still Stands and Delivers."

Newsweek: 58–59.

Mehrens, W.A., and I.J. Lehmann. 1984. *Measurement and Evaluation in Education and Psychology.* New York: Holt, Rinehart & Winston.

Menges, R.J., and B.C. Mathis. 1988. *Key Resources on Teaching, Learning, Curriculum, and Faculty Development.* San Francisco: Jossey-Bass.

Menges, R.J., and M.D. Svinicki. 1991. *College Teaching: From Theory to Practice.* New Directions for Teaching and Learning No. 45. San Francisco: Jossey-Bass.

Mentkowski, M., et al. 1991. *Understanding Abilities, Learning, and Development through College Outcome Studies: What Can We Expect from Higher Education Assessment?* Symposium conducted at a meeting of the American Educational Research Association, April, Chicago, Illinois. ED 342 296. 162 pp. MF–01; PC–07.

Mentkowski, M., and M.J. Strait. 1983. *A Longitudinal Study of Student Change in Cognitive Development, Learning Styles, and Generic Abilities in an Outcome-Centered Liberal Arts Curriculum.* Research Report No. 6, Final Report to the National Institute of Education. Milwaukee: Alverno College, Office of Research and Evaluation. ED 239 562. 394 pp. MF–01; PC–16.

Mercer, J. 12 August 1992. "Education Commission of the States Discusses Radical Change for Colleges." *Chronicle of Higher Education:* A20.

Mestre, J. Summer 1987. "Why Should Mathematics and Science Teachers Be Interested in Cognitive Research Findings?" *Academic Connections:* 3–5+.

Metzner, B.S. 1989. "Perceived Quality of Academic Advising: The Effect on Freshman Attrition." *American Educational Research Journal* 26(3): 422–42.

Meyers, C. 1986. *Teaching Students to Think Critically.* San Francisco: Jossey-Bass.

Michaelsen, L.K. 1992. "Team Learning: A Comprehensive Approach for Harnessing the Power of Small Groups in Higher Education." *To Improve the Academy* 11: 107–22.

"Michigan State Women Protest Campus Climate." 17 March 1995. *Chronicle of Higher Education:* A6.

Millis, B.J. 1991. "Fulfilling the Promise of the 'Seven Principles' through Cooperative Learning: An Action Agenda for the University Classroom." *Journal on Excellence in College Teaching* 2: 139–44.

Milton, O. 1982. *Will That Be on the Final?* Springfield, Ill.: Charles C Thomas.

Milton, O., and J.W. Edgerly. 1976. "The Testing and Grading of Students." A *Change* Policy Paper.

Milton, O., H.R. Pollio, and J.A. Eison. 1986. *Making Sense of Col-*

lege Grades. San Francisco: Jossey-Bass.

Mingle, J.R. 1993. "Faculty Work and the Costs/Quality/Access Collision." *AAHE Bulletin* 45(7): 3–6+.

Moffatt, M. 1989. *Coming of Age in New Jersey: College and American Culture.* New Brunswick, N.J.: Rutgers Univ. Press.

———. 1990. "Undergraduate Cheating." New Brunswick, N.J.: Rutgers Univ., Dept. of Anthropology.

Monaghan, P. 21 September 1988. "Veterinary Educators, Saying Changes Are Overdue, Expect to See Reforms This Year." *Chronicle of Higher Education:* A39.

Mooney, C.J. 16 January 1991. "The Dissertation Is Still a Valuable Requirement, Survey Finds, but Graduate Students Say They Need Better Faculty Advising." *Chronicle of Higher Education:* A15.

Moore, M. 1991. *Cheating 101: The Benefits and Fundamentals of Earning the Easy "A."* Hopewell, N.J.: Moore Publishing.

Moore, W.S. 1987. "The Learning Environment Preferences: Establishing the Preliminary Reliability and Validity for an Objective Measure of the Perry Scheme of Intellectual and Ethical Development." Doctoral dissertation, Univ. of Maryland–College Park.

———. 1988. *The Learning Environment Preferences: An Instrument Manual.* Olympia, Wash.: Center for the Study of Intellectual Development.

———. 1989. "The Learning Environment Preferences: Exploring the Construct Validity of an Objective Measure of the Perry Scheme of Intellectual Development." *Journal of College Student Development* 30: 504–14.

———. 1991a. "The Perry Scheme of Intellectual and Ethical Develop-ment: An Introduction to the Model and Major Assessment Approaches." Paper presented at a meeting of the American Edu-cational Research Association, April 3–7, Chicago, Illinois.

———. 1991b. "Understanding and Assessing Students' Meaning-Making: The Perry Scheme of Intellectual and Ethical Development. Part 1. Overview and Context." Workshop material prepared for the American Association for Higher Education National Conference on Assessment, June 11, San Francisco, California.

Morrill, R.L. 1980. *Teaching Values in College.* San Francisco: Jossey-Bass.

Myers, I.B., and M.H. McCaulley. 1985. *A Guide to the Development and Use of the Myers-Briggs Type Indicator.* Palo Alto, Cal.: Consulting Psychologists Press.

Myers, I.B., and P.B. Myers. 1980. *Gifts Differing.* Palo Alto, Cal.: Consulting Psychologists Press.

Naisbitt, J. 1982. *Megatrends: Ten New Directions Transforming Our Lives.* New York: Warner.

National Center for Education Statistics. 1993. *Pocket Projections: Projections of Educational Statistics to 2003*. NCE 93-194. Washington, D.C.: U.S. Dept. of Education, Office of Educational Research and Improvement.

National Commission on Excellence in Education. 1983. *A Nation at Risk: The Imperative of Education Reform*. A report to the Nation and the Secretary of Education. Washington, D.C.: Author.

National Education Goals Panel. 1994. *The National Education Goals Report: Building a Nation of Learners, 1994*. Washington, D.C.: Author.

National Task Force for Minority Achievement in Higher Education. 1990. *Achieving Campus Diversity: Policies for Change*. Denver: Education Commission of the States.

Nettles, M.T. 1991. *Assessing Progress in Minority Access and Achievement in American Higher Education*. Denver: Education Commission of the States. ED 340 289. 43 pp. MF–01; PC–02.

Neumann, A. 1992. "Double Vision: The Experience of Institutional Stability." *Review of Higher Education* 15(4): 417–47.

"New Poll: Ivy League Students Fail Current Affairs Test." 4 April 1993. Washington, D.C.: Luntz-Weber.

Newman, J.H. 1959. *The Idea of a University*. Garden City, N.Y.: Doubleday.

Nicklin, J.L. 7 February 1990. "Studies Reveal Widespread Abuse of Medical Students during Education." *Chronicle of Higher Education*: A2.

Noble, J. 1988. "What Students Think of Academic Advising." In *The Status and Future of Academic Advising: Problems and Promise*, edited by W.R. Habley. ACT National Center for the Advancement of Educational Priorities.

Noel, L. 1985. "Increasing Student Retention: New Challenges and Potential." In *Increasing Student Retention*, edited by L. Noel, R. Levitz, D. Saluri, and Associates. San Francisco: Jossey-Bass.

Noel, L., R. Levitz, D. Saluri, and Associates. 1985. *Increasing Student Retention*. San Francisco: Jossey-Bass.

Norman, M. 20 April 1988. "Lessons: Honesty Is Not the Best-Respected Policy, Survey on College Cheating Finds." *New York Times*.

North Dakota State Board of Higher Education. n.d. *Total Quality Management: A Guide for the North Dakota University System*. Author.

Nowlis, V., K.E. Clark, and M. Rock. 1969. *The Graduate Student as Teacher*. Washington, D.C: American Council on Education.

Nucci, L., and E.T. Pascarella. 1987. "The Influence of College on Moral Development." In *Higher Education: Handbook of Theory and Research*, edited by J.C. Smart. Vol. 3. New York: Agathon.

Nyquist, J.D., R.D. Abbott, D.H. Wulff, and J. Sprague. 1991. *Preparing the Professoriate of Tomorrow to Teach: Selected Readings in TA Training*. Dubuque, Ia.: Kendall/Hunt.

Olson, L. 28 May 1986. "Carnegie Report: A 'Powerful Synthesis' That Raises Both Hopes and Questions." *Education Week:* 1+.

Osborne, D., and T. Gaebler. 1992. *Reinventing Government: How the Entrepreneurial Spirit Is Transforming the Public Sector*. New York: Penguin.

Pace, C.R. 1984. *Measuring the Quality of College Student Experiences: An Account of the Development and Use of the College Student Experiences Questionnaire*. Los Angeles: Univ. of California Graduate School of Education, Higher Education Research Institute. ED 255 099. 142 pp. MF–01; PC not available EDRS.

———. 1990. *The Undergraduates: A Report of Their Activities and Progress in College in the 1980s*. Los Angeles: Univ. of California, Center for the Study of Evaluation. ED 375 701. 164 pp. MF–01; PC–07.

Palmer, P.J. 1987. "Community, Conflict, and Ways of Knowing: Ways to Deepen Our Educational Agenda." *Change* 19(5): 20–25.

Panel on the General Professional Education of the Physician and College Preparation for Medicine. 1984. *Physicians for the Twenty-first Century: The GPEP Report*. Washington, D.C.: Association of American Medical Colleges. ED 252 102. 61 pp. MF–01; PC–03.

Parker, C.A., ed. 1978. *Encouraging Development in College Students*. Minneapolis: Univ. of Minnesota Press.

Parrett, J.L. 1987. "A Ten-Year Review of TA Training Programs: Trends, Patterns, and Common Practices." In *Institutional Responsibilities and Responses in the Employment and Education of Teaching Assistants: Readings from a National Conference*, edited by N.V. Chism. Columbus: Ohio State Univ., Center for Teaching Excellence.

Pascarella, E.T. 1985. "College Environmental Influences on Learning and Cognitive Development: A Critical Review and Synthesis." In *Higher Education: Handbook of Theory and Research*, edited by J. Smart. Vol. 1. New York: Agathon.

Pascarella, E.T., and P.T. Terenzini. 1991. *How College Affects Students: Findings and Insights from Twenty Years of Research*. San Francisco: Jossey-Bass.

Paul, R.W. 1995. *Critical Thinking: How to Prepare Students for a Rapidly Changing World*. Santa Rosa, Cal.: Foundation for Critical Thinking.

Perry, W.G., Jr. 1970. *Forms of Intellectual and Ethical Development in the College Years: A Scheme*. New York: Holt, Rinehart, Winston.

———. 1981. "Cognitive and Ethical Growth: The Making of

Meaning." In *The Modern American College,* edited by A.W. Chickering and Associates. San Francisco: Jossey-Bass.

Peterson, M.W., K.S. Cameron, L.A. Mets, P. Jones, and D. Ettington. 1986. *The Organizational Context for Teaching and Learning: A Review of the Research Literature.* Ann Arbor: Univ. of Michigan, National Center for Research to Improve Postsecondary Teaching and Learning.

Pew Higher Education Research Program. 1989. "The Business of the Business." *Policy Perspectives* 1(3): 1–6.

———. 1990. "Breaking the Mold." *Policy Perspectives* 2(2): 1.

Pfundt, H., and R. Duit. 1991. "Bibliography: Students' Alternative Frameworks and Science Education." Kiel, Germany: Univ. of Kiel, Institute for Science Education.

"Ph.D. under Attack." 10 June 1966. *Time:* 75.

Piaget, J. 1972. "Intellectual Evolution from Adolescence to Adulthood." *Human Development* 15: 1–12.

Pintrich, P.R., and G.R. Johnson. 1990. "Assessing and Improving Students' Learning Strategies." In *The Changing Face of College Teaching,* edited by M.D. Svinicki. New Directions for Teaching and Learning No. 42. San Francisco: Jossey-Bass.

Pintrich, P.R., D.A.F. Smith, T. Garcia, and W.J. McKeachie. 1991. *A Manual for the Use of the Motivated Strategies for Learning Questionnaire (MSLQ).* Technical Report No. 91-B-004. Ann Arbor: Univ. of Michigan, National Center for Research to Improve Postsecondary Teaching and Learning. ED 338 122. 76 pp. MF–01; PC–04.

"Plagiarism Is Rampant, a Survey Finds." 1 April 1990. *New York Times.*

Plater, W.M. 1995. "Future Work: Faculty Time in the 21st Century." *Change* 27(3): 22–33.

Plomin, R. 13 April 1990. "The Role of Inheritance in Behavior." *Science* 248: 183–88.

Ponemon, L.A., and D.R.L. Gabhart. 1994. "Ethical Reasoning Research in the Accounting and Auditing Professions." In *Moral Development in the Professions: Psychology and Applied Ethics,* edited by J.R. Rest and D. Narváez. Hillsdale, N.J.: Erlbaum.

Pool, R. 27 April 1990. "Who Will Do Science in the 1990s?" *Science* 248: 433–35.

Porter, O.F. 21 March 1990. "Clarifying Study of Graduation Rates." *Chronicle of Higher Education:* B6.

Povlacs-Lunde, J., and M.M. Healy. 1991. *Doing Faculty Development by Committee.* Stillwater, Okla.: New Forums Press.

"PreHealth Highlights: Placement." September 1988. New Orleans: Xavier Univ. of Louisiana.

Price, H.B. 12 May 1993. "Teacher Professional Development: It's about Time." *Education Week:* 32.

Prichard, K.W., and R.M. Sawyer, eds. 1994. *Handbook of College Teaching: Theory and Applications.* Westport, Conn.: Greenwood Press.

Project on the Future of Journalism and Mass Communication Education. 1984. "Planning for Curricular Change." Eugene: Univ. of Oregon, School of Journalism.

Project on Liberal Education and the Sciences. 1990. "The Liberal Art of Science: Agenda for Action." Washington, D.C.: American Association for the Advancement of Science.

Project on Liberal Learning, Study-in-Depth, and the Arts and Sciences Major. 1991. *Liberal Learning and the Arts and Sciences Major.* Vol. 2. *Reports from the Fields.* Washington, D.C.: Association of American Colleges.

Project on Redefining the Meaning and Purpose of Baccalaureate Degrees. 1985. *Integrity in the College Curriculum: A Report to the Academic Community.* Washington, D.C.: Association of American Colleges. ED 251 059. 62 pp. MF–01; PC not available EDRS.

Provost, J.A. 1984. *A Casebook: Applications of the Myers-Briggs Type Indicator in Counseling.* Gainesville, Fla.: Center for Application of Psychological Types.

Provost, J.A., and S. Anchors, eds. 1987. *Applications of the Myers-Briggs Type Indicator in Higher Education.* Palo Alto, Cal.: Consulting Psychologists Press.

Quinlan, K.M. 1991. "About Teaching and Learning Centers." *AAHE Bulletin* 44(2): 11–16.

Ratcliff, J.L., and Associates. *n.d.* "Determining the Effect of Different Coursework Patterns on General Student Learned Abilities." Working paper. University Park: Pennsylvania State Univ., Center for the Study of Higher Education.

———. 1990. *Determining the Effect of Different Coursework Patterns on the General Learned Abilities of College Students.* Working Paper OR 90-524. Washington, D.C.: U.S. Dept. of Education.

Raymond, C. 16 January 1991. "Despite Their Growing Support of Racial Equality, a Substantial Proportion of White Americans Continues to Hold Negative Stereotypes of Blacks, Hispanics, Asians, and Other Minority Groups." *Chronicle of Higher Education:* A8.

Reboy, L.M., and G.B. Semb. 1991. "PSI and Critical Thinking: Compatibility or Irreconcilable Differences?" *Teaching of Psychology* 18(4): 212–15.

Rendon, L.I. 1994. "Validating Culturally Diverse Students: Toward a New Model of Learning and Student Development." *Innovative Higher Education* 19(1): 33–51.

Rest, J.R. 1979. *Development in Judging Moral Issues*. Minneapolis: Univ. of Minnesota Press.

————. 1984. "The Major Components of Morality." In *Morality, Moral Behavior, and Moral Development,* edited by W.M. Kurtines and J.L. Gewirtz. New York: John Wiley & Sons.

————. 1986. *Moral Development: Advances in Research and Theory*. New York: Praeger.

————. 1994a. "Background: Theory and Research." In *Moral Development in the Professions: Psychology and Applied Ethics,* edited by J.R. Rest and D. Narváez. Hillsdale, N.J.: Erlbaum.

————. 1994b. "Summary: What's Possible?" In *Moral Development in the Professions: Psychology and Applied Ethics,* edited by J.R. Rest and D. Narváez. Hillsdale, N.J.: Erlbaum.

Rest, J.R., and D. Narváez, eds. 1994. *Moral Development in the Professions: Psychology and Applied Ethics*. Hillsdale, N.J.: Erlbaum.

Rich, J.M., and J.L. DeVitis. 1985. *Theories of Moral Development*. Springfield, Ill.: Charles C Thomas.

————. 1992. *Competition in Education*. Springfield, Ill.: Charles C Thomas.

Richardson, R.C., Jr., D.A. Matthews, and J.E. Finney. 1992. *Improving State and Campus Environments for Quality and Diversity: A Self-Assessment*. Denver: Education Commission of the States. ED 349 914. 47 pp. MF–01; PC–02.

Richardson, R.C., Jr., and E.F. Skinner. 1991. *Achieving Quality and Diversity: Universities in a Multicultural Society*. New York: ACE/Macmillan.

Richlin, L., ed. 1993. *Preparing Faculty for New Conceptions of Scholarship*. New Directions for Teaching and Learning No. 54. San Francisco: Jossey-Bass.

Robbins, R.R. 1981. "Improving Student Reasoning Skills in Science Classes." *Engineering Education* 72: 208–12.

Rodgers, R.F. 1989. "Student Development." In *Student Services: A Handbook for the Profession,* edited by U. Delworth, G.R. Hanson, and Associates. San Francisco: Jossey-Bass.

Rothman, R. 16 January 1991. "Schools Are Called Partly Responsible for Drop in Self-Esteem among Girls." *Education Week:* 6.

Rothwell, W.J., and H.C. Kazanas. 1992. *Mastering the Instructional Design Process: A Systematic Approach*. San Francisco: Jossey-Bass.

Ruskin, R.S., ed. 1976. *An Evaluative Review of the Personalized System of Instruction*. Washington, D.C.: Georgetown Univ., Center for Personalized Instruction.

Russell, J.D., and K.A. Johanningsmeier. 1981. *Improving Competence through Modular Instruction*. Dubuque, Ia.: Kendall/Hunt.

Sale, K. 1980. *Human Scale*. New York: Coward, McCann &

Geoghegan.

Saluri, D. 1985. "Case Studies and Successful Programs." In *Increasing Student Retention,* edited by L. Noel, R. Levitz, D. Saluri, and Associates. San Francisco: Jossey-Bass.

Sandler, B.R. 1986. *The Campus Revisited: Chilly for Women Faculty, Administrators, and Graduate Students.* Washington, D.C.: Association of American Colleges. ED 298 837. 112 pp. MF–01; PC–05.

Sands, R.G., L.A. Parson, and J. Duane. 1991. "Faculty Mentoring Faculty in a Public University." *Journal of Higher Education* 62(2): 174–93.

Sanford, N. 1962. "Developmental Status of the Entering Student." In *The American College: A Psychological Social Interpretation of the Higher Learning,* edited by N. Sanford. New York: John Wiley & Sons.

———. 1966. *Self and Society: Social Change and Individual Develop-ment.* New York: Atherton.

Saufley, R.W., K.O. Cowan, and J.H. Blake. 1983. "The Struggles of Minority Students at Predominantly White Institutions." In *Teaching Minority Students,* edited by J.H. Cones III, J.F. Noonan, and D. Janha. New Directions for Teaching and Learning No. 16. San Francisco: Jossey-Bass.

Saul, L.J. 1976. *The Psychodynamics of Hostility.* New York: Aronson.

Saunders, P. Winter 1980. "The Lasting Effects of Introductory Economics Courses." *Journal of Economic Education* 12: 1–14.

Saunders, S.A., and L. Ervin. 1984. "Meeting the Special Advising Needs of Students." In *Developmental Academic Advising,* edited by R.B. Winston, T.K. Miller, S.C. Ender, T.J. Grites, and Associates. San Francisco: Jossey-Bass.

Schaie, K.W., and J. Parr. 1981. "Intelligence." In *The Modern American College,* edited by A.W. Chickering and Associates. San Francisco: Jossey-Bass.

Schmeck, R.R., ed. 1988. *Learning Strategies and Learning Styles.* New York: Plenum.

Schmidt, M.R., and H.Z. Sprandel, eds. 1982. *Helping the Learning-Disabled Student.* New Directions for Student Services No. 18. San Francisco: Jossey-Bass.

Schmidt, P. 5 May 1993. "Students Lack the Guidance to Meet Their 'High Hopes,' Study Reveals." *Education Week:* 1+.

Schroeder, C.C. 1993. "New Students: New Learning Styles." *Change* 25(4): 21–31.

———. 1994. "Developing Learning Communities." In *Realizing the Educational Potential of Residence Halls,* edited by C.C. Schroeder, P. Mable, and Associates. San Francisco: Jossey-Bass.

Schwager, S. 20 April 1990. "Perspectives on Education." *Science* 248: 388.

Seldin, P. 1987. "Research Findings on Causes of Academic Stress."
In *Coping with Faculty Stress,* edited by P. Seldin. New Directions
for Teaching and Learning No. 29. San Francisco: Jossey-Bass.

Self, D.J., and D.C. Baldwin, Jr. 1994. "Moral Reasoning in Medi-
cine." In *Moral Development in the Professions: Psychology and
Applied Ethics,* edited by J.R. Rest and D. Narváez. Hillsdale, N.J.:
Erlbaum.

Self, D.J., M. Olivarez, and D.C. Baldwin, Jr. 1994. "Moral Reasoning
in Veterinary Medicine." In *Moral Development in the Professions:
Psychology and Applied Ethics,* edited by J.R. Rest and D. Narváez.
Hillsdale, N.J.: Erlbaum.

Selvin, P. 13 November 1992. "Math Education: Multiplying the
Meager Numbers." *Science* 258: 1200–1201.

Senge, P.M. 1990. *The Fifth Discipline: The Art and Practice of the
Learning Organization.* New York: Doubleday.

Sevenair, J.P., J.W. Carmichael, S.E. O'Conner, and J.T. Hunter. *n.d.*
"Predictors of Organic Chemistry Grades for Black Americans."
New Orleans: Xavier Univ. of Louisiana.

Seymour, D. 1991. "TQM on Campus: What the Pioneers Are Finding." *AAHE Bulletin* 44(3): 10–13+.

———. 1992. *On Q: Causing Quality in Higher Education.* New
York: ACE/Macmillan.

———. 1993a. "Quality on Campus: Three Institutions, Three Begin-
nings." *Change* 25(3): 14–27.

———. 1993b. "TQM: Focus on Performance, not Resources." *Educational Record* 74(2): 6–14.

Seymour, D., and C. Collett. 1991. *Total Quality Management in
Higher Education: A Critical Assessment.* Methuen, Mass.:
GOAL/QPC.

Shea, C. 14 December 1994. "New Look at College Drinking."
Chronicle of Higher Education: A39.

———. 16 June 1995. "Suicide Signals." *Chronicle of Higher
Education:* A35–A36.

Sherman, T.M. 1985. "Learning Improvement Programs: A Review
of Controllable Influences." *Journal of Higher Education* 56(1):
85–100.

Sherr, L.A., and D.J. Teeter. 1991. *Total Quality Management in
Higher Education.* New Directions for Institutional Research No.
71. San Francisco: Jossey-Bass.

Siegfried, J.J., M. Getz, and K.H. Anderson. 19 May 1995. "The
Snail's Pace of Innovation in Higher Education." *Chronicle of
Higher Education:* A56.

Smith, A. 1976. *An Inquiry into the Nature and Causes of the Wealth
of Nations.* Vol. 2. Chicago: Univ. of Chicago Press.

Smith, D.C. 1983. "Instruction and Outcomes in an Undergraduate

Setting." In *Studies of College Teaching: Experimental Results, Theoretical Interpretations, and New Perspectives,* edited by C.L. Ellner and C.P. Barnes. Lexington, Mass.: D.C. Heath.

Smith, D.G. 1989. *The Challenge of Diversity: Involvement or Alienation in the Academy?* ASHE-ERIC Higher Education Report No. 5. Washington, D.C.: George Washington Univ. ED 314 987. 129 pp. MF–01; PC–06.

Smith, D.G., L.E. Wolf, and D.E. Morrison. 1995. "Paths to Success: Factors Related to the Impact of Women's Colleges." *Journal of Higher Education* 66(3): 245–66.

Smith, D.L. 1992. "Validity of Faculty Judgments: Relationship between Grades and Credits Earned and External Criterion Measures." *Journal of Higher Education* 63(3): 329–40.

Smith, P. 1990. *Killing the Spirit: Higher Education in America.* New York: Viking.

Smock, R., and R. Menges. 1985. "Programs for TAs in the Context of Campus Policies and Priorities." In *Strengthening the Teaching Assistant Faculty,* edited by J.D.W. Andrews. New Directions for Teaching and Learning No. 22. San Francisco: Jossey-Bass.

Snarey, J.R. 1985. "Cross-Cultural Universality of Social-Moral Development: A Critical Review of Kohlbergian Research." *Psychological Bulletin* 97(2): 202–32.

Snow, R.E. 1980. "Intelligence for the Year 2001." *Intelligence* 4: 185–99.

———. 1986. "Individual Differences and the Design of Educational Programs." *American Psychologist* 41(10): 1029–39.

Solmon, L.C. 1989. "Traditional College-Age Students." In *Shaping Higher Education's Future: Demographic Realities and Opportunities, 1990–2000,* edited by A. Levine and Associates. San Francisco: Jossey-Bass.

Sprinthall, N.A. 1994. "Counseling and Social Role Taking: Promoting Moral and Ego Development." In *Moral Development in the Professions: Psychology and Applied Ethics,* edited by J.R. Rest and D. Narváez. Hillsdale, N.J.: Erlbaum.

Stanley, C.A., and N.V. Chism. 1991. "Selected Characteristics of New Faculty: Implications for Faculty Development." *To Improve the Academy* 10: 55–61.

Starch, D., and E.C. Elliott. 1912. "Reliability of the Grading of High School Work in English." *School Review* 20: 442–57.

———. 1913a. "Reliability of Grading Work in History." *School Review* 21: 676–81.

———. 1913b. "Reliability of Grading Work in Mathematics." *School Review* 21: 254–95.

Stark, J.S. 1989. "Seeking Coherence in the Curriculum." In *Improving Undergraduate Education in Large Universities,* edited by C.H.

Pazandak. New Directions for Higher Education No. 66. San Francisco: Jossey-Bass.

Stark, J.S., and M.A. Lowther. 1986. *Designing the Learning Plan.* Ann Arbor: Univ. of Michigan, National Center for Research to Improve Postsecondary Teaching and Learning. ED 287 439. 99 pp. MF–01; PC–04.

Stark, J.S., M.A. Lowther, R.J. Bentley, M.P. Ryan, G.G. Martens, M.L. Genthon, P.A. Wren, and K.M. Shaw. 1990. *Planning Introductory College Courses: Influences on Faculty.* Ann Arbor: Univ. of Michigan: National Center for Research to Improve Postsecondary Teaching and Learning. ED 330 277. 370 pp. MF–01; PC–15.

Stark, J.S., M.A. Lowther, M.P. Ryan, and M. Genthon. 1988. "Faculty Reflect on Course Planning." *Research in Higher Education* 29(3): 219–40.

Stark, J.S., K.M. Shaw, and M.A. Lowther. 1989. *Student Goals for College and Courses: A Missing Link in Assessing and Improving Academic Achievement.* ASHE-ERIC Higher Education Report No. 6. Washington, D.C.: George Washington Univ., School of Education and Human Development. ED 317 121. 132 pp. MF–01; PC–06.

Steele, C.M. April 1992. "Race and the Schooling of Black Americans." *Atlantic Monthly:* 68–78.

Sternberg, R.J. 1985. "Instrumental and Componential Approaches to the Nature and Training of Intelligence." In *Thinking and Learning Skills,* edited by S.F. Chipman and J.W. Segal. Vol 2. *Research and Open Questions.* Hillsdale, N.J.: Erlbaum.

———. 1986. "Inside Intelligence." *American Psychologist* 74: 137–43.

———, ed. 1990. *Wisdom: Its Nature, Origins, and Development.* Cambridge: Cambridge Univ. Press.

Stewart, S.S., and P. Rue. 1983. "Commuter Students: Definition and Distribution." In *Commuter Students: Enhancing Their Educational Experiences,* edited by S.S. Stewart. New Directions for Student Services No. 24. San Francisco: Jossey-Bass.

Stice, J.E., ed. 1987. *Developing Critical Thinking and Problem-Solving Abilities.* New Directions for Teaching and Learning No. 30. San Francisco: Jossey-Bass.

Stimpson, C.R. 15 January 1992. "It Is Time to Rethink Affirmative Action." *Chronicle of Higher Education:* A48.

"Struggling for Standards." 12 April 1995. *Education Week* (Special Report).

Study Group on the Conditions of Excellence in American Higher Education. 1984. *Involvement in Learning: Realizing the Potential of American Higher Education.* Washington, D.C.: National Institute of Education. ED 246 833. 127 pp. MF–01; PC–06.

Sudarkasa, N. 1987. "Affirmative Action or Affirmation of the Status Quo?" *AAHE Bulletin* 39(6): 3–6.

Svinicki, M.D., ed. 1990. *The Changing Face of College Teaching.* New Directions for Teaching and Learning No. 42. San Francisco: Jossey-Bass.

Sykes, C.J. 1988. *ProfScam: Professors and the Demise of Higher Education.* New York: St. Martin's.

Task Force on Assessing the National Goal Relating to Postsecondary Education. 1992. "Report to the National Education Goals Panel." National Education Goals Panel.

Task Force on the Student Experience. 1986. "Attaining Educational Excellence: The Report of the Task Force on the Student Experience." Newark, N.J.: Rutgers Univ., Faculty of Arts and Sciences.

Teeter, D.J., and G.G. Lozier, eds. 1993. *Pursuit of Quality in Higher Education: Case Studies in Total Quality Management.* New Directions for Institutional Research No.78. San Francisco: Jossey-Bass.

"This Year's College Freshmen: Attitudes and Characteristics." 30 January 1991. *Chronicle of Higher Education:* A30–A31.

Thoma, S. 1994. "Moral Judgments and Moral Action." In *Moral Development in the Professions: Psychology and Applied Ethics,* edited by J.R. Rest and D. Narváez. Hillsdale, N.J.: Erlbaum.

Thorndike, R.L., and E.P. Hagen. 1986. *Measurement and Evaluation in Psychology and Education.* New York: Macmillan.

Tinto, V. 1985. "Dropping Out and Other Forms of Withdrawal from College." In *Increasing Student Retention,* edited by L. Noel, R. Levitz, D. Saluri, and Associates. San Francisco: Jossey-Bass.

———. 1987. *Leaving College: Rethinking the Causes and Cures of Student Attrition.* Chicago: Univ. of Chicago.

———. 1993. *Leaving College: Rethinking the Causes and Cures of Student Attrition.* 2d ed. Chicago: Univ. of Chicago.

Tobias, S. 1990. *They're Not Dumb, They're Different: Stalking the Second Tier.* Tucson, Ariz.: Research Corp.

———. 1992. *Revitalizing Undergraduate Science: Why Some Things Work and Most Don't.* Tucson, Ariz.: Research Corp.

Toma, J.D., and J.S. Stark. 1995. "Pluralism in the Curriculum: Understanding Its Foundations and Evolution." *Review of Higher Education* 18(2): 217–32.

Tomlinson-Keasey, C.A. 1978. "Piaget's Theory and College Teaching." In *ADAPT, Multidisciplinary Piagetian-Based Programs for College Freshmen: ADAPT, DOORS, SOAR, STAR, The Cognitive Program, The Fourth R.* Lincoln: Univ. of Nebraska.

Toombs, W., and T. Tierney. 1991. *Meeting the Mandate: Renewing the College and Departmental Curriculum.* ASHE-ERIC Higher Education Report No. 6. Washington, D.C.: George Washington Univ., School of Education and Human Development. ED 345

603. 124 pp. MF–01; PC–05.

Torbert, W.R. 1981. "Interpersonal Competence." In *The Modern American College,* edited by A.W. Chickering and Associates. San Francisco: Jossey-Bass.

Treisman, P.U. 1985. "A Study of the Mathematics Performance of Black Students at the University of California–Berkeley." Berkeley: Author.

Tucker, A. 1992. *Chairing the Academic Department: Leadership among Peers.* New York: ACE/Macmillan.

Turnbull, W.W. 1985. "Are They Learning Anything in College?" *Change* 17(6): 23–26.

"Twice Imagined." 1995. Pew Higher Education Roundtable *Policy Perspectives* 6(1): 1A–11A.

"Universities Need to Take a Hard Look at Their Engineering Programs." 21 April 1995. *Chronicle of Higher Education:* A21.

Upcraft, M.L., J.H. Gardner, and Associates. 1989. *The Freshman-Year Experience: Helping Students Survive and Succeed in College.* San Francisco: Jossey-Bass.

Valuing in Decision Making Competence Division. 1987. "Valuing Education Materials." Milwaukee: Alverno College.

Vandament, W.E. 30 November 1988. "Those Who Would Reform Undergraduate Education Must Recognize the Realities of Academic Governance." *Chronicle of Higher Education:* A52.

Van Doren, M. 1943. *Liberal Education.* New York: Holt.

Van Heuvelen, A. 1991a. "Learning to Think like a Physicist: A Review of Research-Based Instructional Strategies." *American Journal of Physics* 59(10): 891–97.

———. 1991b. "Overview: Case Study Physics." *American Journal of Physics* 59(10): 898–907.

Van Horn, C.E. 1995. *Enhancing the Connection between Higher Education and the Workplace: A Survey of Employers.* Denver: State Higher Education Officers and Education Commission of the States.

Viadero, D. 25 November 1992. "Survey Finds Young People More Likely to Lie, Cheat, Steal." *Education Week:* 5.

"Virginia May Toughen Admission Standards." 18 November 1992. *Chronicle of Higher Education:* A22.

Von Blum, P. 1986. *Stillborn Education: A Critique of the American Research University.* Lanham, Md.: University Press of America.

Wadsworth, E.C., ed. 1988. *A Handbook for New Practitioners.* Stillwater, Okla.: Professional and Organizational Development Network in Higher Education.

Walberg, H.J. 1984. "Improving the Productivity of America's Schools." *Educational Leadership* 41(8): 19–27.

Wales, C.E., and R.A. Stager. 1977. "Guided Design." Morgantown:

Univ. of West Virginia.

Walton, M. 1986. *The Deming Management Method*. New York: Perigee.

Warren, J.R. 1971. *College Grading Practices: An Overview*. Report No. 9. Washington, D.C.: George Washington Univ., ERIC Clearinghouse on Higher Education.

Washington Center News. 1994. Special Ten-Year Anniversary Issue, 8(2).

Weathersby, R.P. 1981. "Ego Development." In *The Modern American College*, edited by A.W. Chickering and Associates. San Francisco: Jossey-Bass.

Webster, D.S. 1985. "Does Research Productivity Enhance Teaching?" *Educational Record* 66: 60–72.

Wechsler, H., C. Deutsch, and G. Dowdall. 14 April 1995. "Too Many Colleges Are Still in Denial about Alcohol Abuse." *Chronicle of Higher Education:* B1–B2.

Weimer, M. 1990. *Improving College Teaching: Strategies for Developing Instructional Effectiveness*. San Francisco: Jossey-Bass.

Weimer, M., M.D. Svinicki, and G. Bauer. 1989. "Designing Programs to Prepare TAs to Teach." In *Teaching Assistant Training in the 1990s*, edited by J.D. Nyquist, R.D. Abbott, and D.H. Wulff. New Directions for Teaching and Learning No. 39. San Francisco: Jossey-Bass.

Weinstein, C.E. 1988a. "Assessment and Training of Student Learning Strategies." In *Learning Strategies and Learning Styles*, edited by R.R. Schmeck. New York: Plenum.

———. 1988b. "Executive Control Processes in Learning: Why Knowing about How to Learn Is Not Enough." *Journal of College Reading and Learning* 21: 48–56.

Weinstein, C.E., and R.E. Mayer. 1986. "The Teaching of Learning Strategies." In *Handbook of Research on Teaching*, edited by M. Wittrock. New York: Macmillan.

Weinstein, C.E., D.R. Palmer, and A. Schulte. 1987. *LASSI: Learning and Study Strategies Inventory*. Clearwater, Fla.: H&H Publishing.

Weinstein, C.E., and V.L. Underwood. 1985. "Learning Strategies: The How of Learning." In *Thinking and Learning Skills*. Vol. 1. *Relating Instruction to Research*, edited by J.W. Segal, S.F. Chipman, and R. Glaser. Hillsdale, N.J.: Erlbaum.

Wells, A.S. 31 May 1989. "For Slow Learners, an Accelerated Curriculum." *New York Times*.

White, G.P., and W.C.C. Coscarelli. 1986. *The Guided Design Guidebook: Patterns in Implementation*. Morgantown: Univ. of West Virginia, National Center for Guided Design.

White, R.W. 1981. "Humanitarian Concern." In *The Modern American College*, edited by A.W. Chickering and Associates. San Francisco: Jossey-Bass.

Whitehead, A.N. 1929. *The Aims of Education and Other Essays.* New York: Free Press.

Whiteley, J.M. 1982. *Character Development in College Students.* Vol. 1. *The Freshman Year.* Schenectady, N.Y.: Character Research Press.

Whiteley, J.M., and N. Yokota. 1988. *Character Development in the Freshman Year and over Four Years of Undergraduate Study.* Monograph Series No. 1. Columbia: Univ. of South Carolina, Center for the Study of the Freshman Year Experience.

Whitman, N.A., D.C. Spendlove, and C.H. Clark. 1986. *Increasing Students' Learning: A Faculty Guide to Reducing Stress among Students.* ASHE-ERIC Higher Education Report No. 4. Washington, D.C.: Association for the Study of Higher Education. ED 274 264. 101 pp. MF–01; PC–05.

Whitt, E.J. 1991. "Hit the Ground Running: Experiences of New Faculty in a School of Education." *Review of Higher Education* 14(2): 177–97.

"Widespread Cheating Found by Survey at Concordia U." 6 May 1987. *Chronicle of Higher Education:* 47.

Widick, C., and D. Simpson. 1978. "Developmental Concepts in College Instruction." In *Encouraging Development in Students,* edited by C.A. Parker. Minneapolis: Univ. of Minnesota Press.

Wilcox, J.R., and S.L. Ebbs. 1992. *The Leadership Compass: Values and Ethics in Higher Education.* ASHE-ERIC Higher Education Report No. 1. Washington, D.C.: George Washington Univ., School of Education and Human Development. ED 347 955. 129 pp. MF–01; PC–06.

Wilshire, B. 1990. *The Moral Collapse of the University: Professionalism, Purity, and Alienation.* Albany: State Univ. of New York Press.

Wingspread Group on Higher Education. 1993. *An American Imperative: Higher Expectations for Higher Education.* Racine, Wis.: The Johnson Foundation.

Winkler, K.J. 6 March 1985. "Rigor Is Urged in Preparation of New Teachers." *Chronicle of Higher Education:* 1.

Winston, R.B., Jr., W.C. Bonney, T.K. Miller, and J.C. Dagney. 1988. *Promoting Student Development through Intentionally Structured Groups: Principles, Techniques, and Applications.* San Francisco: Jossey-Bass.

Winston, R.B., Jr., S.C. Ender, and T.K. Miller, eds. 1982. *Developmental Approaches to Academic Advising.* New Directions for Student Services No. 17. San Francisco: Jossey-Bass.

Winston, R.B., Jr., T.J. Grites, T.K. Miller, and S.C. Ender. 1984. "Epilogue: Improving Academic Advising." In *Developmental Academic Advising,* edited by R.B. Winston, Jr., T.K. Miller, S.C.

Ender, T.J. Grites, and Associates. San Francisco: Jossey-Bass.

Winston, R.B., Jr., T.K. Miller, S.C. Ender, T.J. Grites, and Associates, eds. 1984. *Developmental Academic Advising.* San Francisco: Jossey-Bass.

Winter, D.G., D.C. McClelland, and A.J. Stewart. 1981. *A New Case for the Liberal Arts.* San Francisco: Jossey-Bass.

Wood, L., and B.G. Davis. 1978. *Designing and Evaluating Higher Education Curricula.* AAHE-ERIC Research Report No. 8. Washington, D.C.: American Association for Higher Education.

Woods, D.R. 1987. "How Might I Teach Problem Solving?" In *Developing Critical Thinking and Problem-Solving Abilities,* edited by J.E. Stice. New Directions for Teaching and Learning No. 30. San Francisco: Jossey-Bass.

Working Party on Effective State Action to Improve Undergraduate Education. 1986. *Transforming the State Role in Undergraduate Education: Time for a Different View.* Publication No. PS-86-3. Denver: Education Commission of the States. ED 275 219. 45 pp. MF–01; PC not available EDRS.

Wright, D.J., ed. 1987. *Responding to the Needs of Today's Minority Students.* New Directions for Student Services No. 38. San Francisco: Jossey-Bass.

Wright, W.A., and M.C. O'Neil. 1994. "Teaching Improvement Practices: New Perspectives." *To Improve the Academy* 13: 5–37.

WuDunn, S. 22 May 1995. "Japanese Critics Say Schools Pushed Best and Brightest into Sect's Arms." *New York Times.*

Wyche, J.H., and H.T. Frierson, Jr. 31 August 1990. "Minorities at Majority Institutions." *Science* 249: 989–91.

Wyer, J.C. 1993. "Change Where You Might Least Expect It: Accounting Education." *Change* 25(1): 12–17.

Zemsky, R. 1989. *Structure and Coherence. Measuring the Undergraduate Curriculum.* Washington, D.C.: Association of American Colleges. ED 310 658. 47 pp. MF–01; PC not available EDRS.

Zimmerman, M. 1986. "The Evolution-Creation Controversy: Opinions from Students in a 'Liberal' Liberal Arts College." *Ohio Journal of Science* 86(4): 134–39.

———. 1987. "The Evolution-Creation Controversy: Opinions of Ohio High School Biology Teachers." *Ohio Journal of Science* 87(4): 115–25.

———. January 1988. "Ohio School Board Presidents' Views on the Evolution-Creation Controversy: Part 2." *Newsletter of the Ohio Center for Science Education:* 1+.

INDEX

A

AAAS, new science-as-liberal-art curriculum of, 115
abilities, development of higher order, 50–51
abstract reasoning
      capacity for, 10–12
      development of, 10–12
academic advising. See advising
academic community, need creation of, 146
academic department chair, 138–139
academic practices retarding students abstract thinking, 59
accelerated schools dramatically improve minority learning rate,
  96
accounting
      critiques of college curricula of , 34
      lower scores on moral judgment of majors, 29
ACE-UCLA CIRP survey, 101
active involvement
      need for students to have in learning, 114–115
      sustained, diverse and appropriate required for learning,
  23
actual outcomes, need specific and timely knowledge of, 60
ADAPT Program at the University of Nebraska-Lincoln, 12
administrative and faculty separate views of world, 135–136
advising
      as "a high calling," 88
      Developmental Academic, 120 121
      evaluation of, 90–91
      importance of high-quality, 87
      lack of concern in effectiveness and outcomes , 92
      necessity for training in, 91–92
      need for in undergraduate course selection, 28
      passivity of, 90
      student perceptions differ from faculty and administrators,
  93
affective outcomes desired by college and university faculty, 8
African-American students
      academically oriented males at special risk, 85
      degrees of 80 % received from 20 % of U.S. institutions, 84
      graduation rates, 83, 99
      higher education failing, 82
      liberal arts increased choice of typically white careers, 28
      student perception that less intelligent, 81
      withdrawal from college of, 82–83

California Polytechnic State University-Pomona, 99-100
campus and polity, dissolution of the boundaries between, xi
Campus Climate, classroom central to, 118
campus experiences as developmentally destructive, 105
Campus Life: In Search of Community, 81
Carnegie Foundation for the Advancement of Teaching, 8, 75
challenge need for activities just above current cognitive levels, 23
cheating
        amount by students of, 68–70
        long-term developmental effects of, 70–71
Chickering (1974), 124
CIRP
        respondents organization of time, 53
        survey of first-year students, 87
classroom tests
        facts emphasis may mislead on quality of performance, 58
        reliability of, 63–64
        technical qualities of, 63
        validity of, 63
        what do they measure, 60
Clear Missions and Goals, need for, 107–109
cognitive complexity, development happens slowly, 19
cognitive development
        definition, 22
        necessary but not sufficient for educational system, 111
cognitive dissonance's, development value of, 23
Cognitive Interaction Analysis System, 44
cognitive outcomes
        desired by college and university faculty, 8
        understanding of, 41–42
cognitive requirements, rating for, 42
cognitive and ethical capacities implications, 18–19
coherent curricula, need for, 110–111
collaborative learning, important need for, 114
college classroom
        intellectual climate of, 40–41
        tests usually not questioned in, 64–65
college curricula. *See* curricula
college experience, no strong gains in high or low score's, 32, 33
college withdrawals
        of more than half of students on many campuses, 102
        from students experiences in college than academic
    failure, 101

deficiencies of training of new, 142, 142–143

Development as foundation for Student Development, 139–143

discipline centered model of academic work, xi

performance criteria based upon experience with students, 58

professional literature in higher education don't read, 65

world view separate from that of administration, 135–136

Finkelstein, Martin J., xii, xiii

"fitness for use" student meet criteria of, 89

"formal reasoning" skills

consistent patterns in development of, 12

definition of, 10

students need of assistance from teachers to develop, 10–11

G

Gardiner, Lion, xi–xii

Gaulois Theory course, large percentage of minority students in, 99

gender effects on curriculum, significance of , 30

"general learned abilities," 32

general learning, counts of credits may not be a reliable proxy of, 33

gifted students, campus minority-groups experience of, 82

Gilligan (1977), 17

GIS. *See* New Jersey Test of General Intellectual Skills

goals

national education, 57–58

need for clear and rational, 108

teaching concepts of field as, 37

GPA, question as to meaning of, 65

grades

effect on moral development, 68

how well do they communicate outcomes, 66–68

predictive validity is severely limited, 67

graduate courses, difference from undergraduate courses of, 44–45

Guided Design, group problem solving with, 117

H

Harvard University, 100

nine distinct undergraduates epistemologies at, 12

HBCU provide more graduate school science majors, 84

Jewish students, experience of ethnoviolence, 81–82
jobs requiring education beyond high school, 22% increase in, 1
John Hopkins University, 100
journalism, critiques of college curricula of , 34

K

Kennedy, Donald, 140
Kohlberg and Mayer (1972), 108
Keller plan. See Personalized System of Instruction

L

large classes used recall, 43
large size, need to reduce effect in education of, 113
LASSI tool to assess learning skills, 119
Latino students. See also Mexican-American students
    college degrees of 80 % from 20 % of U.S. institutions, 84
    graduation rates, 83
    success with cooperative learning, 99–100
leadership for quality, basis of, 133
learner-centered model of collegiate education, xi
learning-centered
    management of administrators need shift to, 130
    models visions of desirable, xi
learning society, American higher education as gateway to, xi
learning strategies, need for students to be instructed in, 119
Learning to Learn, 118–119
lecture
    behavior similarity of learning and grade oriented
  students, 45
    benefits consistently only the most formal of students, 12
    educational yield low from, 38
    effective as discussion for low-level factual material, 39
    motivational purposes primary purpose, 116
    principal instructional method, 38
Levin (1991), 96
liberal arts
    practicality of programs of, 28–29
    students show greater gains in moral judgment, 29
    women's gender-atypical careers increased by, 28
library, low use connected with little time spent in studying, 52
life-long learning, need for, 7
listening time. See critical thinking and memorizing
Louisiana State, screening out guns and knives at, 74

M

key cognitive deficiency of, 13
defects of, 14

N

O

P

Pennsylvania State University, 63
"Perry Position," 14
Personalized System of Instruction, 115–116
pervasively developmental culture, 149
"Peter Principled" professionals, educators as, 137
Piagetian stages of cognitive development, 20
Plaget, abstract reasoning not possible until about age 11, 10
post conventional principled ethical reasoning, 19
pre medicine
 cheating in, 70
 critiques of college curricula of, 34
president responsibility for filling university mission, 132
principled ethical reasoning, capacity for, 15–18
problem solving
 essential to success, 50
 lack of improvement in skills for, 51
Process assessment, 125
ProfScam, critique of faculty-centered model, xi
professors fill duty then students will not neglect theirs, if, 53
Project SOAR at Xavier University of Louisiana, 12
prose literacy, deficiencies in, 54–55
psychological climate
 academic performance association with, 73
 student responsibility for high-quality effort produced by,
53
psychological theory, need to use, 111–112
psychometric work, minimal student guidance with regard to, 65
psycho pathology as result of cognitive development, 111
purpose, need for clarity with regard to, 131–132
PSI. See Personalized System of Instruction

Q

Quality improvement
 precondition in schools for, 55–57
 prerequisite of professional development, 134
quality of instruction
 more significant than student's abilities, 97
 teachers perceptions of, 57–59
quality needs
 a campus climate that inspires and supports, 145
 definition meeting or exceeding customers' needs, 131
 to monitor, 129
"quantified gossip," 125

quantitative literacy, lack of, 55

"quiz show" as reinforcement of dualistic epistemology, 40

R

reading more valuable than listing to lectures, 39

Recall

    definition of knowledge as, 41

    level discourse employed by professors in classes , 42

Redesigning Higher Education, xi–xii, 4-5

Relativism as epistemological level, 13

Relativists

    defects of, 14

    few students are, 14

reliability definition, 63

required courses, do they have intended effects, 31–32

research

    of faculty, effect on quality of teaching is minimal, 141

    students should be helped to understand and apply, 111

    using to improve quality of education, 124–128

"rhetoric of conclusions," 59

Rutgers University, xi, 51, 52, 69, 76

    few undergraduates taught how to study, 119

    knowledge gained at to build World Trade center bomb,

112

    no Relativists in sample from, 14

    study of first-year physical science students at, 10

    support of author by, xiv

    Teaching Excellence Center Faculty Seminar, xiii

S

Saint Cloud State University, faculty making racist comments at, 82

Samuel Johnson, critique of lectures by, 40

SAT, college learning assessed through, 32

Schwab, Joseph, 59

self-esteem, cooperative activities effect on, 20

serious learning requires sustained effort outside the classroom, 51

Seton Hall University, xii

skills, tests generally do not assess higher order, 63

small classes used thinking level of analysis , 43

Smith, Adam, 53

Stand and Deliver, 96

standards, need to be set high, 129–131

Stanford University, 100, 140

University of Waterloo (Ontario), consideration of suicide at, 75
UCLA.   See   University of California - Los Angeles

V

veterinary medicine, critiques of college curricula of , 34
vocationally oriented programs and decrement in moral judgment, 29

W

Walberg (1984), 97
waste-generating problems associated with management, 133
waste, cost of, 127-129
"Western University", 27
     students share very little of formal learning at, 30
white males as a increasingly smaller part of the workforce, 1
women
     care-giving in moral issues, 17
     emphasize interpersonal relationships, 17
     increase of number on campus of, 77
     overt sex violence against, 79
     students receive less encouragement than men, 78
     development, peer culture has devastating effect on, 80
women's liberal arts colleges
     decrease in numbers of, 78
     gender-atypical careers increased by attending, 28
Workshop
     Physics reduction of course content by 30 %, 115
     low value in professional development of, 138, 141
World Trade Center, bombing of, 112

X

Xavier University of Louisiana, 12, 100

ASHE-ERIC HIGHER EDUCATION REPORTS

Since 1983, the Association for the Study of Higher Education (ASHE) and the Educational Resources Information Center (ERIC) Clearinghouse on Higher Education, a sponsored project of the Graduate School of Education and Human Development at The George Washington University, have cosponsored the *ASHE-ERIC Higher Education Report* series. The 1994 series is the twenty-third overall and the sixth to be published by the School of Education and Human Development at the George Washington University.

Each monograph is the definitive analysis of a tough higher education problem, based on thorough research of pertinent literature and institutional experiences. Topics are identified by a national survey. Noted practitioners and scholars are then commissioned to write the reports, with experts providing critical reviews of each manuscript before publication.

Eight monographs (10 before 1985) in the ASHE-ERIC Higher Education Reports series are published each year and are available on individual and subscription basis. To order, use the order form on the last page of this book.

Qualified persons interested in writing a monograph for the ASHE-ERIC Higher Education Reports are invited to submit a proposal to the National Advisory Board. As the preeminent literature review and issue analysis series in higher education, we can guarantee wide dissemination and national exposure for accepted candidates. Execution of a monograph requires at least a minimal familiarity with the ERIC database, including *Resources in Education* and *Current Index to Journals in Education*. The objective of these Reports is to bridge conventional wisdom with practical research. Prospective authors are strongly encouraged to call Dr. Fife at 800-773-3742.

For further information, write to
  ASHE-ERIC Higher Education Reports
  The George Washington University
  1 Dupont Circle, Suite 630
  Washington, DC 20036
Or phone (202) 296-2597, toll-free: 800-773-ERIC.
  Write or call for a complete catalog.

ADVISORY BOARD

Barbara E. Brittingham
University of Rhode Island

Mildred Garcia
Montclair State College

Rodolfo Z. Garcia
North Central Association of Colleges and Schools

James Hearn
University of Georgia

Bruce Anthony Jones
University of Pittsburgh

L. Jackson Newell
Deep Springs College

Carolyn Thompson
State University of New York-Buffalo

CONSULTING EDITORS

Robert J. Barak
State Board of Regents, Iowa

E. Grady Bogue
The University of Tennessee

John M. Braxton
Vanderbilt University

John A. Centra
Syracuse University

Robert A. Cornesky
Cornesky and Associates, Inc.

Peter Ewell
National Center for Higher Education Management Systems

John Folger
Institute for Public Policy Studies

George Gordon
University of Strathclyde

Jane Halonen
Alverno College

Dean L. Hubbard
Northwest Missouri State University

Thomas F. Kelley
Binghamton University

George D. Kuh
Indiana UniversityBloomington

Daniel T. Layzell
University of Wisconsin System

Frances Lucas-Tauchar
Emory University

Laurence R. Marcus
New Jersey Department of Higher Education

L. Jackson Newell
University of Utah

C. Robert Pace
University of California-Los Angeles

James Rhem
The National Teaching & Learning Forum

Gary Rhoades
University of Arizona

G. Jeremiah Ryan
Harford Community College

Karl Schilling
Miami University

Charles Schroeder
University of Missouri

Lawrence A. Sherr
University of Kansas

Patricia A. Spencer
Riverside Community College

Frances Stage
Indiana University-Bloomington

David Sweet
OERI, U.S. Dept. of Education

Barbara E. Taylor
Association of Governing Boards

Sheila L. Weiner
Board of Overseers of Harvard College

Wesley K. Willmer
Biola University

Manta Yorke
Liverpool John Moores University

REVIEW PANEL

Charles Adams
University of MassachusettsAmherst

Louis Albert
American Association for Higher Education

Richard Alfred
University of Michigan

Henry Lee Allen
University of Rochester

Philip G. Altbach
Boston College

Marilyn J. Amey
University of Kansas

Kristine L. Anderson
Florida Atlantic University

Karen D. Arnold
Boston College

Robert J. Barak
Iowa State Board of Regents

Alan Bayer
Virginia Polytechnic Institute and State University

John P. Bean
Indiana UniversityBloomington

John M. Braxton
Peabody College, Vanderbilt University

Ellen M. Bricr
Tennessee State University

Barbara E. Brittingham
The University of Rhode Island

Dennis Brown
University of Kansas

Peter McE. Buchanan
Council for Advancement and
    Support of Education

Patricia Carter
University of Michigan

John A. Centra
Syracuse University

Arthur W. Chickering
George Mason University

Darrel A. Clowes
Virginia Polytechnic Institute and State University

Deborah M. DiCroce
Piedmont Virginia Community College

Cynthia S. Dickens
Mississippi State University

Sarah M. Dinham
University of Arizona

Kenneth A. Feldman
State University of New YorkStony Brook

Dorothy E. Finnegan
The College of William & Mary

Mildred Garcia
Montclair State College

Rodolfo Z. Garcia
Commission on Institutions of Higher Education

Kenneth C. Green
University of Southern California

James Hearn
University of Georgia

Edward R. Hines
Illinois State University

Deborah Hunter
University of Vermont

Philo Hutcheson
Georgia State University

Bruce Anthony Jones
University of Pittsburgh

Elizabeth A. Jones
The Pennsylvania State University

Kathryn Kretschmer
University of Kansas

Marsha V. Krotseng
State College and University Systems of West Virginia

George D. Kuh
Indiana UniversityBloomington

Daniel T. Layzell
University of Wisconsin System

Patrick G. Love
Kent State University

Cheryl D. Lovell
State Higher Education Executive Officers

Meredith Jane Ludwig
American Association of State Colleges and Universities

Dewayne Matthews
Western Interstate Commission for Higher Education

Mantha V. Mehallis
Florida Atlantic University

Toby Milton
Essex Community College

James R. Mingle
State Higher Education Executive Officers

John A. Muffo
Virginia Polytechnic Institute and State University

L. Jackson Newell
Deep Springs College

James C. Palmer
Illinois State University

Robert A. Rhoads
The Pennsylvania State University

G. Jeremiah Ryan
Harford Community College

Mary Ann Danowitz Sagaria
The Ohio State University

Daryl G. Smith
The Claremont Graduate School

William G. Tierney
University of Southern California

Susan B. Twombly
University of Kansas

Robert A. Walhaus
University of IllinoisChicago

Harold Wechsler
University of Rochester

Elizabeth J. Whitt
University of IllinoisChicago

Michael J. Worth
The George Washington University

RECENT TITLES

1994 ASHE-ERIC Higher Education Reports

1. The Advisory Committee Advantage: Creating an Effective Strategy for Programmatic Improvement
   Lee Teitel

2. Collaborative Peer Review: The Role of Faculty in Improving College Teaching
   Larry Keig and Michael D. Waggoner

3. Prices, Productivity, and Investment: Assessing Financial Strategies in Higher Education
   Edward P. St. John

4. The Development Officer in Higher Education: Toward an Understanding of the Role
   Michael J. Worth and James W. Asp, II

5. The Promises and Pitfalls of Performance Indicators in Higher Education
   Gerald Gaither, Brian P. Nedwek, and John E. Neal

6. A New Alliance: Continuous Quality and Classroom Effectiveness
   Mimi Wolverton

1993 ASHE-ERIC Higher Education Reports

1. The Department Chair: New Roles, Responsibilities and Challenges
   Alan T. Seagren, John W. Creswell, and Daniel W. Wheeler

2. Sexual Harassment in Higher Education: From Conflict to Community
   Robert O. Riggs, Patricia H. Murrell, and JoAnn C. Cutting

3. Chicanos in Higher Education: Issues and Dilemmas for the 21st Century
   Adalberto Aguirre, Jr., and Ruben O. Martinez

4. Academic Freedom in American Higher Education: Rights, Responsibilities, and Limitations
   Robert K. Poch

5. Making Sense of the Dollars: The Costs and Uses of Faculty Compensation
   Kathryn M. Moore and Marilyn J. Amey

6. Enhancing Promotion, Tenure and Beyond: Faculty Socialization as a Cultural Process
   William G. Tierney and Robert A. Rhoads

7. New Perspectives for Student Affairs Professionals: Evolving Realities, Responsibilities and Roles
   Peter H. Garland and Thomas W. Grace

8. Turning Teaching Into Learning: The Role of Student Responsibility in the Collegiate Experience
   Todd M. Davis and Patricia Hillman Murrell

1992 ASHE-ERIC Higher Education Reports

1. The Leadership Compass: Values and Ethics in Higher Education
   John R. Wilcox and Susan L. Ebbs

2. Preparing for a Global Community: Achieving an International Perspective in Higher Education
   Sarah M. Pickert

3. Quality: Transforming Postsecondary Education
   Ellen Earle Chaffee and Lawrence A. Sherr

4. Faculty Job Satisfaction: Women and Minorities in Peril
   Martha Wingard Tack and Carol Logan Patitu

5. Reconciling Rights and Responsibilities of Colleges and Students: Offensive Speech, Assembly, Drug Testing, and Safety
   Annette Gibbs

6. Creating Distinctiveness: Lessons from Uncommon Colleges and Universities
   Barbara K. Townsend, L. Jackson Newell, and Michael D. Wiese

7. Instituting Enduring Innovations: Achieving Continuity of Change in Higher Education
   Barbara K. Curry

8. Crossing Pedagogical Oceans: International Teaching Assistants in U.S. Undergraduate Education
   Rosslyn M. Smith, Patricia Byrd, Gayle L. Nelson, Ralph Pat Barrett, and Janet C. Constantinides

1991 ASHE-ERIC Higher Education Reports

1. Active Learning: Creating Excitement in the Classroom
   Charles C. Bonwell and James A. Eison

2. Realizing Gender Equality in Higher Education: The
   Need to Integrate Work/Family Issues
   Nancy Hensel

3. Academic Advising for Student Success: A System of
   Shared Responsibility
   Susan H. Frost

4. Cooperative Learning: Increasing College Faculty
   Instructional Productivity
   *David W. Johnson, Roger T. Johnson, and Karl A.
   Smith*

5. High SchoolCollege Partnerships: Conceptual Models,
   Programs, and Issues
   Arthur Richard Greenberg

6. Meeting the Mandate: Renewing the College and
   Departmental Curriculum
   William Toombs and William Tierney

7. Faculty Collaboration: Enhancing the Quality of
   Scholarship and Teaching
   Ann E. Austin and Roger G. Baldwin

8. Strategies and Consequences: Managing the Costs in
   Higher Education
   John S. Waggaman

1990 ASHE-ERIC Higher Education Reports

1. The Campus Green: Fund Raising in Higher Education
   Barbara E. Brittingham and Thomas R. Pezzullo

2. The Emeritus Professor: Old Rank - New Meaning
   James E. Mauch, Jack W. Birch, and Jack Matthews

3. "High Risk" Students in Higher Education: Future
   Trends
   Dionne J. Jones and Betty Collier Watson

4. Budgeting for Higher Education at the State Level:
   Enigma, Paradox, and Ritual
   Daniel T. Layzell and Jan W. Lyddon

8. Renewing Civic Capacity: Preparing College Students for Service and Citizenship
   Suzanne W. Morse

1988 ASHE-ERIC Higher Education Reports

1. The Invisible Tapestry: Culture in American Colleges and Universities
   George D. Kuh and Elizabeth J. Whitt

2. Critical Thinking: Theory, Research, Practice, and Possibilities
   Joanne Gainen Kurfiss

3. Developing Academic Programs: The Climate for Innovation
   Daniel T. Seymour

4. Peer Teaching: To Teach is To Learn Twice
   Neal A. Whitman

5. Higher Education and State Governments: Renewed Partnership, Cooperation, or Competition?
   Edward R. Hines

6. Entrepreneurship and Higher Education: Lessons for Colleges, Universities, and Industry
   James S. Fairweather

7. Planning for Microcomputers in Higher Education: Strategies for the Next Generation
   Reynolds Ferrante, John Hayman, Mary Susan Carlson, and Harry Phillips

8. The Challenge for Research in Higher Education: Harmonizing Excellence and Utility
   Alan W. Lindsay and Ruth T. Neumann

*Out-of-print. Available through EDRS. Call 1-800-443-ERIC.

ORDER FORM 94-7

Quantity   **Amount**

_____ Please begin my subscription to the 1995 *ASHE-ERIC Higher Education Reports* at $98.00, 31% off the cover price, starting with Report 1, 1994. Includes shipping. _____

_____ Please send a complete set of the 1994 *ASHE-ERIC Higher Education Reports* at $98.00, 31% off the cover price. Please add shipping charge, below. _____

Individual reports are available at the following prices:
1993 and 1994, $18.00; 1988–1992, $17.00; 1980–1987, $15.00

SHIPPING CHARGES
For orders of more than 50 books, please call for shipping information.

	1st three books	*Ea. addl. book*
U.S., 48 Contiguous States		
Ground:	$3.75	$0.15
2nd Day*:	8.25	1.10
Next Day*:	18.00	1.60
Alaska & Hawaii (2nd Day Only)*:	13.25	1.40

U.S. Territories and Foreign Countries: Please call for shipping information.
*Order will be shipping within 24 hours of request.
All prices shown on this form are subject to change.

PLEASE SEND ME THE FOLLOWING REPORTS:

Quantity	Report No.	Year	Title	Amount

Please check one of the following:
☐ Check enclosed, payable to GWU–ERIC.
☐ Purchase order attached ($45.00 minimum).
☐ Charge my credit card indicated below:
    ☐ Visa   ☐ MasterCard

Subtotal: _____
Shipping: _____
Total Due: _____

Expiration Date _____

Name _____

Title _____

Institution _____

Address _____

City _____ State _____ Zip _____

Phone _____ Fax _____ Telex _____

Signature _____ Date _____

SEND ALL ORDERS TO: ASHE-ERIC Higher Education Reports
The George Washington University
One Dupont Cir., Ste. 630, Washington, DC 20036-1183
Phone: (202) 296-2597 • Toll-free: 800-773-ERIC